MathFlare

Name: ___________________

Class: __________

Teacher: ___________________

Introduction

As parents and educators, we recognize the pivotal role mathematics plays in shaping a child's academic journey and future success. Yet, the path to mathematical proficiency can often seem daunting, fraught with challenges and complexities. That's where the transformative power of MathFlare Workbooks shine through, illuminating the way forward with clarity, precision, and purpose.

Introducing MathFlare Workbooks – a beacon of guidance, a testament to excellence, and a catalyst for achievement. Crafted with meticulous care and expertise, MathFlare Workbooks stand as paragons of educational excellence, designed to nurture young minds, ignite a passion for learning, and develop a deep-rooted understanding of mathematical concepts.

Picture this: your child eagerly delves into the pages of Mathflare Workbook, greeted by a step-by-step guide illuminated with vivid examples that demystify complex mathematical concepts. With each turn of the page, they embark on a journey of discovery, encountering thoughtfully curated practice questions that reinforce learning and hone problem-solving skills. And when they unveil the answers to those very questions, a sense of accomplishment blossoms within them – a tangible reward for their hard work and dedication.

But MathFlare Workbooks are more than just tools for learning; they are pathways to comprehension, fostering a deep-seated understanding of mathematical concepts through a sequential, logical flow. From fundamental principles to advanced problem-solving strategies, every chapter builds upon the last, ensuring a robust foundation upon which future knowledge can be constructed.

As parents, we yearn for nothing more than to see our children thrive, to witness the spark of inspiration ignited within them as they conquer academic challenges with confidence and poise. MathFlare Workbooks serve as partners in this noble endeavor, offering not just practice questions, but the keys to unlocking a world of opportunity.

And for teachers, MathFlare Workbooks stand as invaluable allies in the quest to cultivate mathematical proficiency in the classroom. With answers readily available, instructors can focus on guiding and nurturing their students, confident in the knowledge that MathFlare Workbooks provide a solid framework upon which to build.

In the pages of MathFlare Workbooks, we find not just the promise of academic excellence, but the seeds of a brighter tomorrow. So let us embrace the power of mathematics, let us champion the journey of learning, and let us pave the way for a generation of young minds poised to shape the world. With MathFlare Workbooks as our guide, the possibilities are infinite, and the future, bright.

Table of Contents

MathFlare
Grade 2
MATH WORKBOOK
Step by Step Guide and Essential Practice with Answers
Addition Subtraction
Multiplication
Place Value and Expanded Notations
Geometry
MathFlare Publishing

MathFlare
Grade 2-3
MATH WORKBOOK
Step by Step Guide and Essential Practice with Answers
Addition Subtraction
Multiplication and Division
Place Value and Expanded Notations
Geometry
MathFlare Publishing

MathFlare
Grade 3
MATH WORKBOOK
Step by Step Guide and Essential Practice with Answers
Multiplication and Division
Decimals
Place Value and Expanded Notations
Fractions and Geometry
MathFlare Publishing

MathFlare
Grade 1
MATH WORKBOOK
Step by Step Guide and Essential Practice with Answers
Counting and Numbers
Addition and Subtraction
Place Value and Expanded Notations
Understanding Time
MathFlare Publishing

MathFlare
Grade 1-2
MATH WORKBOOK
Step by Step Guide and Essential Practice with Answers
Counting and Numbers
Addition and Subtraction
Place Value and Expanded Notations
Understanding Time
MathFlare Publishing

MathFlare
Grade 3-4
MATH WORKBOOK
Step by Step Guide and Essential Practice with Answers
Addition Subtraction
Multiplication Division
Place Value and Expanded Notations
Fractions and Geometry
MathFlare Publishing

MathFlare
Grade 4
MATH WORKBOOK
Step by Step Guide and Essential Practice with Answers
Addition Subtraction
Multiplication Division
Place Value and Expanded Notations
Fractions and Geometry
MathFlare Publishing

MathFlare
Grade 4-5
MATH WORKBOOK
Step by Step Guide and Essential Practice with Answers
Multiplication Division
Place Value and Expanded Notations
Fractions and Geometry
Unit Conversion
MathFlare Publishing

MathFlare
MATH WORKBOOK
5
Step by Step Guide and Essential Practice with Answers
Multiplication Division
Place Value and Expanded Notations
Fractions and Geometry
Unit Conversion
MathFlare Publishing

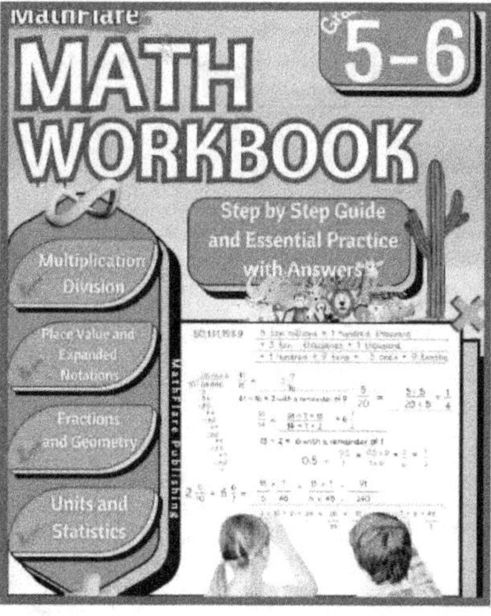
MathFlare
MATH WORKBOOK
5-6
Step by Step Guide and Essential Practice with Answers
Multiplication Division
Place Value and Expanded Notations
Fractions and Geometry
Units and Statistics
MathFlare Publishing

MathFlare
MATH WORKBOOK
6
Step by Step Guide and Essential Practice with Answers
Integers and Statistics
Arithmetic and Pre-Algebra
Fractions and Geometry
Ratio and Percentage
MathFlare Publishing

MathFlare
MATH WORKBOOK
6-7
Step by Step Guide and Essential Practice with Answers
Arithmetic and Pre-Algebra
Ratio, Percent Proportion
Geometry
Statistics
MathFlare Publishing

MathFlare
MATH WORKBOOK
7
Step by Step Guide and Essential Practice with Answers
Pre-Algebra
Ratio, Percent Proportion
Geometry
Statistics
MathFlare Publishing

MathFlare
MATH WORKBOOK
7-8
Step by Step Guide and Essential Practice with Answers
Pre-Algebra
Ratio, Percent Proportion
Geometry and Cartesian Plane
Statistics
MathFlare Publishing

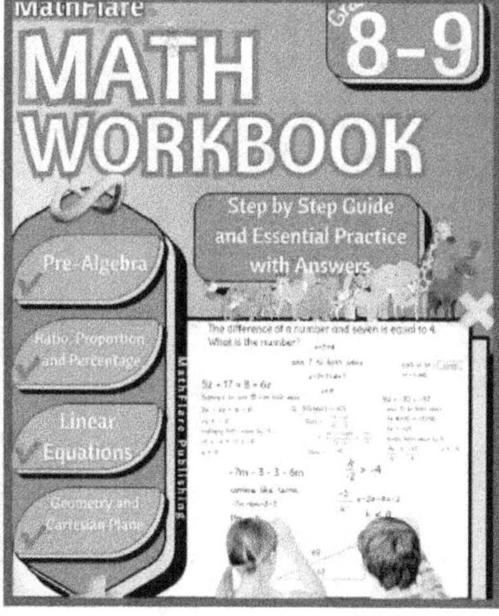
MathFlare
MATH WORKBOOK
8-9
Step by Step Guide and Essential Practice with Answers
Pre-Algebra
Ratio, Proportion and Percentage
Linear Equations
Geometry and Cartesian Plane
MathFlare Publishing

MathFlare
MATH WORKBOOK
8
Step by Step Guide and Essential Practice with Answers
Pre-Algebra
Percentage
Linear Equations
Geometry
MathFlare Publishing

Chapter. 01

Multiplication and Division

Multiplication

Multiplication is an easy way of adding numbers together quickly. Instead of adding the same number repeatedly, we use multiplication to find the total much faster.

For instance, rather than adding 2 + 2 + 2 + 2 + 2, we can multiply 2 by 5 to get the same result: 2 x 5 = 10.

Here, the first number (2) is called the multiplicand, second number (5) is the multiplier. The answer we get, in this case, 10, is called the product.

Let's think of multiplication as repeated addition.

Take 2 x 5, for example. It means adding 2 together five times, which we can illustrate as: 2 + 2 + 2 + 2 + 2 = 10

Multiplication can also be visualized as groups of objects. Imagine we have 2 groups, each containing 5 oranges.

To find the total number of oranges, we multiply the number of groups (2) by the number of oranges in each group (5):

2 groups of 5 oranges = 10 oranges

Expressed as multiplication: 2 x 5 = 10

In summary, multiplication offers various ways to approach it: through repeated addition or by envisioning groups of objects. It's a powerful tool that makes solving math problems much quicker and more efficient!

We can also use the following table to quickly remember multiplication facts. The intersection of two points shows the product of two numbers.

For instance, the product of 5 x 6 = 30, or 6 x 5 = 30.

	1	2	3	4	5	6	7	8	9	10
1	1	2	3	4	5	6	7	8	9	10
2	2	4	6	8	10	12	14	16	18	20
3	3	6	9	12	15	18	21	24	27	30
4	4	8	12	16	20	24	28	32	36	40
5	5	10	15	20	25	30	35	40	45	50
6	6	12	18	24	30	36	42	48	54	60
7	7	14	21	28	35	42	49	56	63	70
8	8	16	24	32	40	48	56	64	72	80
9	9	18	27	36	45	54	63	72	81	90
10	10	20	30	40	50	60	70	80	90	100

Long Division and Remainders

Division is like the opposite of multiplication. It's all about sharing or distributing items equally among a certain number of groups or people.

When we divide one number by another, we're essentially splitting a number into equal parts. We're figuring out how many groups of a certain size can be made from that number.

For instance, let's divide 20 by 4.

When we divide 20 by 4, we're essentially asking, "How many groups of size 4 can we make from 20?"

Now, there are several parts or terms involved in the division process:

- **Dividend:** This is the number being divided, which in this case, is 20.

- **Divisor:** This is the number we're dividing by, which is 4.

- **Quotient:** This is the answer we get after dividing. It tells us how many groups of divisors can be made from the dividend. In this case, the answer is 5.

- **Remainder:** when the divisor doesn't evenly divide the dividend, we get the remainder.

So, when we divide 20 by 4, we found out that 5 groups of 4 can be made from 20.

Let's solve problems from exercises:

$$\begin{array}{r} 08{,}464.6 \\ 10\overline{)\,84{,}646} \\ -0 \\ \hline 84 \\ -80 \\ \hline 46 \\ -40 \\ \hline 64 \\ -60 \\ \hline 46 \\ -40 \\ \hline 60 \\ -60 \\ \hline 0 \end{array}$$

$$\begin{array}{r} 8{,}965 \text{ R1} \\ 9\overline{)\,80{,}686} \\ -72 \\ \hline 86 \\ -81 \\ \hline 58 \\ -54 \\ \hline 46 \\ -45 \\ \hline 1 \end{array}$$

Multi Digit Multiplication

$$\begin{array}{r} 70{,}278 \\ \times \quad 2{,}965 \\ \hline +\quad 351390 \\ +\quad 421668 \\ +\ 632502 \\ +140556 \\ \hline =208374270 \end{array}$$

Multiplying Decimals

Multiplying decimals is a lot like multiplying whole numbers, but we need to be careful about where we put the decimal point in the answer.

> **Step 1:** Start by multiplying the numbers together, just like we do with whole numbers. Ignore the decimals for now.

Step 2: Count how many decimal places there are in the numbers we're multiplying. This will tell us how many decimal places our answer should have.

Step 3: Put the decimal point in the answer by starting from the right side of the number. Move the decimal point to the left as many places as there are in the total number of decimal places.

For example, let's multiply 4.5 by 2.5:

Step 1: Multiply the numbers as if they were whole numbers:

$$25 \times 45 = 1125.$$

Step 2: There is one decimal place in 2.5 and one in 4.5, making a total of two decimal places.

Step 3: Starting from the right side of the answer, count two places to the left and put the decimal point there.

So, the final answer is 11.25.

Remember to pay close attention to where the decimal point goes in the answer.

Let's solve a problem:

$$
\begin{array}{r}
379.75 \\
\times \quad 33.75 \\
\hline
+ \quad 189875 \\
+ \ 265825 \\
+ \ 113925 \\
+113925 \\
\hline
=12816.5625
\end{array}
$$

Dividing Decimals

Dividing decimals is a lot like dividing whole numbers, but we need to be careful about placement of decimal point in the answer.

Steps to follow:

1. **Set up the division problem:** Write the dividend (the number being divided) and the divisor (the number you're dividing by) as you would in a long division problem.

$$1.7\overline{)1.6}$$

2. **Move the decimal:** Move the decimal point to the right in the dividend and divisor by the same number of places.

$$17\overline{)16}$$

3. **Perform the division:** Divide as you would with whole numbers.

```
        0 0.9 4
  17)1 6
     - 0
     1 6
     - 0
     1 6 0
   - 1 5 3
         7 0
       - 6 8
           2
```

4. **Place the decimal point:** Place the decimal point in the quotient directly above its position in the dividend.

So, the quotient is 0.94.

Let's solve another problem:

$$9\overline{)98.69} = 10.97$$

$$
\begin{array}{r}
10.97 \\
9\overline{)98.69} \\
-9 \\
\hline
08 \\
-0 \\
\hline
86 \\
-81 \\
\hline
59 \\
-54 \\
\hline
5
\end{array}
$$

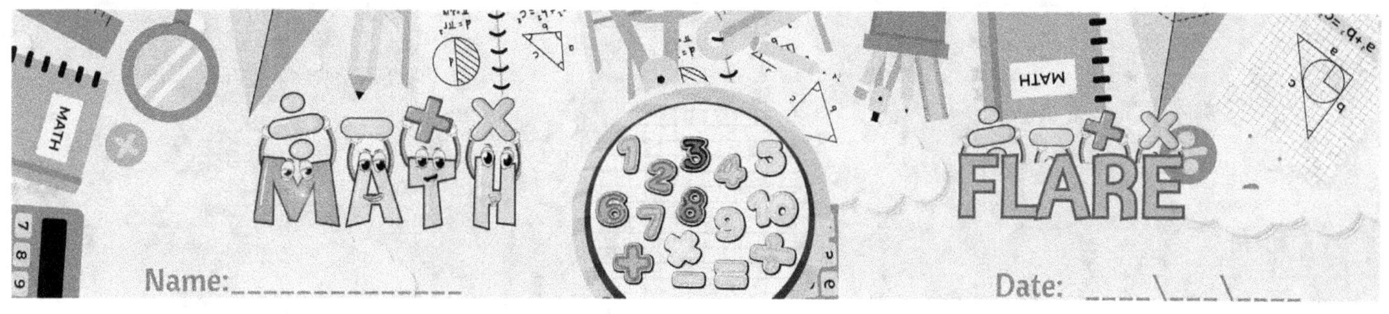

Long Division: Remainders

Find the quotient.

1)
$$9{,}248 \text{ R}1$$
$$9\overline{)83{,}233}$$
$$-\ 81$$
$$\quad 22$$
$$-\ 18$$
$$\quad 43$$
$$-\ 36$$
$$\quad 73$$
$$-\ 72$$
$$\quad 1$$

2)
$$17\overline{)27{,}813}$$

3)
$$10\overline{)29{,}542}$$

4)
$$6\overline{)24{,}015}$$

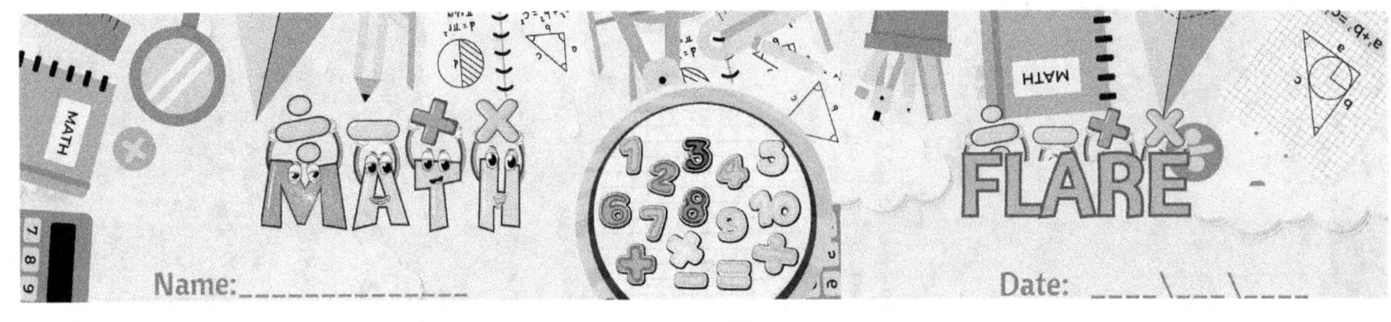

5)

$$9 \overline{)32{,}929}$$

6)

$$14 \overline{)46{,}977}$$

7)

$$15 \overline{)98{,}765}$$

8)

$$7 \overline{)14{,}818}$$

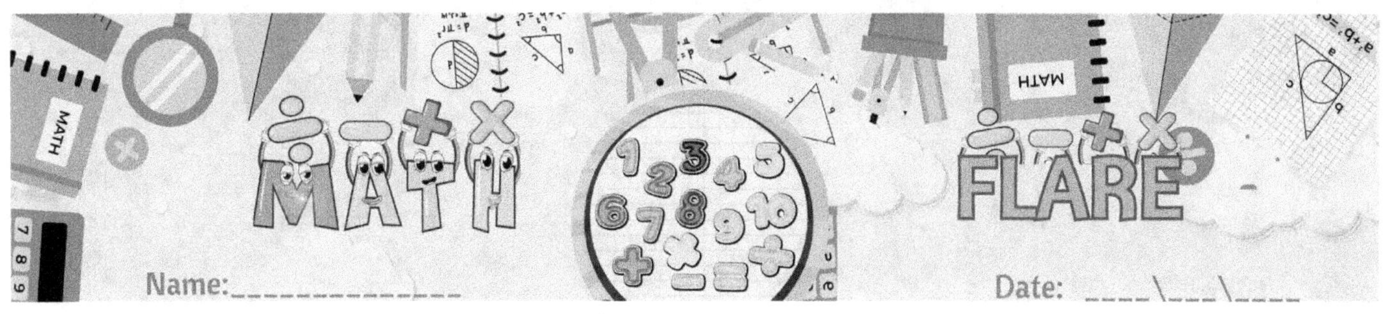

9)

$$4 \overline{)13{,}077}$$

10)

$$18 \overline{)14{,}811}$$

11)

$$19 \overline{)66{,}656}$$

12)

$$20 \overline{)74{,}410}$$

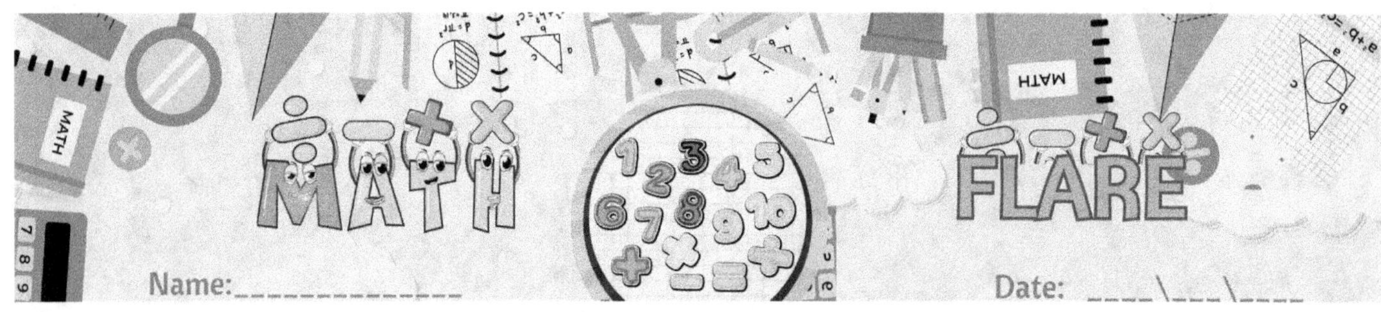

13)

$$6 \overline{) 51{,}099}$$

14)

$$4 \overline{) 71{,}128}$$

15)

$$7 \overline{) 21{,}914}$$

16)

$$13 \overline{) 83{,}740}$$

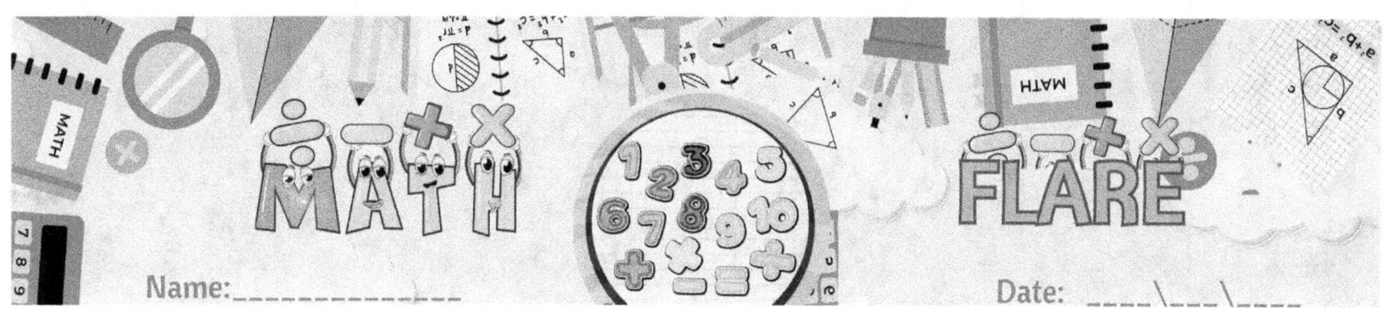

17)

4 ⟌ 54,493

18)

17 ⟌ 72,884

19)

13 ⟌ 54,498

20)

3 ⟌ 29,008

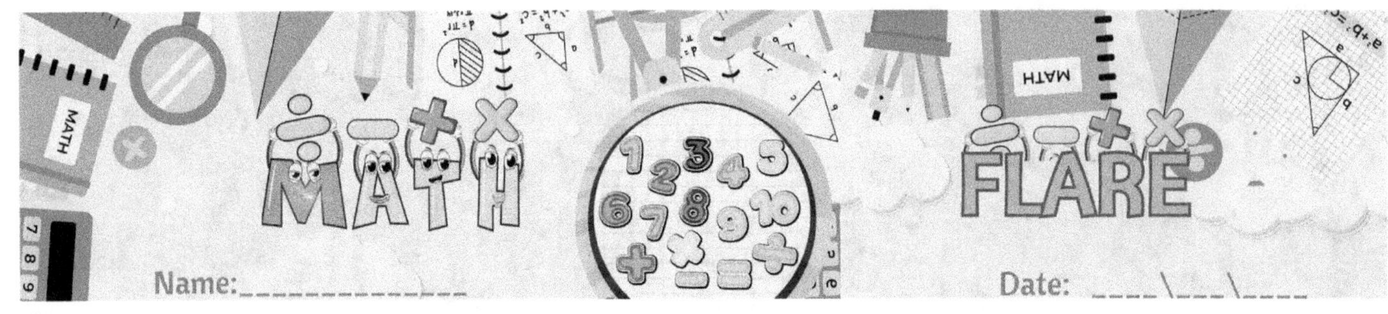

21)

$$12 \overline{)\, 62{,}479}$$

22)

$$20 \overline{)\, 82{,}262}$$

23)

$$10 \overline{)\, 19{,}199}$$

24)

$$6 \overline{)\, 92{,}289}$$

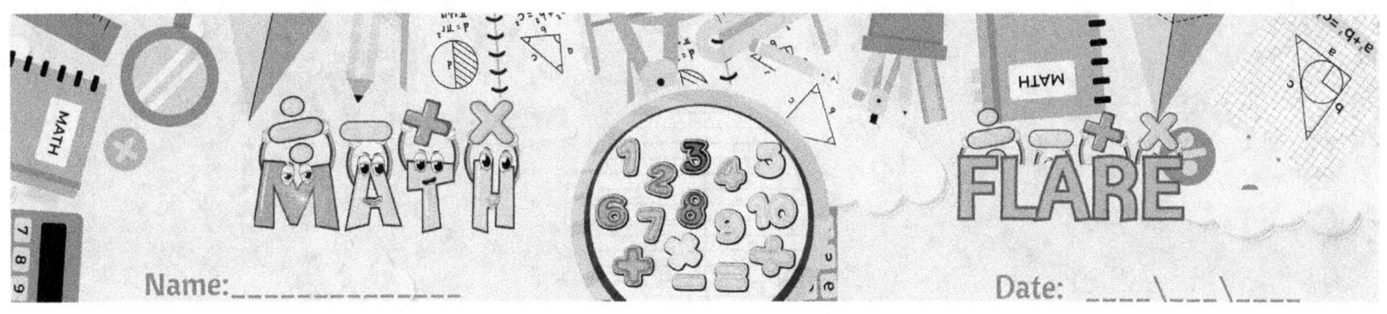

25)

$$3 \overline{)73{,}951}$$

26)

$$6 \overline{)32{,}657}$$

27)

$$8 \overline{)92{,}649}$$

28)

$$17 \overline{)44{,}040}$$

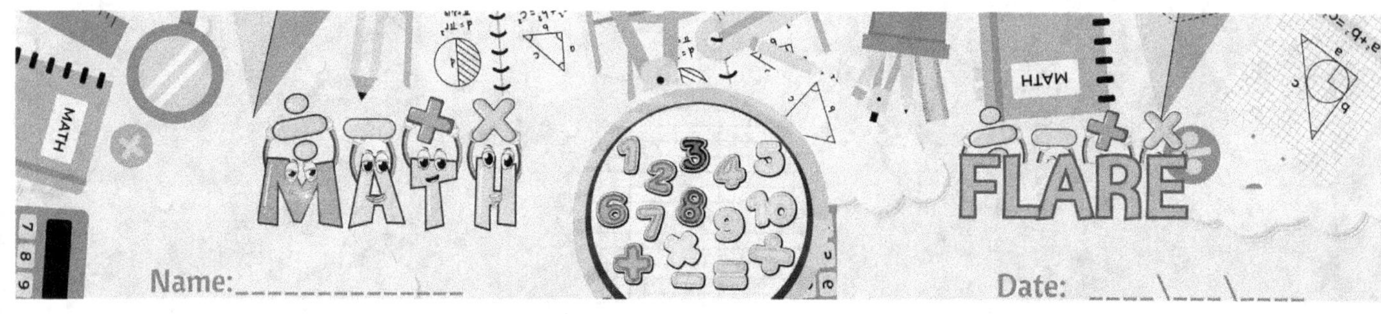

Multi Digit Multiplication

Find the product.

1) 70,278
× 2,965
+ 351390
+ 421668
+ 632502
+140556
=208374270

2) 41,508
× 1,018

3) 77,102
× 1,517

4) 16,528
× 9,648

5) 60,893
× 8,249

6) 24,034
× 8,990

7) 12,007
× 2,971

8) 80,254
× 4,561

9) 89,783
× 1,020

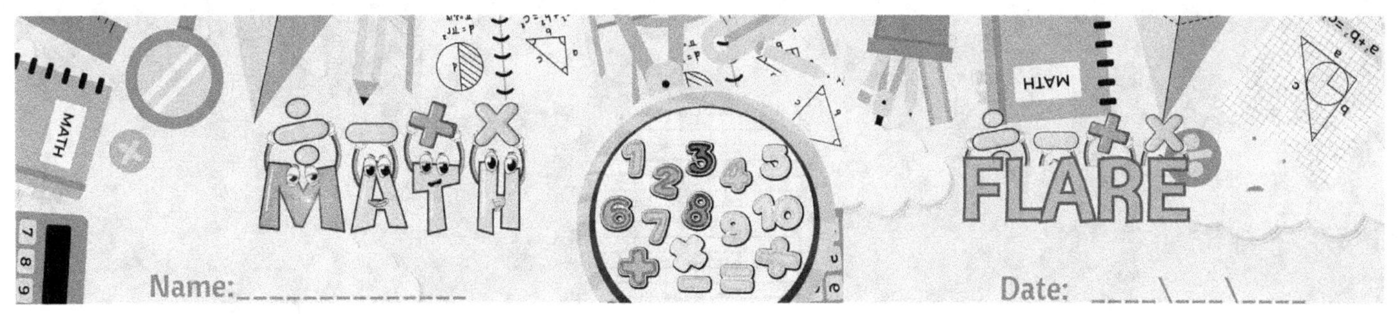

10)   39,396
     ×   1,661

11)   23,777
     ×   7,602

12)   88,957
     ×   9,866

13)   37,068
     ×   5,094

14)   44,884
     ×   1,749

15)   13,781
     ×   6,282

16)   71,821
     ×   2,371

17)   74,818
     ×   8,569

18)   24,815
     ×   3,485

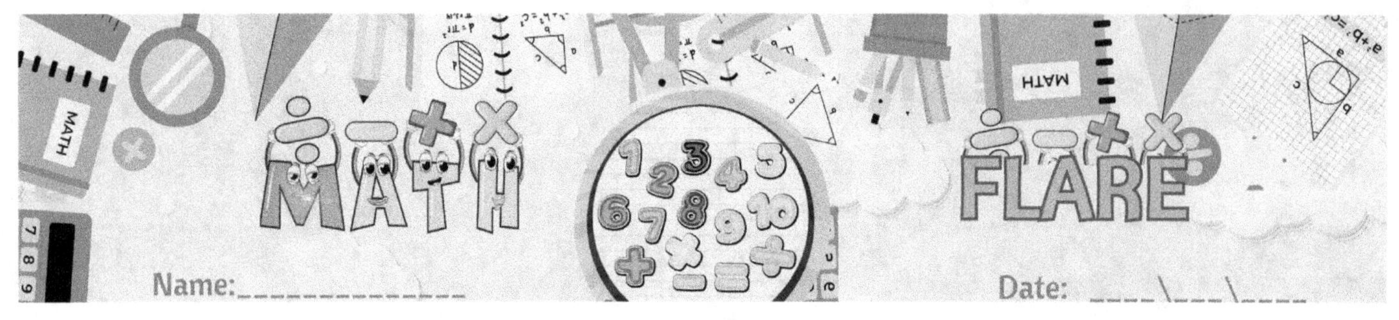

19) 35,946
   × 2,883

20) 37,502
   × 5,731

21) 53,517
   × 8,577

22) 47,485
   × 3,670

23) 38,399
   × 1,239

24) 28,181
   × 5,424

25) 34,158
   × 8,703

26) 41,128
   × 9,245

27) 11,383
   × 3,743

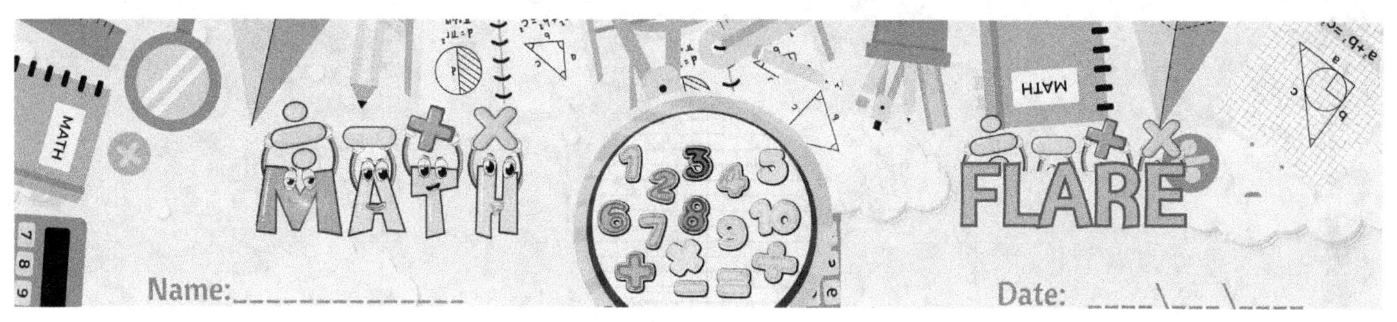

28) 73,407
   × 9,425

29) 40,679
   × 4,284

30) 73,097
   × 3,616

31) 70,277
   × 9,903

32) 92,699
   × 9,806

33) 20,666
   × 1,032

34) 25,079
   × 2,631

35) 14,899
   × 5,540

36) 19,668
   × 7,095

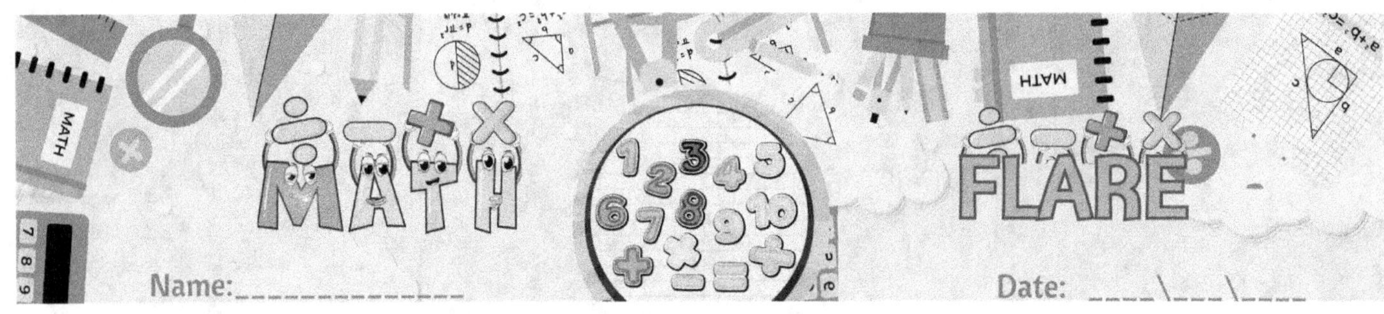

Multi Digit Multiplication: Decimals

Find the product.

1) 379.75
  × 33.75
  + 189875
  + 265825
  + 113925
  +113925
  =12816.5625

2) 553.40
  × 92.56

3) 322.57
  × 11.35

4) 505.57
  × 97.13

5) 112.54
  × 29.04

6) 242.45
  × 48.75

7) 643.29
  × 13.95

8) 759.22
  × 67.06

9) 134.56
  × 59.08

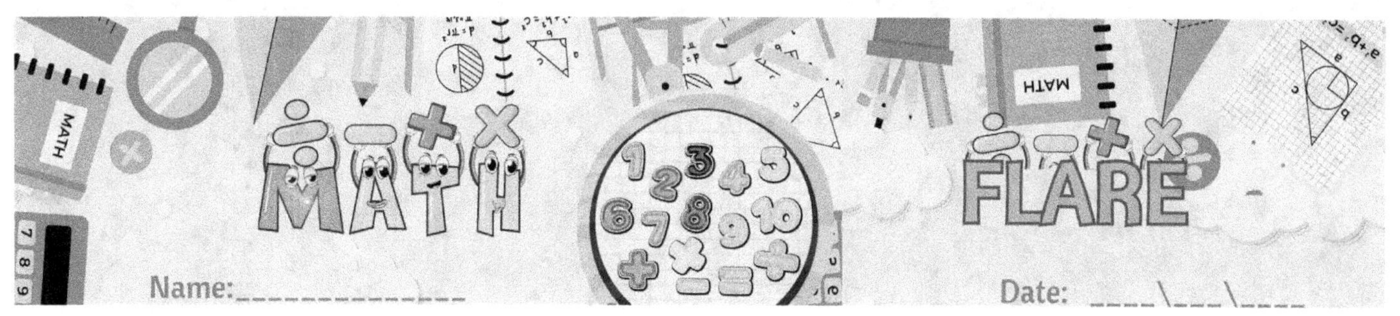

10) 640.99
  ×   68.73
  ____

11) 920.50
  ×   81.57
  ____

12) 685.61
  ×   84.85
  ____

13) 280.41
  ×   35.94
  ____

14) 279.78
  ×   25.09
  ____

15) 524.24
  ×   46.48
  ____

16) 849.09
  ×   74.95
  ____

17) 341.87
  ×   89.18
  ____

18) 942.24
  ×   97.63
  ____

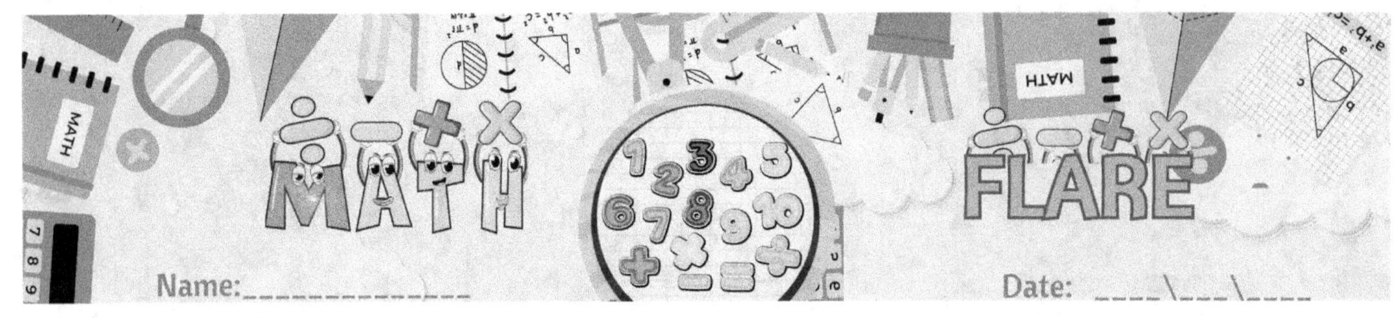

19)   483.63
     ×   45.19

20)   805.74
     ×   50.46

21)   923.63
     ×   68.80

22)   357.68
     ×   74.55

23)   382.09
     ×   11.13

24)   681.72
     ×   25.02

25)   417.32
     ×   52.84

26)   108.36
     ×   71.01

27)   947.28
     ×   76.61

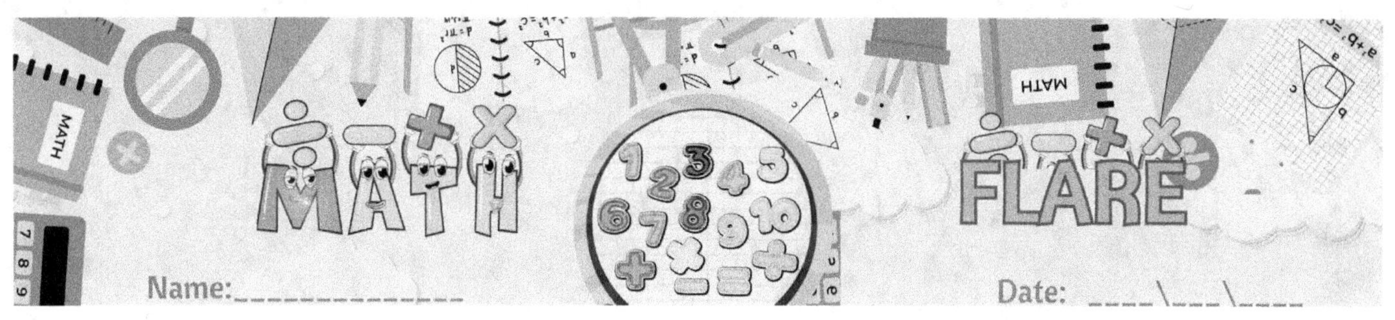

28) 449.38
   × 56.40
   ⎯⎯⎯⎯⎯⎯

29) 651.82
   × 70.48
   ⎯⎯⎯⎯⎯⎯

30) 745.22
   × 96.31
   ⎯⎯⎯⎯⎯⎯

31) 833.65
   × 35.47
   ⎯⎯⎯⎯⎯⎯

32) 547.02
   × 64.76
   ⎯⎯⎯⎯⎯⎯

33) 441.19
   × 49.29
   ⎯⎯⎯⎯⎯⎯

34) 245.58
   × 75.14
   ⎯⎯⎯⎯⎯⎯

35) 197.18
   × 78.28
   ⎯⎯⎯⎯⎯⎯

36) 286.96
   × 68.25
   ⎯⎯⎯⎯⎯⎯

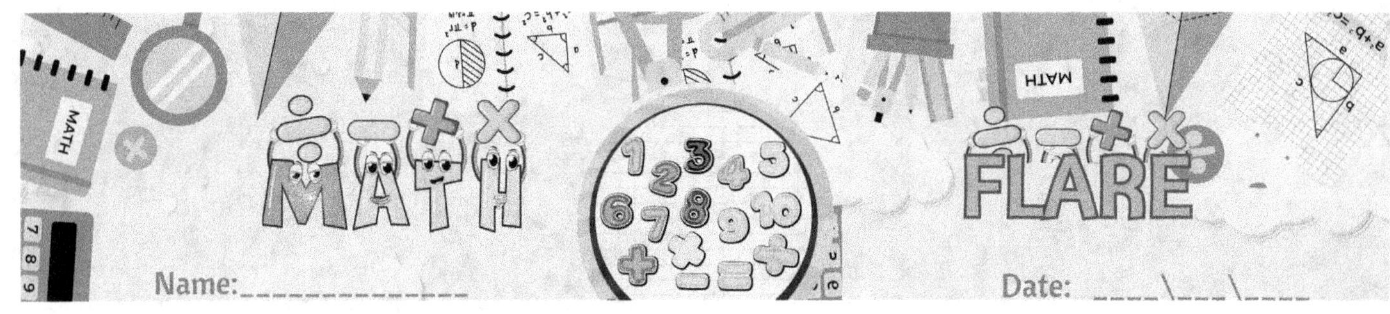

Dividing Decimals

Find the quotient.

1)
$$9 \overline{)98.69} = 10.97$$

```
       10.97
   9)  98.69
      -9
       08
       -0
        86
       -81
         59
        -54
          5
```

2)
$$8 \overline{)11.41}$$

3)
$$3 \overline{)32.23}$$

4)
$$4 \overline{)15.68}$$

5)
$$7 \overline{)73.05}$$

6)
$$5 \overline{)92.08}$$

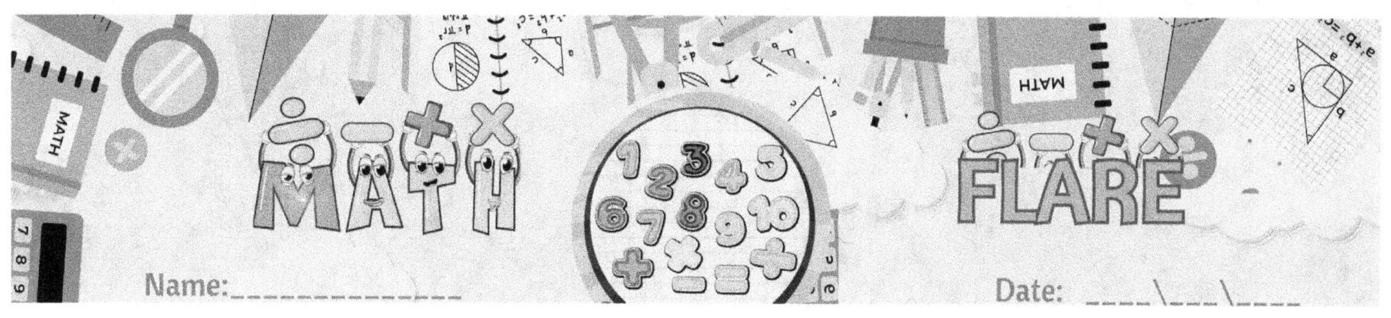

7)

$9\overline{)12.31}$

8)

$8\overline{)82.62}$

9)

$2\overline{)64.63}$

10)

$10\overline{)79.06}$

11)

$8\overline{)26.02}$

12)

$6\overline{)39.46}$

13)

$10\overline{)39.14}$

14)

$4\overline{)33.51}$

15)

$5\overline{)93.39}$

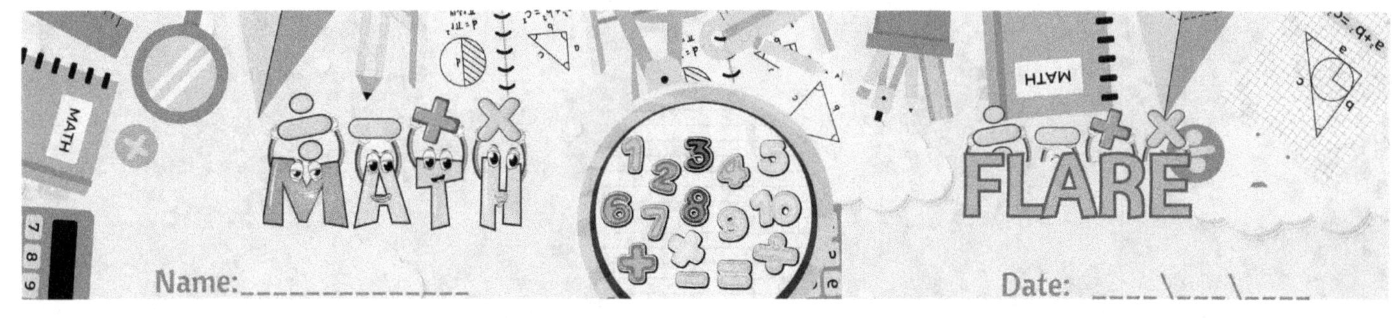

16)

8)27.13

17)

7)45.94

18)

8)21.22

19)

7)76.28

20)

8)77.21

21)

10)83.59

22)

1)22.33

23)

4)19.58

24)

8)43.35

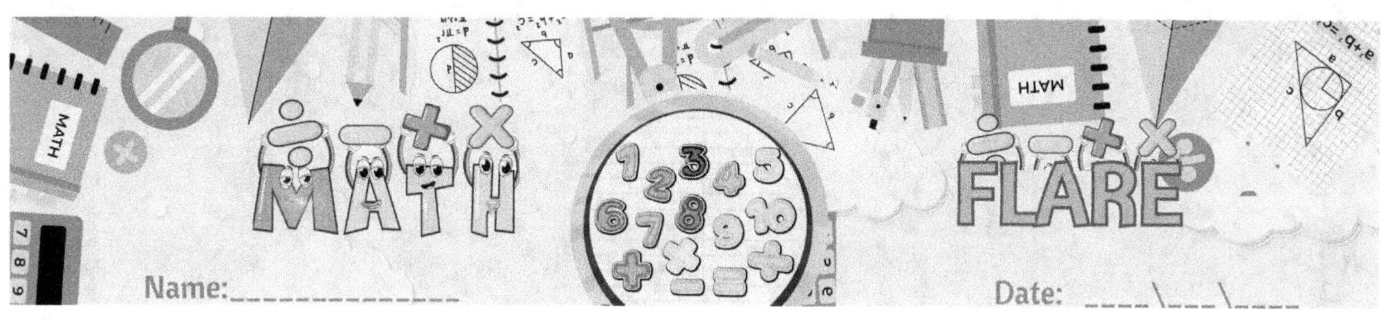

25)

$$5 \overline{)84.19}$$

26)

$$3 \overline{)50.93}$$

27)

$$7 \overline{)48.70}$$

28)

$$3 \overline{)87.01}$$

29)

$$5 \overline{)64.49}$$

30)

$$4 \overline{)46.68}$$

31)

$$7 \overline{)96.67}$$

32)

$$3 \overline{)48.97}$$

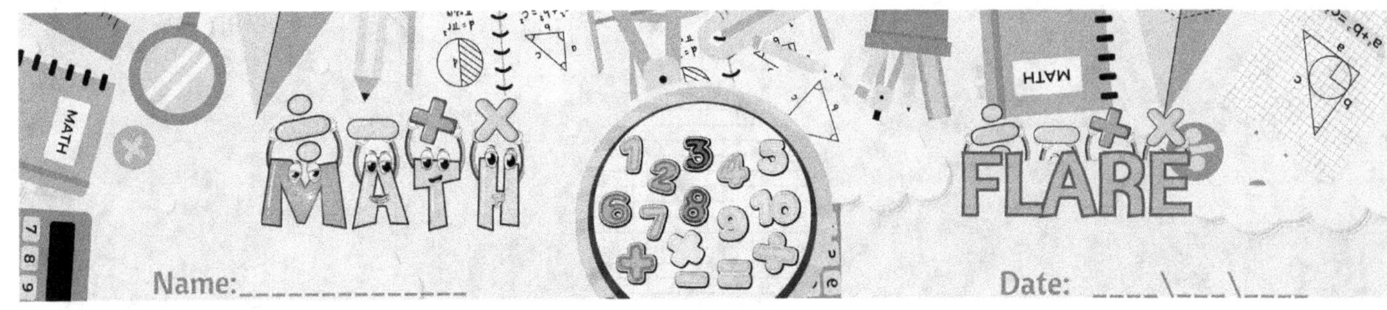

Multiplication Word Problems

1) Christopher can ride 17 miles in one hour. How far can he ride in 20 hours?

$$
\begin{array}{r}
17 \\
\times\ 2\,0 \\
\hline
+\,0\,0\,0 \\
+\,3\,4 \\
\hline
=\,3\,4\,0
\end{array}
$$

17 miles in one hour
how many miles in 20 hours?

So, Christopher can ride 340 miles in 20 hours

2) Lily has 17 jars of jam. Each jar has 11 ounces of jam. How many ounces of jam does Lily have in all?

3) A garden has 12 rows of flowers and 13 flowers in each row. How many flowers are there in total?

4) Camila baked 20 batches of cookies. Each batch had 14 cookies. How many cookies did Camila bake in all?

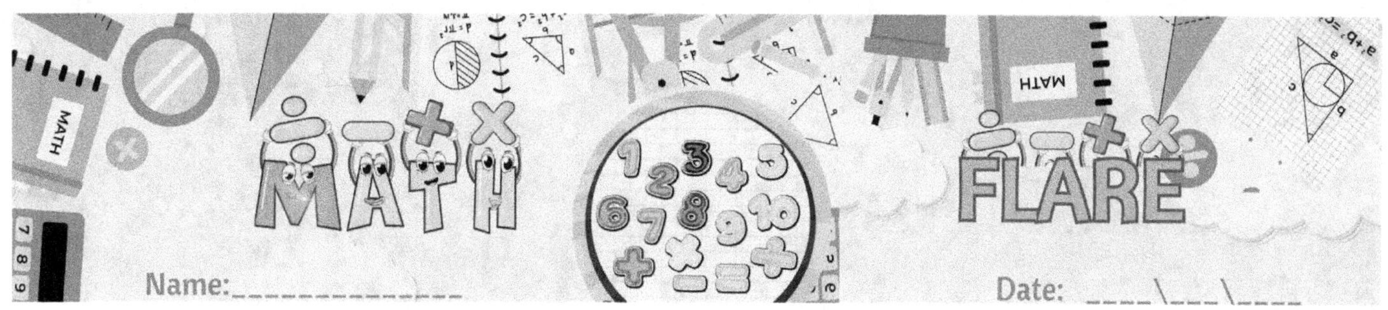

5) Joseph can make 19 sandwiches in 1 hour. How many sandwiches can he make in 19 hour?

6) Colton can lift 18 pounds of weight. How many pounds of weight can he lift in seven repetitions?

7) Caroline has 11 books on each shelf, and there are 20 shelves. How many books does Caroline have in total?

8) If Chase can paint 17 square feet of wall in one hour, how many square feet of wall can he paint in five hours?

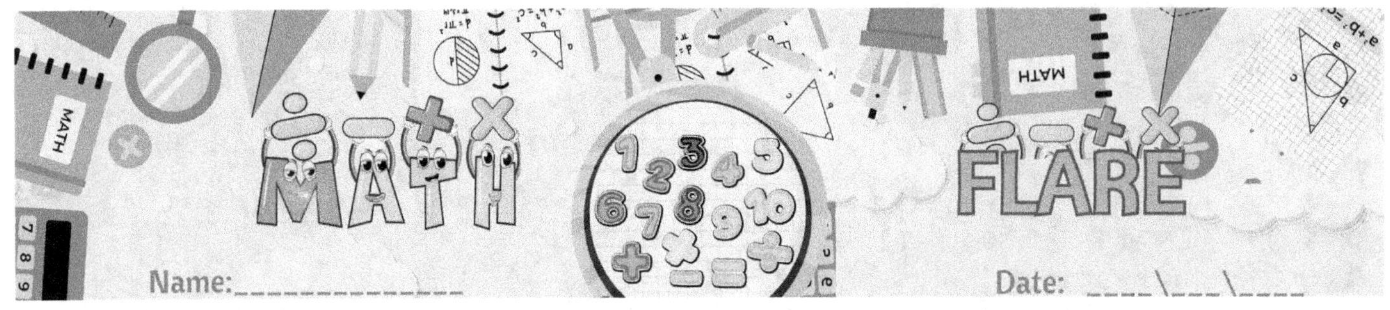

9) A bookshelf can hold six books. If there are 10 bookshelves in a room, how many books can the room hold in total?

10) There are three pencils in each bag. If Harper buys nine bags, how many pencils will Harper have?

11) If a boat travels at eight miles per hour for six hours, how far will it go?

12) There are 16 bananas in each bunch. If Everleigh buys 11 bunches, how many bananas will Everleigh have?

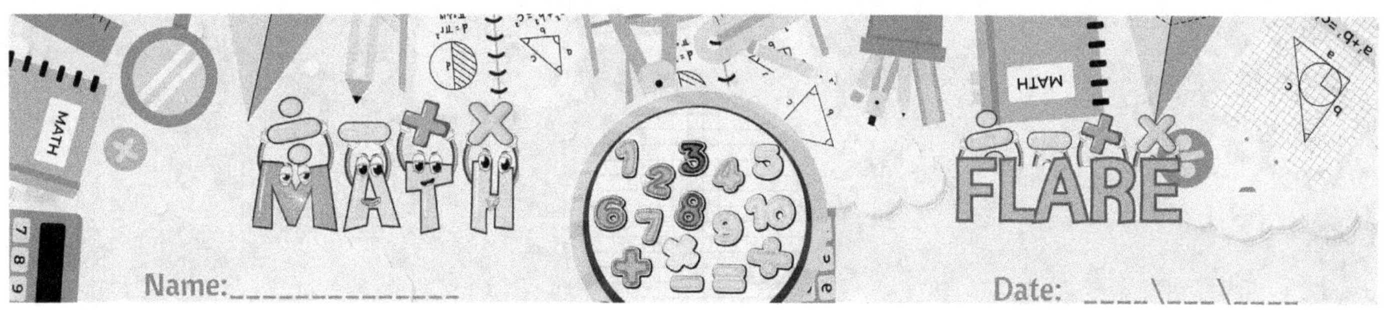

13) Reagan has three yards of fabric, and each dress requires 17 yards of fabric. How many dresses can Reagan make?

14) Lincoln can run two laps in 1 hour. How many laps can Lincoln run in two hour?

15) James can solve 15 math problems in one hour. How many math problems can James solve in 18 hours?

16) There are three pencils in each pack. If Maria buys two packs, how many pencils will Maria have?

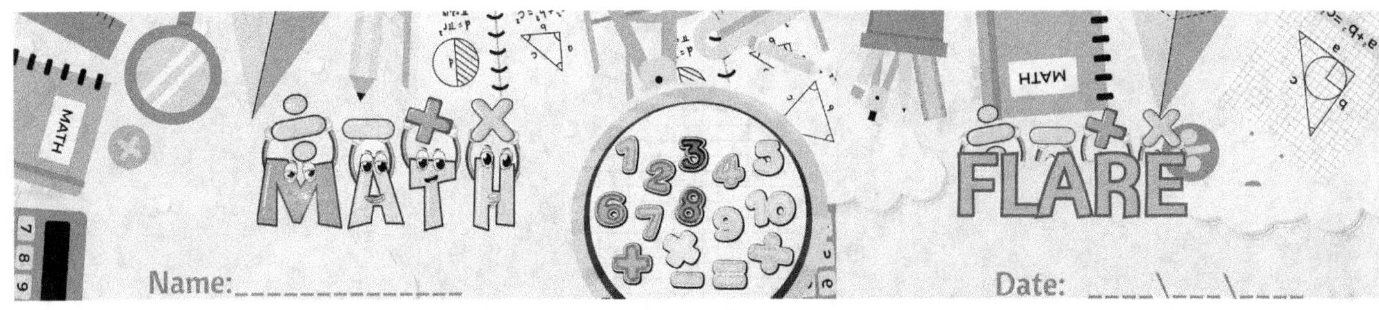

17) There are 12 students in a class. If each student needs seven pencils, how many pencils are needed for the class in total?

18) If a car travels at 18 miles per hour for 11 hours, how far will it go?

19) There are 11 pages in a book. If six books are needed for a class, how many pages are there in total?

20) Easton sells 18 cakes each day at his bakery. If he works 20 days, how many cakes does he sell?

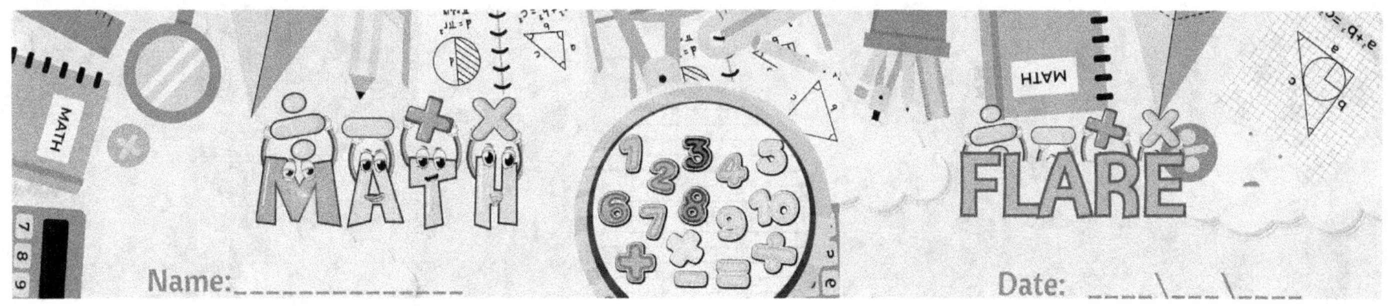

Division Word Problems

1) Jordan is reading a book with 901 pages. If Jordan wants to read the same number of pages every day, how many pages would Jordan have to read each day to finish in 17 days?

$$\begin{array}{r} 97 \\ 17\,\overline{)901} \\ -85 \\ \hline 51 \\ -51 \\ \hline 0 \end{array}$$

Jordan must read 97 pages to finish the book in 17 days.

2) If a box contains 192 chocolates and each person can have eight chocolates, how many people can be served from that box?

3) Scarlett has 1,692 papers. If Scarlett divides them evenly among 18 children, how many papers will each child get?

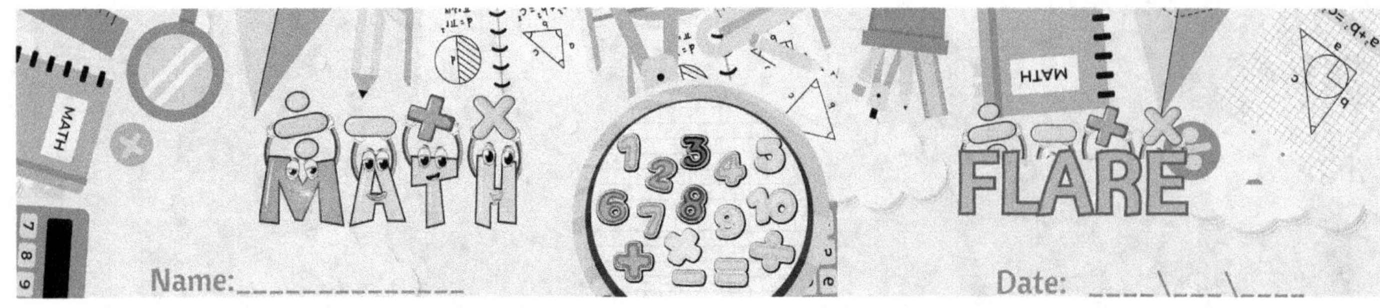

4) Lila is packing 1,920 cupcakes into boxes. Each box can hold 20 cupcakes. How many boxes will Lila need?

5) Isaac has 290 pages of homework to do. If he wants to finish his homework in five days, how many pages does he need to do each day?

6) If Genesis has 539 Sunglassess and wants to distribute them equally to 11 students, how many Sunglassess will each student get?

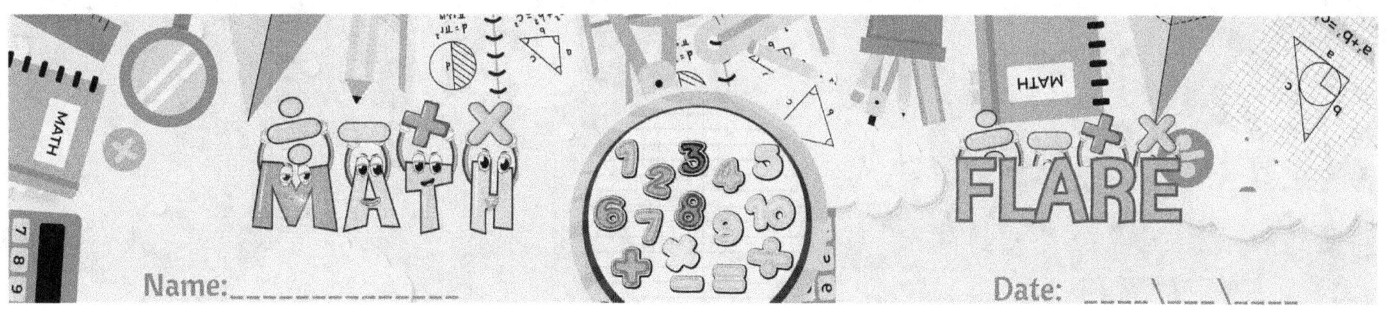

7) Ryder read a book that had 722 pages in 19 days. If he read the same number of pages each day, how many pages did he read per day?

8) If a garden is 180 feet long and it is divided into nine equal parts, how long is each part?

9) If Nathan has 1,314 Balls and wants to share them equally among 18 friends, how many Balls will each friend get?

10) If a store sells nine Kites for $423 how much will each Kites cost?

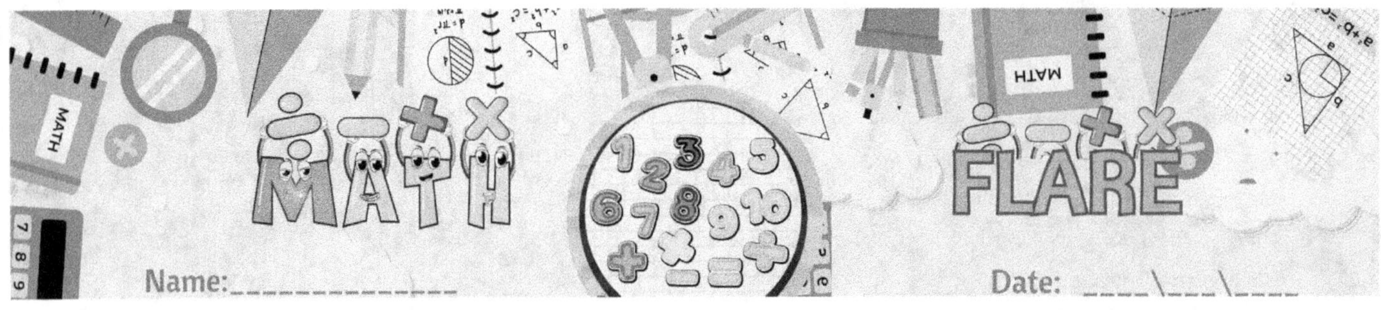

11) Peyton has 1,840 purses and wants to divide them equally among 20 children. How many purses will each child get?

12) Penelope has 378 glasses and wants to divide them equally among nine people. How many glasses will each person get?

13) A pool is 12 meters long. If it is divided into three equal parts, how long is each part?

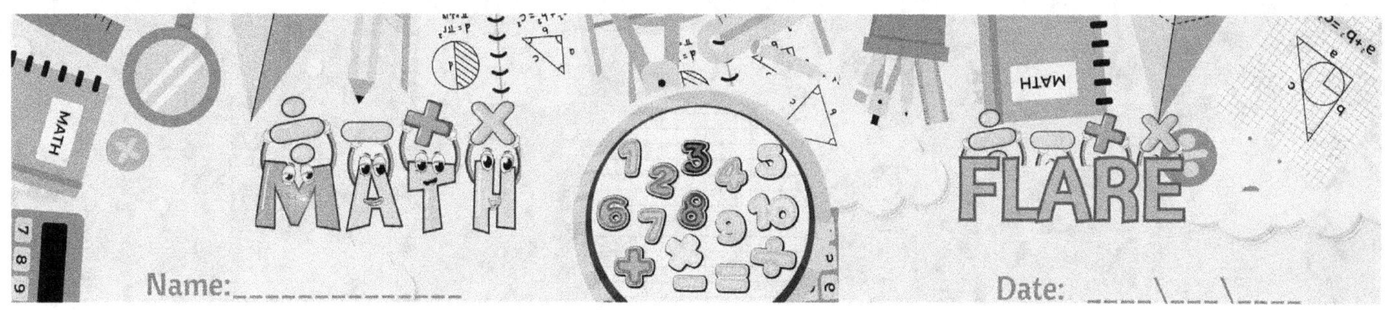

14) At a restaurant, four friends decided to divide the bill equally. If each person paid $95, then what was the total bill?

15) You have 448 Cameras and want to share them equally with 14 people. How many Cameras would each person get?

16) If a field is 1,560 acres and it is divided into 20 equal parts, how many acres is each part?

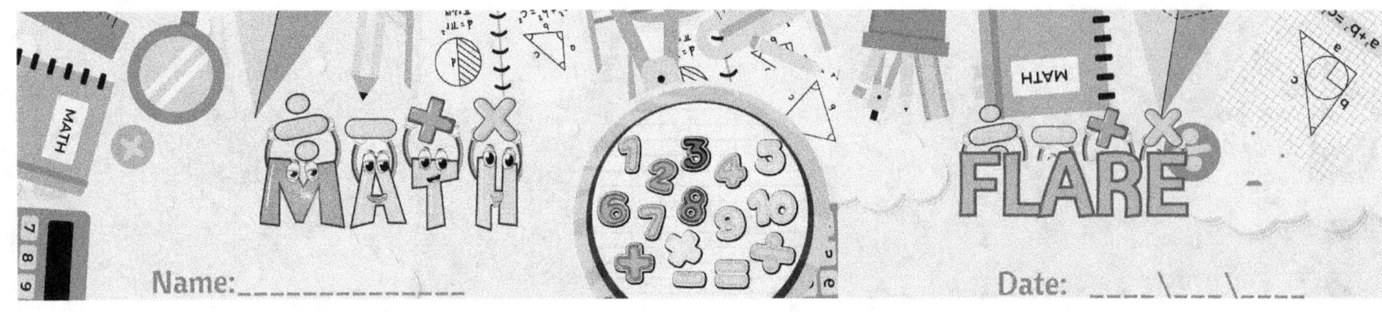

17) A box of Socks has 1,065 Socks. If 15 children each get an equal number of Socks, how many Socks will each child get?

18) Lincoln scored 273 points in three games. What is his average score per game?

19) How many 14 cm pieces of pipe can you cut from a pipe that is 504 cm long?

20) Grace bought three soaps for a total of $279. How much did each soaps cost?

Chapter. 02

Place Value and Expanded Notations

Place value tells us the value of a digit in a number based on where it's placed.

Imagine we have the number 35,987,647.52843. It has 13 digits.

Now, each digit holds a special place. Let's break down the number 35,987,647.52843:

- The digit 3 is in the ten millions place. Its value is 3 × 1,000,000=30,000,000.

- The digit 5 is in the millions place. Its value is 5 × 1,000,000=5,000,000.

- The digit 9 is in the hundred thousands place. Its value is 9×100,000=900,000.

- The digit 8 is in the ten thousands place. Its value is 8×10,000=80,000.

- The digit 7 is in the thousands place. Its value is 7×1,000=7,000.

- The digit 6 is in the hundreds place. Its value is 6×100=600.

- The digit 4 is in the tens place. Its value is 4×10=40.

- The digit 7 is in the ones place. Its value is 7×1=7.

- The digit 5 is in the tenths place. Its value is $5 \times \frac{1}{10} = 0.5$.

- The digit 2 is in the hundredths place. Its value is $2 \times \frac{1}{100} = 0.02$.

- The digit 8 is in the thousandths place. Its value is $8 \times \frac{1}{1000} = 0.008$.

- The digit 4 is in the ten thousandths place. Its value is $4 \times \frac{1}{10,000} = 0.0004$.

- The digit 3 is in the hundred thousandths place. Its value is $3 \times \dfrac{1}{100,000} = 0.00003$.

When we add these values together, we find the value of the entire number:

$$30,000,000 + 5,000,000 + 900,000 + 80,000 + 7,000 + 600 + 40 + 7 + 0.5 + 0.02$$
$$+ 0.008 + 0.0004 + 0.00003 = 35,987,647.52843$$

Let's solve some problems:

Place value of the underlined digit:

$$49,477,31\underline{3}.593 = \underline{\quad 3 \text{ ones} \quad}$$

Expanded notations:

$86,951,328.0$	8 ten millions + 6 millions + 9 hundred thousands + 5 ten thousands + 1 thousand + 3 hundreds + 2 tens + 8 ones
$2,897,917.886$	2,000,000 + 800,000 + 90,000 + 7,000 + 900 + 10 + 7 + 0.8 + 0.08 + 0.006
$614,537,541.1$	6 hundred millions + 1 ten million + 4 millions + 5 hundred thousands + 3 ten thousands + 7 thousands + 5 hundreds + 4 tens + 1 one + 1 tenth

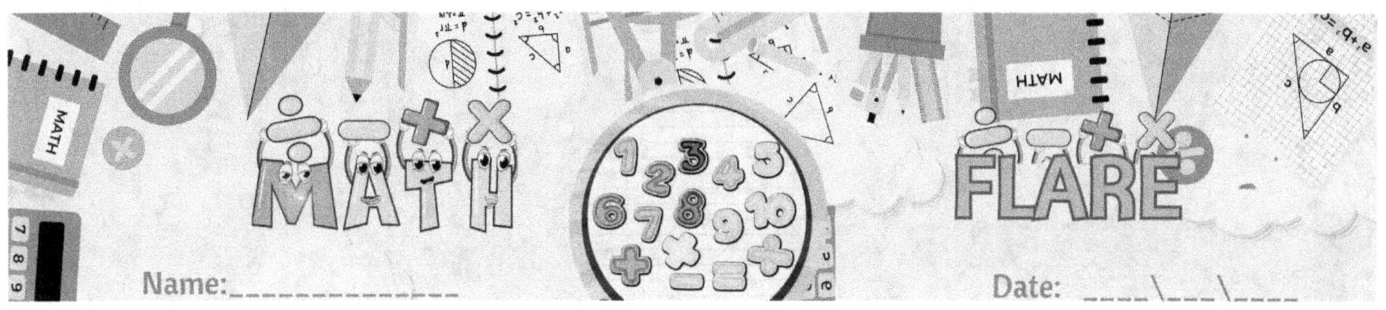

Place Value

Determine the place value of the underlined digit.

1) 49,477,313.593 = _3 ones_

2) 4,446,858,715.4 = ________________

3) 196,238,701.37 = ________________

4) 6,140,691,512.3 = ________________

5) 2,488,844,784.2 = ________________

6) 45,564,398.954 = ________________

7) 61,526,427,651 = ________________

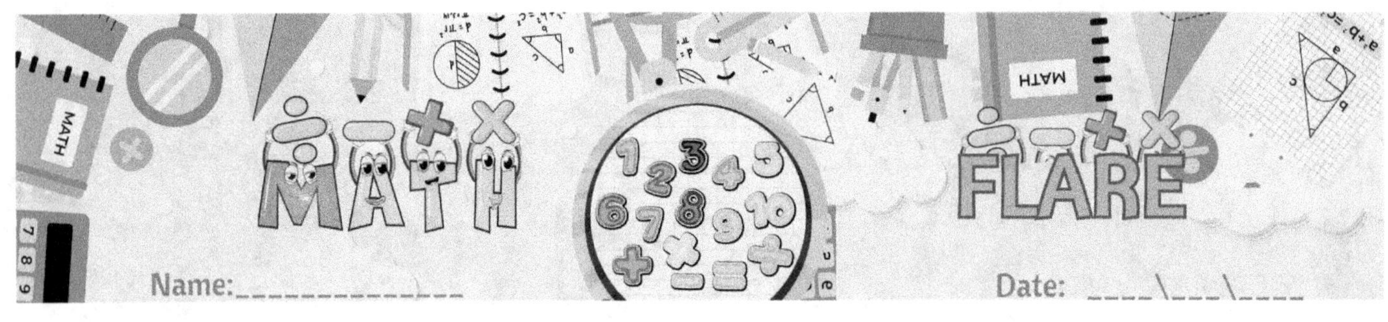

8) 597,015,647.44 = _______________________________

9) 480,638.31393 = _______________________________

10) 6,897,170,850.9 = _______________________________

11) 55,391,669,676 = _______________________________

12) 682,230.03474 = _______________________________

13) 35,532,924.954 = _______________________________

14) 67,466,888.878 = _______________________________

15) 6,069,075.312 = _______________________________

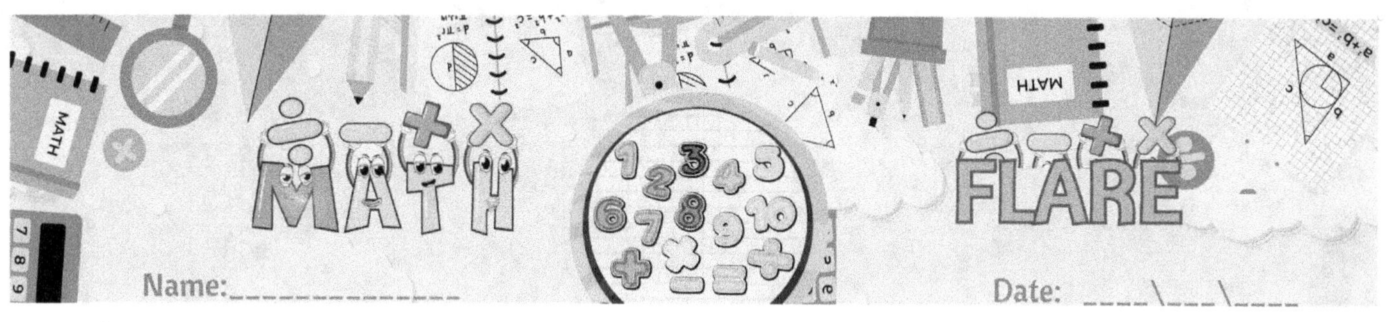

16) 139,839.097<u>7</u>8 = _______________________

17) <u>7</u>4,678,396.654 = _______________________

18) 194,197.<u>7</u>2974 = _______________________

19) 35,8<u>5</u>3,263,231 = _______________________

20) 2,3<u>1</u>5,159.5212 = _______________________

21) 7,904,71<u>5</u>,300.9 = _______________________

22) 757,09<u>6</u>,376.24 = _______________________

23) 50,176,63<u>7</u>,442 = _______________________

24) 110,685.37673 = _______________________________

25) 5,112,365.4745 = _______________________________

26) 69,579,944,833 = _______________________________

27) 90,498,035.005 = _______________________________

28) 3,395,824.2621 = _______________________________

29) 491,958,835.25 = _______________________________

30) 21,004,221.104 = _______________________________

Place Value and Expanded Notation

1)   86,951,328.0 ______________   8 ten millions + 6 millions + 9 hundred thousands + 5 ten thousands + 1 thousand + 3 hundreds + 2 tens + 8 ones

2)   ______________________   4 hundred millions + 2 ten millions + 7 millions + 9 hundred thousands + 5 ten thousands + 3 thousands + 2 hundreds + 6 tens + 2 ones

3)   ______________________   7 hundred millions + 2 ten millions + 1 million + 7 hundred thousands + 3 ten thousands + 9 thousands + 8 hundreds + 1 ten + 7 ones

4) ______________________ 7 hundred thousands + 8 ten thousands + 4 thousands + 4 hundreds + 1 ten + 1 one + 6 tenths + 5 hundredths + 6 thousandths

5) ______________________ 5 millions + 7 hundred thousands + 5 ten thousands + 2 thousands + 7 hundreds + 6 tens + 8 ones + 5 tenths + 2 hundredths

6) ______________________ 4 ten millions + 5 millions + 3 hundred thousands + 8 ten thousands + 5 thousands + 9 hundreds + 6 tens + 2 ones + 5 tenths

7) ______________________ 9 hundred thousands + 5 ten thousands + 6 hundreds + 3 ones + 9 tenths + 4 hundredths + 3 thousandths

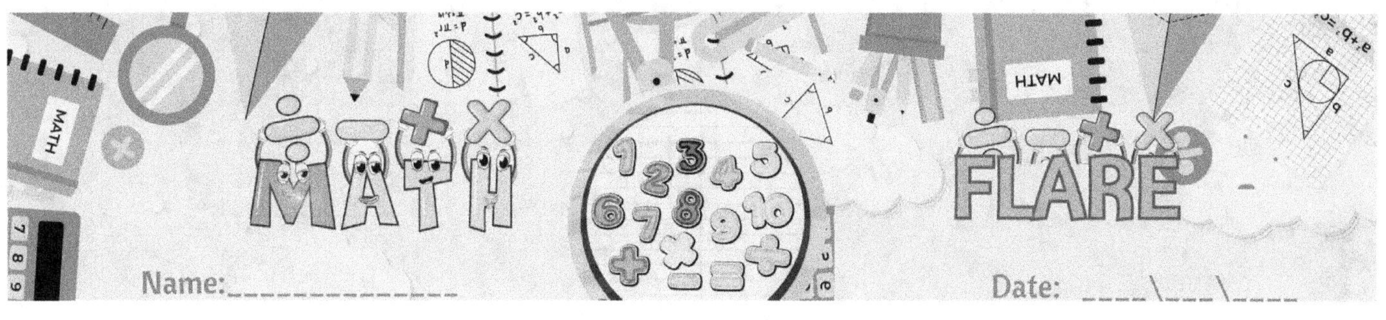

8) _________________________________ 3 hundred thousands + 7 ten thousands + 3 thousands + 2 hundreds + 5 tens + 3 ones + 2 tenths + 8 hundredths + 9 thousandths

9) _________________________________ 4 ten millions + 5 millions + 6 hundred thousands + 4 ten thousands + 8 thousands + 1 hundred + 7 tens + 3 ones + 3 tenths

10) _________________________________ 2 millions + 9 hundred thousands + 6 ten thousands + 7 thousands + 8 tens + 4 ones + 8 tenths + 5 hundredths

11) _________________________________ 5 hundred millions + 3 ten millions + 9 millions + 6 hundred thousands + 5 ten thousands + 1 ten + 7 ones

12) _______________________ 4 hundred thousands + 4 ten thousands + 4 thousands + 5 hundreds + 8 tens + 3 ones + 3 tenths + 8 hundredths + 5 thousandths

13) _______________________ 2 hundred thousands + 7 ten thousands + 5 thousands + 4 hundreds + 6 tens + 3 ones + 5 tenths + 3 thousandths

14) _______________________ 7 millions + 9 hundred thousands + 1 ten thousand + 2 thousands + 7 hundreds + 2 tens + 2 ones + 9 tenths

15) _______________________ 4 millions + 6 hundred thousands + 6 ten thousands + 4 thousands + 3 hundreds + 5 tens + 1 one + 5 tenths + 1 hundredth

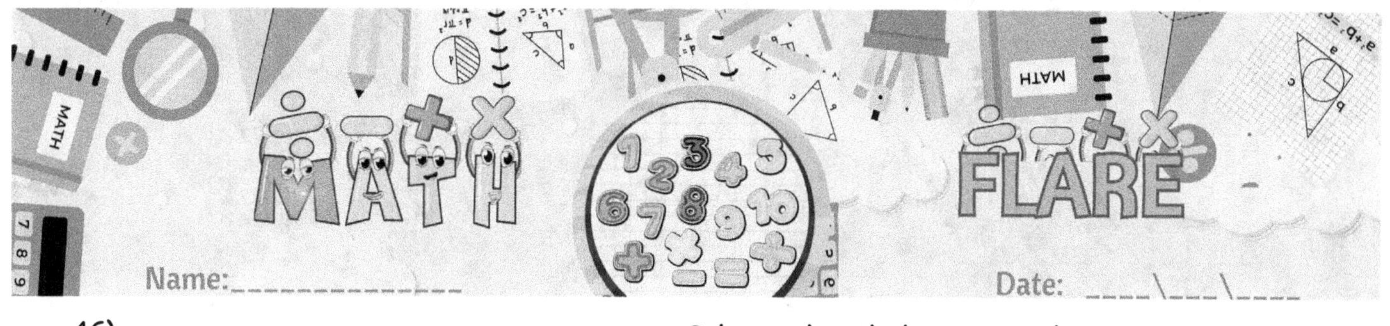

16) _________________________________ 2 hundred thousands + 8 ten thousands + 2 thousands + 8 hundreds + 6 tens + 7 ones + 9 tenths + 1 hundredth + 1 thousandth

17) _________________________________ 8 millions + 1 hundred thousand + 1 ten thousand + 5 thousands + 5 hundreds + 7 tens + 8 tenths + 6 hundredths

18) _________________________________ 7 hundred thousands + 9 ten thousands + 2 thousands + 5 hundreds + 4 tens + 5 ones + 3 tenths + 5 hundredths + 7 thousandths

19) _________________________________ 9 millions + 9 hundred thousands + 2 ten thousands + 7 thousands + 9 hundreds + 5 ones + 2 tenths

20) _______________________________ 8 millions + 6 thousands + 7 hundreds + 6 tens + 2 ones + 3 tenths + 4 hundredths

21) _______________________________ 7 ten millions + 3 millions + 4 hundred thousands + 9 ten thousands + 2 thousands + 1 ten + 7 ones + 8 tenths

22) _______________________________ 9 hundred millions + 8 ten millions + 7 millions + 1 hundred thousand + 8 ten thousands + 6 thousands + 1 hundred + 6 tens + 6 ones

23) _______________________________ 6 hundred thousands + 9 thousands + 3 tens + 8 ones + 8 tenths + 6 hundredths + 6 thousandths

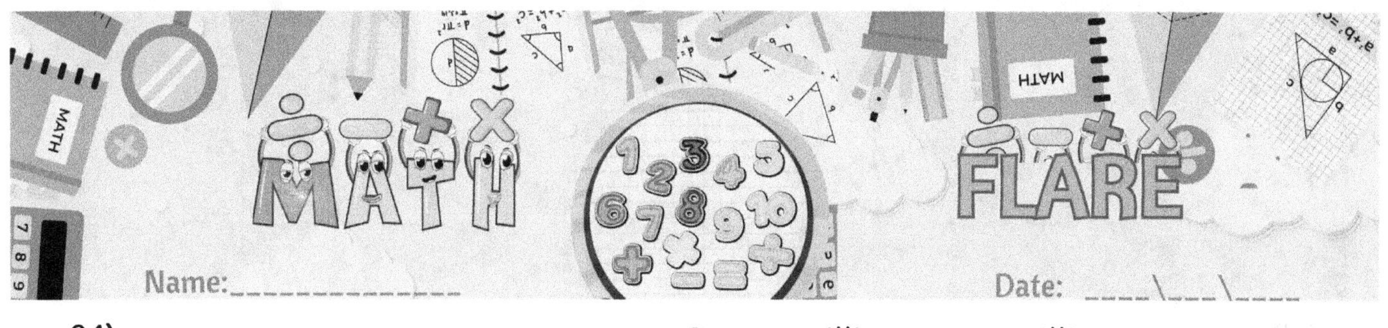

24) _________________________________ 9 ten millions + 4 millions + 2 hundred thousands + 2 ten thousands + 4 thousands + 8 hundreds + 2 tens + 1 one + 5 tenths

25) _________________________________ 2 ten millions + 6 millions + 9 hundred thousands + 8 ten thousands + 7 thousands + 4 hundreds + 1 ten + 1 one + 6 tenths

26) _________________________________ 1 hundred million + 6 ten millions + 8 millions + 6 hundred thousands + 7 ten thousands + 4 thousands + 5 hundreds + 1 ten

27) _________________________________ 2 ten millions + 8 millions + 7 hundred thousands + 2 ten thousands + 5 thousands + 3 hundreds + 7 ones + 4 tenths

28) _________________________ 8 ten millions + 5 millions + 7 hundred thousands + 2 ten thousands + 6 thousands + 5 hundreds + 4 ones + 8 tenths

29) _________________________ 5 hundred millions + 8 ten millions + 2 millions + 5 hundred thousands + 8 ten thousands + 8 hundreds + 1 ten + 2 ones

30) _________________________ 3 hundred thousands + 2 ten thousands + 8 thousands + 9 hundreds + 3 tens + 2 ones + 9 tenths + 8 hundredths + 4 thousandths

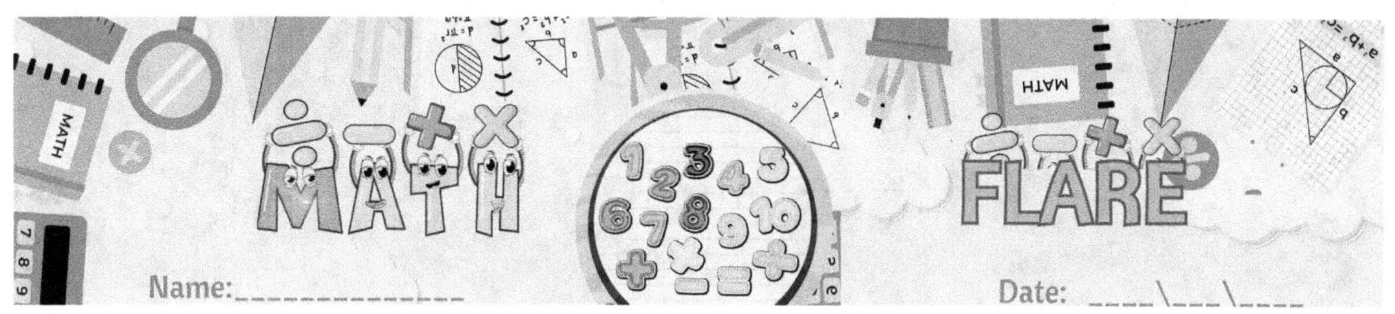

Place Value and Expanded Notation

1) _2,897,917.886_

2,000,000 + 800,000 + 90,000 + 7,000 + 900 + 10 + 7 + 0.8 + 0.08 + 0.006

2) _______________

9,000,000,000 + 600,000,000 + 10,000,000 + 6,000,000 + 600,000 + 60,000 + 7,000 + 300 + 40 + 1

3) _______________

200,000,000 + 20,000,000 + 7,000,000 + 500,000 + 6,000 + 500 + 60 + 2 + 0.2

4) _______________

900,000,000 + 20,000,000 + 1,000,000 + 500,000 + 90,000 + 9,000 + 3 + 0.1

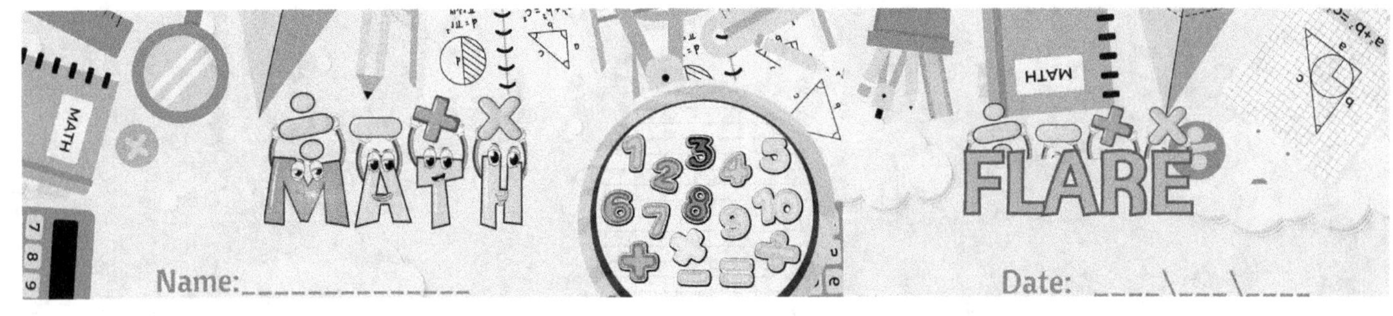

5) _______________________________

10,000,000 + 3,000,000 + 500,000 + 1,000 + 300 + 80 + 7 + 0.6 + 0.07

6) _______________________________

20,000,000 + 1,000,000 + 50,000 + 9,000 + 100 + 90 + 3 + 0.5 + 0.06

7) _______________________________

40,000,000 + 3,000,000 + 400,000 + 90,000 + 7,000 + 400 + 60 + 9 + 0.7 + 0.04

8) _______________________________

8,000,000,000 + 900,000,000 + 50,000,000 + 9,000,000 + 900,000 + 900 + 10 + 6

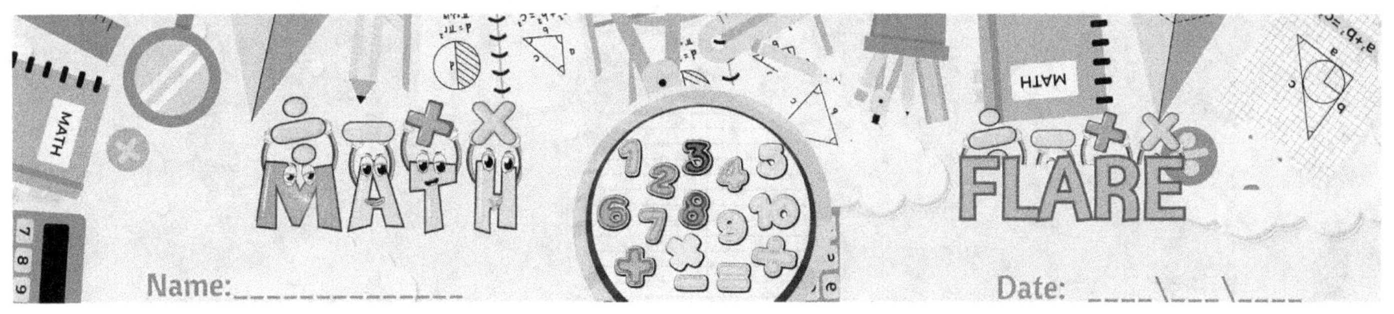

9) _________________________ 8,000,000,000 +
400,000,000 + 20,000,000 +
2,000,000 + 200,000 + 4

10) _________________________ 3,000,000,000 +
400,000,000 + 20,000,000 +
6,000,000 + 100,000 +
70,000 + 3,000 + 100 + 60 + 4

11) _________________________ 30,000,000 + 6,000,000 +
400,000 + 4,000 + 100 + 8 +
0.8 + 0.07

12) _________________________ 30,000,000 + 5,000,000 +
900,000 + 80,000 + 8,000 +
200 + 50 + 2 + 0.5 + 0.06

13) _______________________________ 1,000,000 + 400,000 + 20,000 + 1,000 + 400 + 80 + 0.6 + 0.07 + 0.008

14) _______________________________ 500,000,000 + 40,000,000 + 900,000 + 60,000 + 8,000 + 200 + 70 + 4 + 0.9

15) _______________________________ 50,000,000 + 300,000 + 20,000 + 6,000 + 900 + 40 + 7 + 0.9 + 0.07

16) _______________________________ 7,000,000,000 + 400,000,000 + 9,000,000 + 600,000 + 90,000 + 9,000 + 300 + 90 + 4

17) _________________________________

9,000,000 + 200,000 + 70,000 + 3,000 + 600 + 90 + 1 + 0.002

18) _________________________________

7,000,000,000 + 600,000,000 + 10,000,000 + 8,000,000 + 100,000 + 20,000 + 7,000 + 300 + 90 + 4

19) _________________________________

1,000,000 + 800,000 + 40,000 + 2,000 + 200 + 80 + 4 + 0.8 + 0.07 + 0.007

20) _________________________________

1,000,000 + 900,000 + 20,000 + 8,000 + 100 + 30 + 9 + 0.3 + 0.09 + 0.005

21) _______________________________ 3,000,000,000 + 900,000,000 + 30,000,000 + 4,000,000 + 900,000 + 90,000 + 7,000 + 200 + 50 + 8

22) _______________________________ 50,000,000 + 7,000,000 + 800,000 + 5,000 + 70 + 4 + 0.4 + 0.09

23) _______________________________ 1,000,000 + 70,000 + 6,000 + 500 + 90 + 1 + 0.02 + 0.003

24) _______________________________ 70,000,000 + 3,000,000 + 700,000 + 90,000 + 1,000 + 900 + 10 + 9 + 0.4 + 0.04

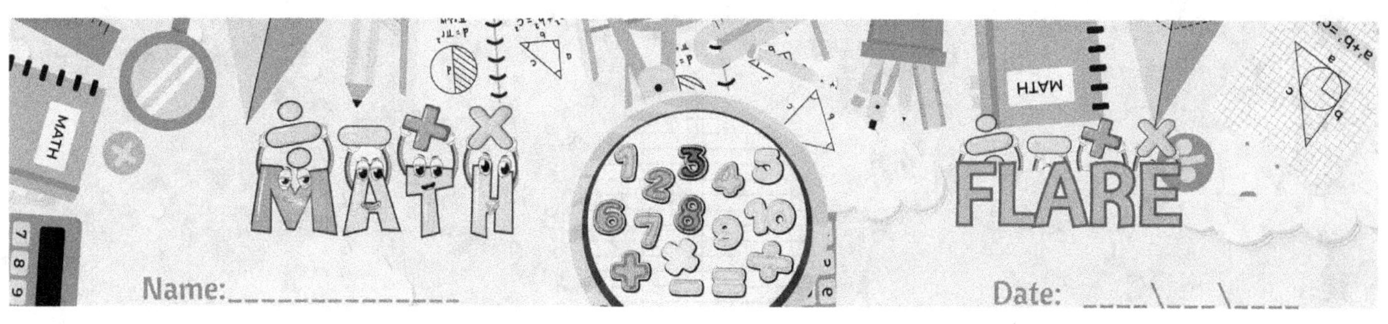

25) _________________________________ 6,000,000 + 700,000 + 90,000 + 2,000 + 500 + 30 + 8 + 0.6 + 0.01 + 0.008

26) _________________________________ 800,000,000 + 80,000,000 + 2,000,000 + 300,000 + 20,000 + 7,000 + 100 + 10 + 3 + 0.8

27) _________________________________ 800,000,000 + 10,000,000 + 8,000,000 + 900,000 + 10,000 + 4,000 + 300 + 90 + 6 + 0.1

28) _________________________________ 7,000,000 + 700,000 + 90,000 + 4,000 + 900 + 10 + 6 + 0.01 + 0.009

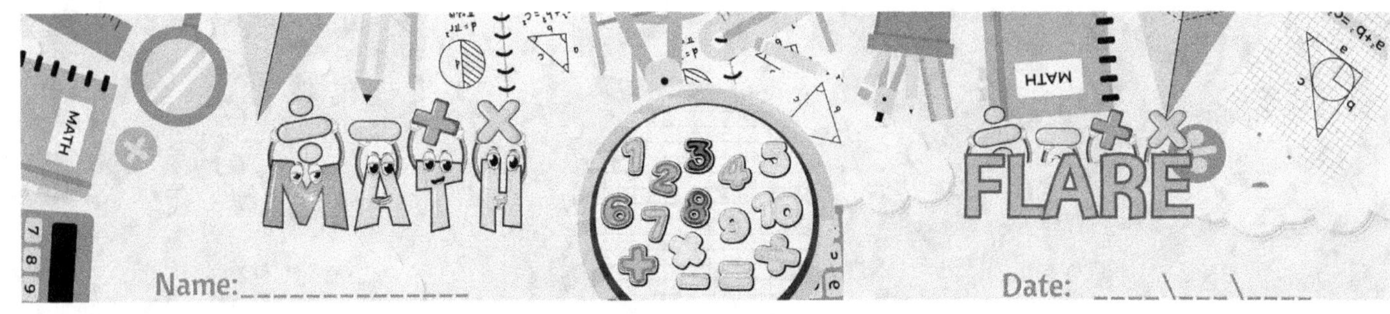

Place Value and Expanded Notation

1) 614,537,541.1   6 hundred millions + 1 ten million + 4 millions
+ 5 hundred thousands + 3 ten thousands
+ 7 thousands + 5 hundreds + 4 tens
+ 1 one + 1 tenth

2) 5,066,023.423

3) 266,606,550.9

4) 1,933,388,948

5) 79,067,247.69

6) 227,548,749.1

7) 1,069,166,962

8) 5,779,832.831

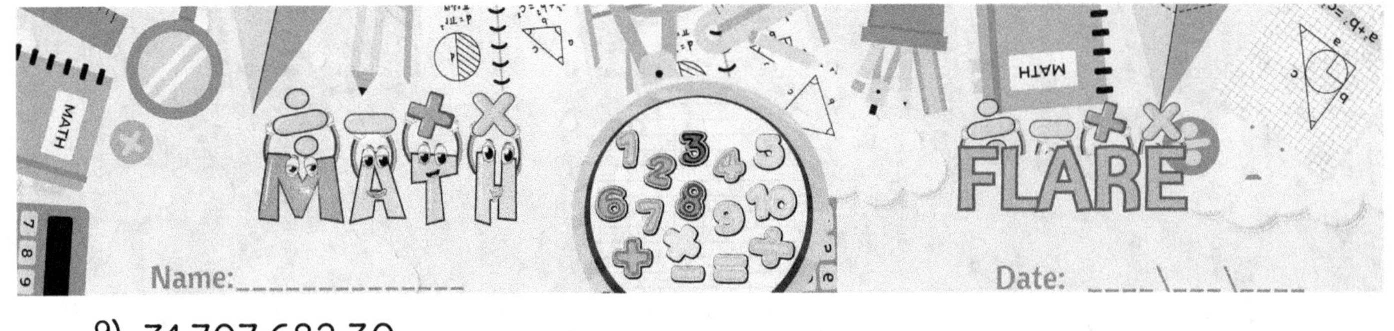

9) 31,707,682.30 _______________________

10) 353,864,500.2 _______________________

11) 7,562,584.138 _______________________

12) 35,584,321.61 _______________________

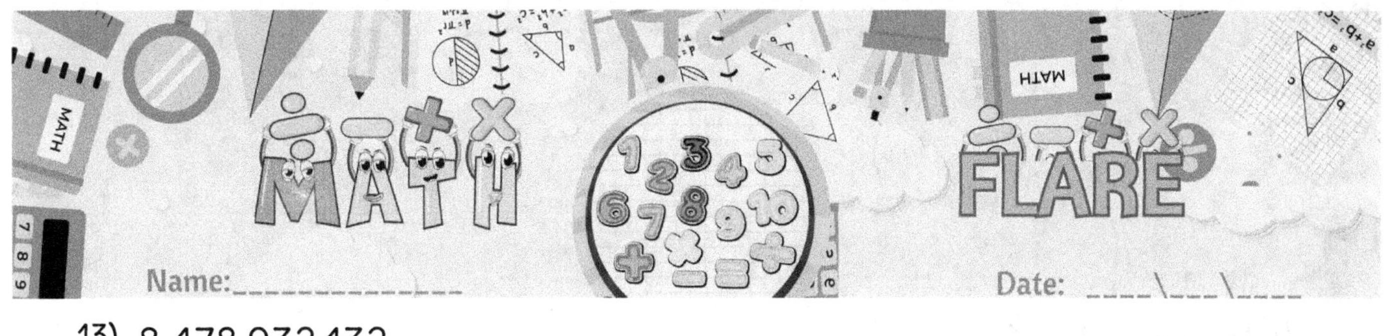

13) 8,478,932.132 ______________________

14) 9,155,669,946 ______________________

15) 950,325,357.3 ______________________

16) 75,017,320.41 ______________________

17) 53,663,514.61

____
____
____
____

18) 4,750,376.532

____
____
____
____

19) 9,450,380.993

____
____
____
____

20) 168,070,591.5

____
____
____
____

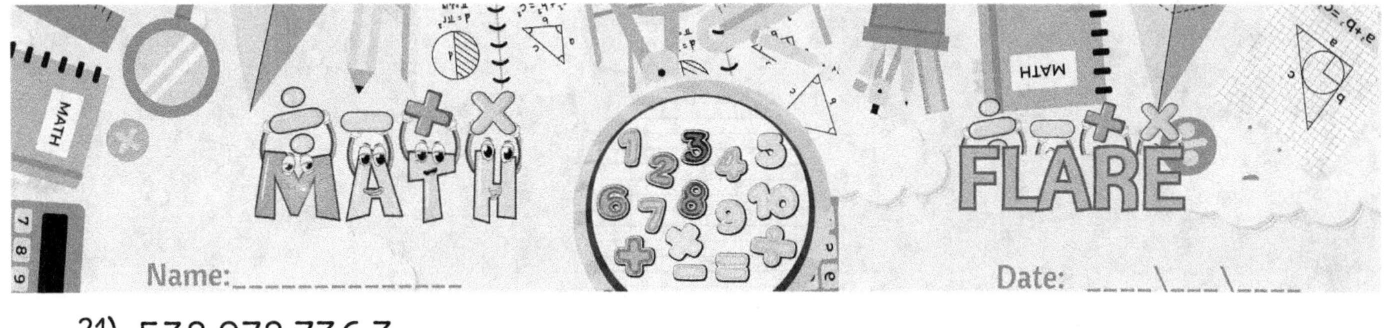

21) 538,978,736.3

22) 528,904,176.5

23) 241,305,409.8

24) 5,254,403.349

25) 7,730,365.612

26) 48,976,687.28

27) 935,433,258.5

28) 7,117,410,436

Chapter. 03

Factors and Multiples

Factors and multiples are two fundamental concepts in mathematics.

Factors:

- Factors are numbers that divide another number without leaving a remainder.

- For example, the factors of 12 are 1, 2, 3, 4, 6, and 12 because these numbers can divide 12 evenly.

- Factors always come in pairs, except for perfect squares.

Multiples:

- Multiples are the result of multiplying a number by an integer.

- For example, the multiples of 3 are 3, 6, 9, 12, 15, and so on because these numbers are obtained by multiplying 3 by 1, 2, 3, 4, 5, and so on.

- Every number has an infinite number of multiples.

Every factor of a number is a divisor of that number, and every multiple of a number is divisible by that number.

Let's solve some problems:

Factors of **44**

2, 4, 11, 22

Multiples of **77**

77, 154, 231, 308, 385

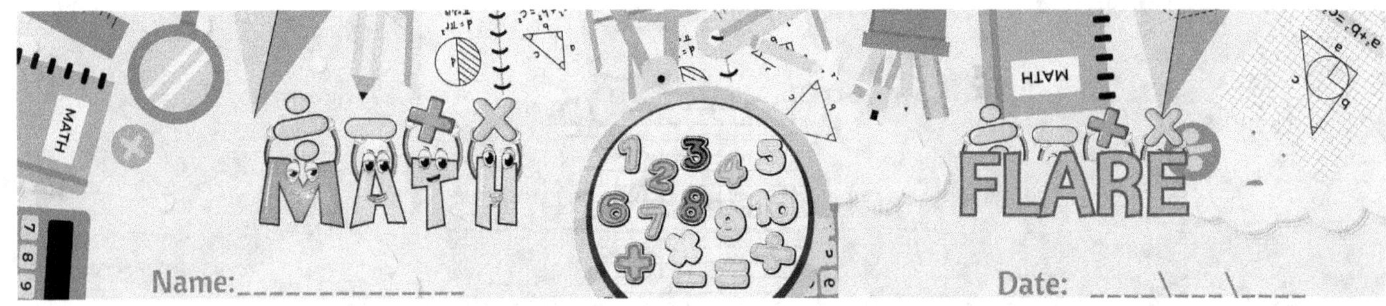

Factors

1) 44   2, 4, 11, 22 _______________________________

2) 2   _______________________________

3) 6   _______________________________

4) 4   _______________________________

5) 91   _______________________________

6) 92   _______________________________

7) 67   _______________________________

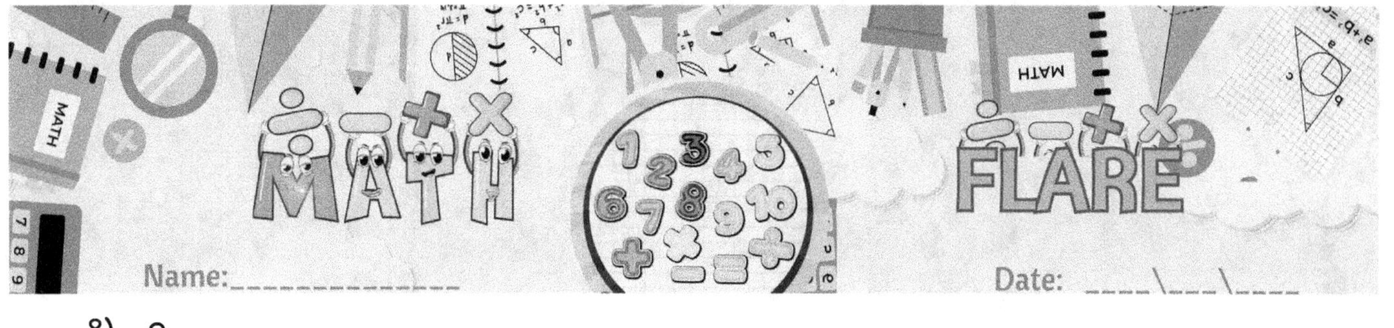

8) 8 ____________________________________

9) 35 ____________________________________

10) 3 ____________________________________

11) 73 ____________________________________

12) 1 ____________________________________

13) 7 ____________________________________

14) 40 ____________________________________

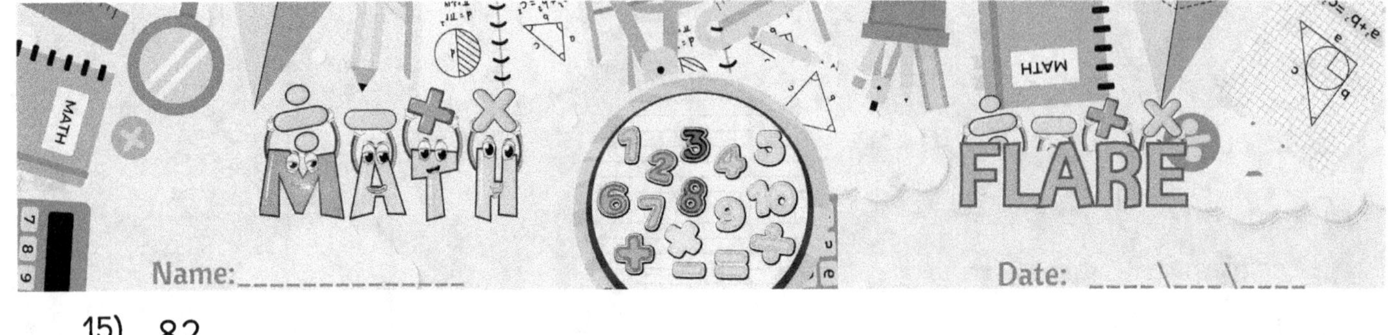

15) 82 ______________________________

16) 22 ______________________________

17) 61 ______________________________

18) 36 ______________________________

19) 5 ______________________________

20) 94 ______________________________

21) 29 ______________________________

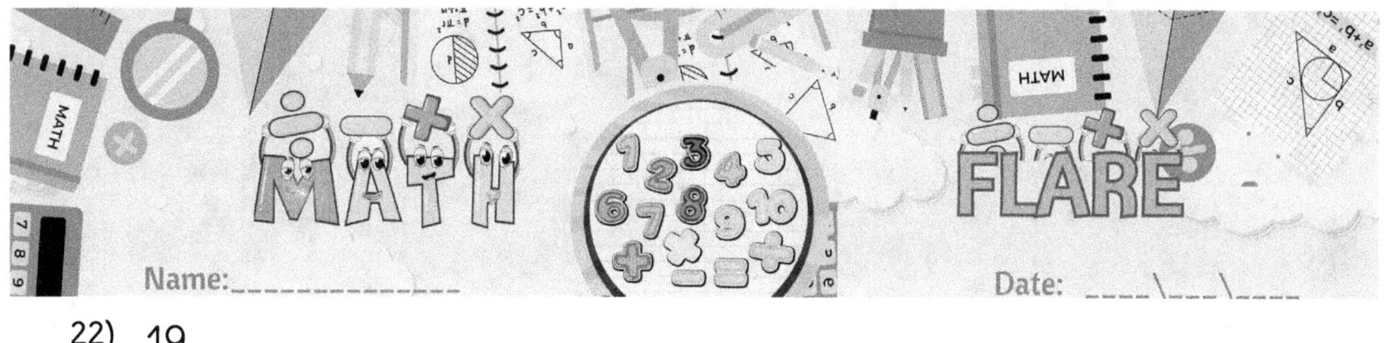

22) 19 ______________________________________

23) 16 ______________________________________

24) 69 ______________________________________

25) 50 ______________________________________

26) 93 ______________________________________

27) 9 ______________________________________

28) 97 ______________________________________

29) 38 ____

30) 33 ____

31) 49 ____

32) 68 ____

33) 42 ____

34) 66 ____

35) 72 ____

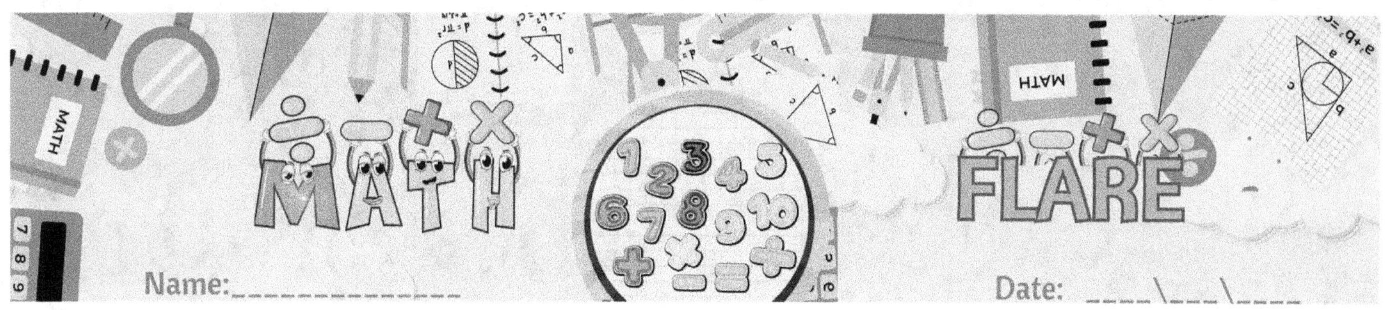

Multiples

1) 77   77, 154, 231, 308, 385

2) 23

3) 1

4) 2

5) 32

6) 9

7) 22

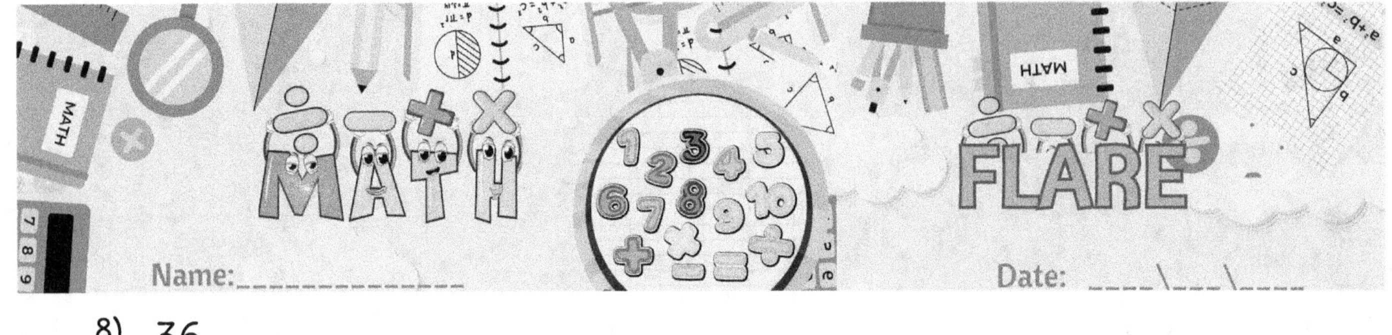

8) 36 ____

9) 83 ____

10) 3 ____

11) 60 ____

12) 24 ____

13) 66 ____

14) 79 ____

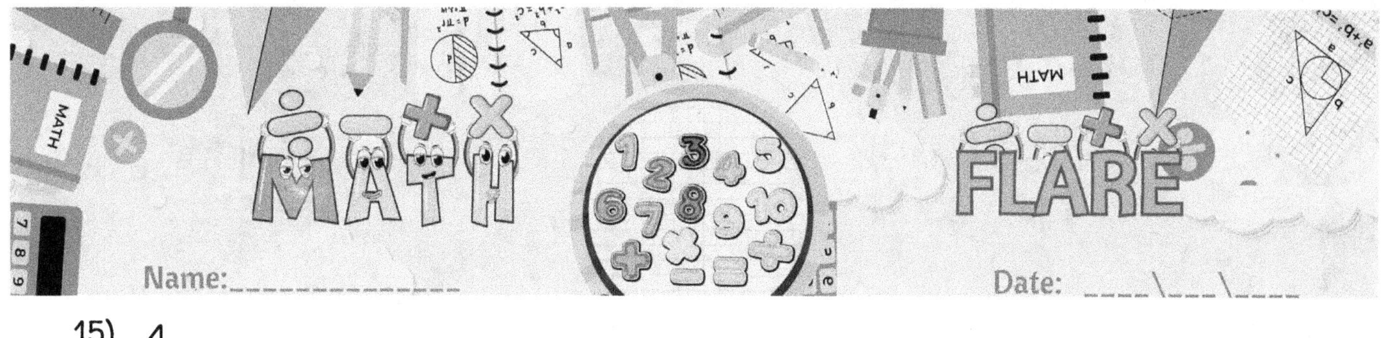

15) 4 ____

16) 91 ____

17) 98 ____

18) 20 ____

19) 6 ____

20) 67 ____

21) 7 ____

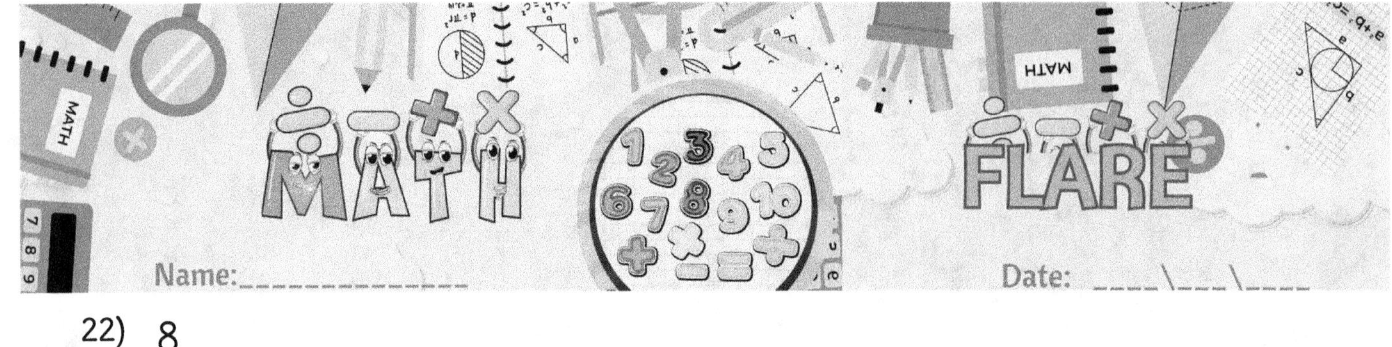

22) 8 ____

23) 34 ____

24) 25 ____

25) 76 ____

26) 5 ____

27) 75 ____

28) 93 ____

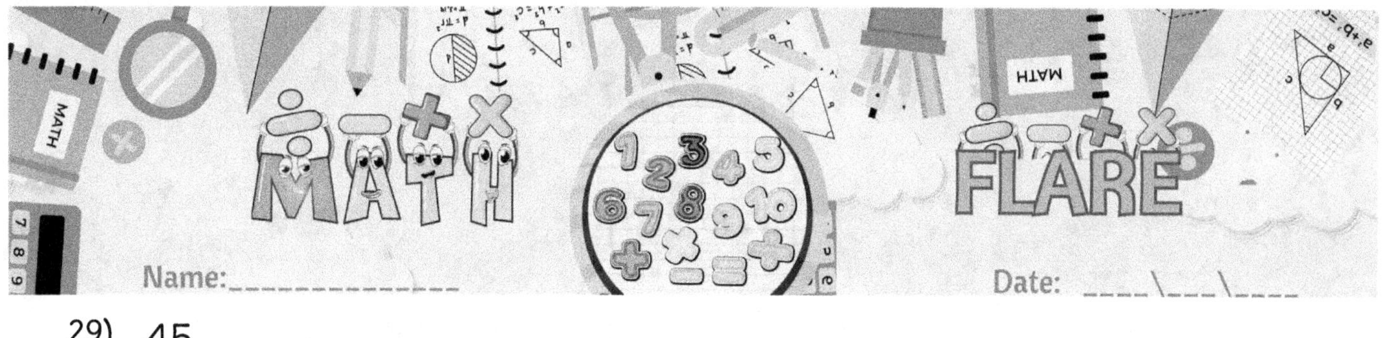

Name:________________   Date: ____________

29) 45 _______________________________________

30) 59 _______________________________________

31) 42 _______________________________________

32) 18 _______________________________________

33) 50 _______________________________________

34) 10 _______________________________________

35) 37 _______________________________________

Chapter. 04

Fractions

Fractions represent parts of a whole. They consist of a numerator (the number on top) and a denominator (the number on the bottom).

For example: we have an orange, and we divide it into 5 equal slices. Each slice represents $\frac{1}{5}$ of the orange. Now, if we take 3 of those slices, we have taken $\frac{3}{5}$ of the orange.

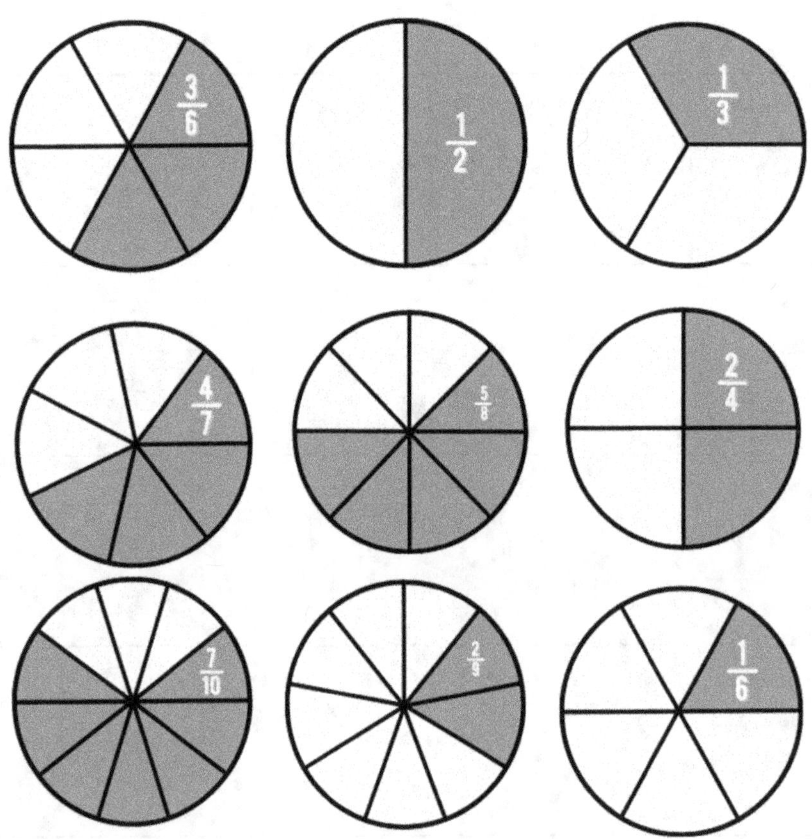

<u>Equivalent Fractions</u>

Equivalent fractions are fractions that represent the same value or part of a whole, even though they may look different.

To find equivalent fractions, you can:

- Multiply or divide both the numerator and denominator by the same nonzero number.
- Simplify fractions to their simplest form.

$\frac{1}{2}$ and $\frac{2}{4}$ are equivalent fractions because if you multiply the numerator and denominator of $\frac{1}{2}$ by 2, you get $\frac{2}{4}$. Similarly, if you divide both the numerator and denominator of $\frac{2}{4}$ by 2, you get $\frac{1}{2}$.

Let's solve a problem:

$$\frac{}{8} = \frac{15}{40}$$

To solve the missing numerator, we can cross multiply.

$$40x = 8 \times 15$$

$$40x = 120$$

$$x = \frac{120}{40} = x = 3$$

$$\frac{3}{8} = \frac{15}{40}$$

Convert Fractions and Decimals

Fraction to Decimal

To transform a fraction into a decimal, we divide the numerator by the denominator.

For instance, $\frac{1}{4}$ equals 0.25 because when we divide 1 by 4, we get 0.25.

In certain cases, the resulting decimal repeats infinitely, like $\frac{1}{3}$, which equals 0.3333...
In such instances, we round the decimal to a specific number of decimal places.

$$\frac{498}{500} = \frac{498 \div 2}{500 \div 2} = \frac{249}{250} = 0.996$$

Decimal to Fraction

Step 1: Write down the decimal as a fraction with the decimal part in the numerator and the place value of the last digit in the denominator.

Step 2: Simplify the fraction if possible.

For example,

$$0.68 = \frac{\frac{17}{25}}{}$$

$$\frac{0.68}{1} = \frac{0.68 \times 100}{1 \times 100} = \frac{68}{100} = \frac{68 \div 4}{100 \div 4}$$

Least Common Multiple (LCM)

The Lowest Common Multiple (LCM) of two or more numbers is the smallest multiple that is divisible by each of the numbers.

There are several methods to find the LCM; however, we will focus on only two:

Listing Multiples: List the multiples of each number until you find a common multiple. For example:

$$
\begin{array}{r|l}
8 & 8,\ 16,\ 24,\ 32,\ 40,\ 48,\ 56 \\
\hline
7 & 7,\ 14,\ 21,\ 28,\ 35,\ 42,\ 49,\ 56
\end{array}
\quad,\ \text{LCM} = \underline{56}
$$

Division Method: Divide each number with the smallest prime number that divides at least one of the numbers evenly. The product of all the divisors and quotients is the LCM. For example:

$$
\begin{array}{c|cc}
2 & 7 & 8 \\
\hline
2 & 7 & 4 \\
\hline
2 & 7 & 2 \\
\hline
7 & 7 & 1 \\
\hline
 & 1 & 1
\end{array}
$$

$$\text{LCM} = 2 \times 2 \times 2 \times 7 = \underline{56}$$

Both methods have their advantages. For big numbers, using the division way is usually faster. But if we are working with smaller numbers or like seeing patterns, listing multiples might make more sense.

Mixed Numbers: Mixed into Improper

Mixed numbers and improper fractions are two different ways to represent the same value of a fraction.

1. **Mixed Number:** A mixed number is a combination of a whole number and a proper fraction. For example, $2\frac{1}{3}$ is a mixed number, where 2 is the whole number part and $\frac{1}{3}$ is the fraction part.

2. **Improper Fraction:** An improper fraction is a fraction where the numerator is greater than or equal to the denominator. For example, $\frac{7}{3}$ is an improper fraction because 6 is greater than 3.

To convert a mixed number to an improper fraction, you multiply the whole number by the denominator of the fraction, add the numerator, and then write the result over the original denominator. For example:

$$2\frac{1}{3} = \frac{2 \times 3 + 1}{3} = \frac{7}{3}$$

To convert an improper fraction to a mixed number, we divide the numerator by the denominator. The quotient becomes the whole number part, and the remainder becomes the numerator of the fraction. For example:

$$\frac{7}{3} = 2\frac{1}{3}$$

Let's solve some problems:

$$2\frac{10}{20} = \begin{matrix} 20 \times 2 = 40 \\ 40 + 10 = 50 \end{matrix} = \frac{50}{20} = \frac{5}{2}$$

$$\frac{91}{14} = \begin{matrix} 91 \div 7 = 13 \\ 14 \div 7 = 2 \end{matrix} = 6\frac{1}{2}$$

$$13 \div 2 = 6 \text{ with a remainder of } 1$$

Mixed Numbers: Addition and Subtraction

To add or subtract mixed numbers, we follow similar steps as when adding or subtracting regular fractions. For instance:

Addition:

- <u>Add the whole numbers:</u> Add the whole number parts of the mixed numbers together.
- <u>Add the fractions:</u> Add the fractions parts of the mixed numbers together.
- <u>Simplify (if needed):</u> If the fraction part of the sum is an improper fraction, simplify it by converting it to a mixed number.

Subtraction:

- <u>Subtract the whole numbers:</u> Subtract the whole number part of the second mixed number from the whole number part of the first mixed number.
- <u>Subtract the fractions:</u> Subtract the fraction part of the second mixed number from the fraction part of the first mixed number.
- <u>Simplify (if needed):</u> If the fraction part of the difference is a negative fraction, borrow from the whole number part or simplify it by converting it to a mixed number.

Let's solve some problems:

$$3\frac{4}{8} + 7\frac{1}{3} = \frac{4}{8} + \frac{1}{3} = \frac{4\times3 + 8\times1}{8\times3} = \frac{12 + 8}{24} = \frac{20}{24} = 10\frac{5}{6}$$

$$3 + 7 = 10$$

$$7\frac{4}{6} - 2\frac{3}{8} = \frac{4}{6} - \frac{3}{8} = \frac{4\times8 - 6\times3}{6\times8} = \frac{32 - 18}{48} = \frac{14}{48} = 5\frac{7}{24}$$

$$7 - 2 = 5$$

MathFlare - Math Workbook 5th and 6th Grade

Mixed Numbers: Multiplication and Division

To multiply or divide mixed numbers, we follow these steps:

Multiplication:

- Convert the mixed numbers to improper fractions: Multiply the whole number by the denominator of the fraction, then add the numerator. Write the result over the original denominator.
- Multiply the fractions: Multiply the numerators together to get the new numerator and multiply the denominators together to get the new denominator.
- Simplify (if needed): If the result is an improper fraction, simplify it by converting it back to a mixed number.

Division:

- Convert the mixed numbers to improper fractions:
- Invert the divisor: Flip the second fraction (the one you're dividing by) so that the division becomes multiplication.
- Multiply the fractions: Multiply the numerators together to get the new numerator and multiply the denominators together to get the new denominator.
- Simplify (if needed): If the result is an improper fraction, simplify it by converting it back to a mixed number.

Let's solve some problems:

$$1\frac{2}{4} \times 3\frac{1}{6} = \frac{3}{2} \times \frac{19}{6} = \frac{3 \times 19}{2 \times 6} = \frac{57}{12} = 4\frac{3}{4}$$

$$1 \times 4 + 2 = 6 = \frac{6}{2} = \frac{3}{2} \qquad 3 \times 8 + 1 = \frac{19}{6}$$

$$2\frac{6}{10} \div 6\frac{6}{7} = \frac{\dfrac{13}{5} \times \dfrac{7}{48}}{} = \frac{13 \times 7}{5 \times 48} = \frac{91}{240}$$

$$2 \times 10 + 6 = 26 = \frac{26}{10} = \frac{13}{5} \qquad 6 \times 7 + 6 = 48 = \frac{48}{7}$$

Multiplication with whole numbers

To multiply a fraction by a whole number, we simply multiply the numerator of the fraction by the whole number while keeping the denominator the same.

For example, if we have $\frac{2}{3}$ and we want to multiply it by 5:

$$5 \times \frac{2}{3} = \frac{5 \times 2}{3} = \frac{10}{3}$$

Let's solve a problem:

$$1 \times \frac{8}{10} = \frac{1 \times 8}{10} = \frac{8 \div 2}{10 \div 2} = \frac{4}{5}$$

Simplify Fractions

To simplify a fraction means to rewrite it in its simplest form, where the numerator and denominator have no common factors other than 1. We follow these steps:

- **Identify the Greatest Common Divisor (GCD):** Find the largest number that divides both the numerator and the denominator evenly.
- **Divide by the GCD:** Divide both the numerator and denominator by their GCD.

For example, let's simplify. $\frac{12}{18}$

Identify the GCD: The factors of 12 are 1, 2, 3, 4, 6, and 12. The factors of 18 are 1, 2, 3, 6, 9, and 18. The largest number that divides both 12 and 18 evenly is 6. So, the GCD is 6.

MathFlare - Math Workbook 5th and 6th Grade

Divide by the GCD: Divide both the numerator and denominator by 6.

$$\frac{12}{18} \div \frac{6}{6} = \frac{2}{3}$$

Another way to simplify fractions is to factorize the numerator and denominator completely, and then cancel out common factors. This method is particularly useful when dealing with larger numbers or algebraic fractions.

Name:________________   Date: ______________

Convert Fractions and Decimals

Convert Fractions to Decimals and Decimals to Fractions.

1) $\dfrac{498}{500} = \dfrac{498 \div 2}{500 \div 2} = \dfrac{249}{250} = 0.996$

2) $0.7 = $ ________________

3) $0.68 = \dfrac{17}{25}$

$\dfrac{0.68}{1} = \dfrac{0.68 \times 100}{1 \times 100} = \dfrac{68}{100} = \dfrac{68 \div 4}{100 \div 4}$

4) $0.725 = $ ________________

5) $0.105 = $ ________________

6) $0.156 = $ ________________

7) $0.955 = $ ________________

8) $0.333 = $ ________________

9) $\dfrac{3}{4} = $ ________________

10) $\dfrac{15}{16} = $ ________________

11) $\dfrac{10}{17} = $ ________________

12) $\dfrac{11}{20} = $ ________________

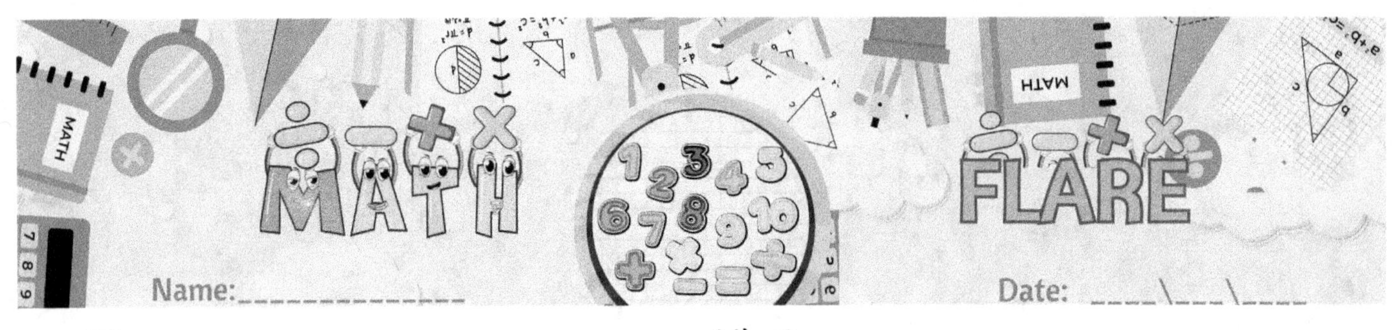

13) 0.278 = _______________

14) $\frac{8}{11}$ = _______________

15) $\frac{1}{4}$ = _______________

16) 0.667 = _______________

17) 0.2 = _______________

18) 0.417 = _______________

19) $\frac{5}{10}$ = _______________

20) 0.158 = _______________

21) 0.014 = _______________

22) $\frac{13}{14}$ = _______________

23) 0.9 = _______________

24) $\frac{4}{8}$ = _______________

25) $\frac{19}{22}$ = _______________

26) $\frac{8}{12}$ = _______________

Mixed Numbers: Improper Fractions

1) $\dfrac{91}{14}$ = _______________

2) $9\dfrac{2}{38}$ = _______________

3) $8\dfrac{2}{10}$ = _______________

4) $8\dfrac{2}{4}$ = _______________

5) $5\dfrac{14}{18}$ = _______________

6) $9\dfrac{3}{4}$ = _______________

7) $\dfrac{124}{20}$ = _______________

8) $5\dfrac{3}{12}$ = _______________

9) $\dfrac{120}{16}$ = _______________

10) $9\dfrac{3}{6}$ = _______________

11) $\dfrac{39}{22}$ = _______________

12) $2\dfrac{25}{34}$ = _______________

13) $5\dfrac{10}{13}$ = _______________

14) $6\dfrac{19}{30}$ = _______________

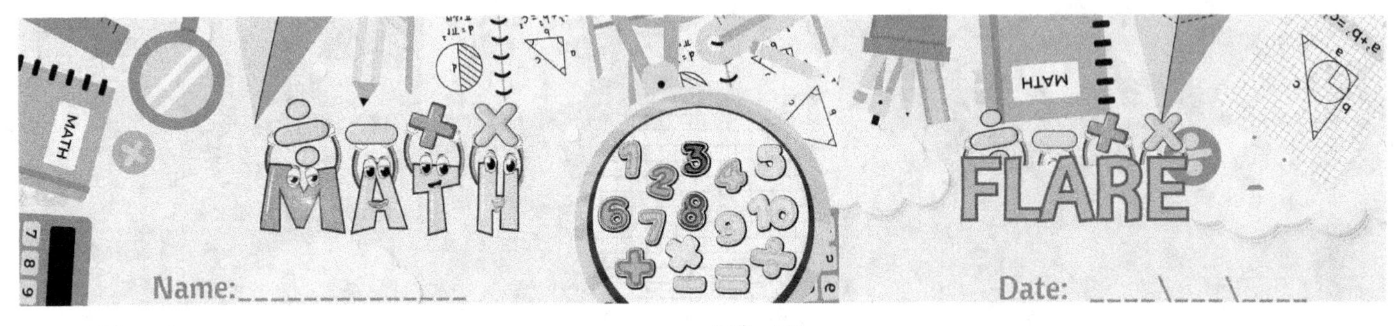

15) $\dfrac{22}{7}$ = _________________

16) $\dfrac{51}{6}$ = _________________

17) $2\dfrac{15}{20}$ = _________________

18) $\dfrac{226}{30}$ = _________________

19) $\dfrac{25}{13}$ = _________________

20) $\dfrac{135}{16}$ = _________________

21) $7\dfrac{2}{3}$ = _________________

22) $2\dfrac{2}{11}$ = _________________

23) $3\dfrac{17}{24}$ = _________________

24) $5\dfrac{22}{34}$ = _________________

25) $\dfrac{64}{9}$ = _________________

26) $7\dfrac{9}{11}$ = _________________

27) $\dfrac{38}{4}$ = _________________

28) $6\dfrac{16}{19}$ = _________________

29) $4\dfrac{6}{24}$ = _________________

30) $5\dfrac{1}{10}$ = _________________

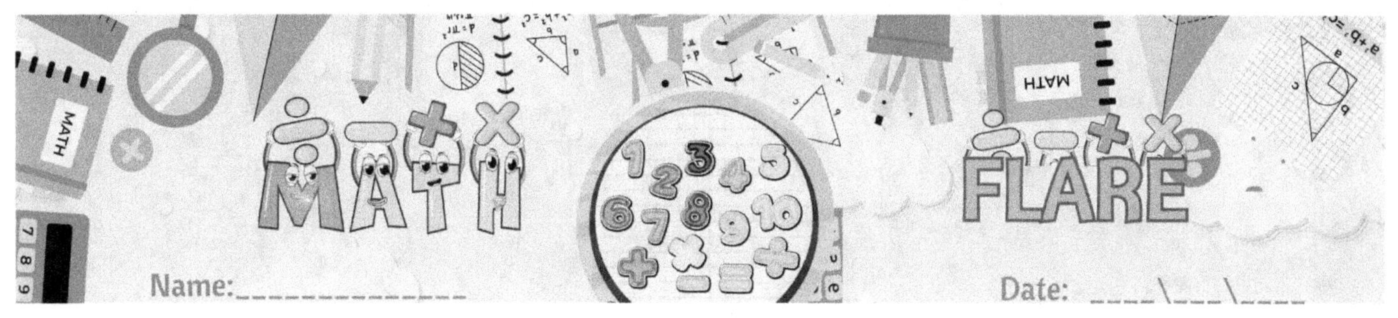

31) $6\frac{6}{26} =$ _______________

32) $2\frac{1}{2} =$ _______________

33) $9\frac{8}{20} =$ _______________

34) $\frac{70}{12} =$ _______________

35) $\frac{23}{4} =$ _______________

36) $3\frac{22}{28} =$ _______________

37) $7\frac{5}{11} =$ _______________

38) $\frac{230}{32} =$ _______________

39) $\frac{111}{16} =$ _______________

40) $4\frac{8}{10} =$ _______________

41) $3\frac{8}{9} =$ _______________

42) $\frac{64}{7} =$ _______________

43) $3\frac{1}{12} =$ _______________

44) $6\frac{5}{8} =$ _______________

45) $2\frac{2}{3} =$ _______________

46) $\frac{50}{18} =$ _______________

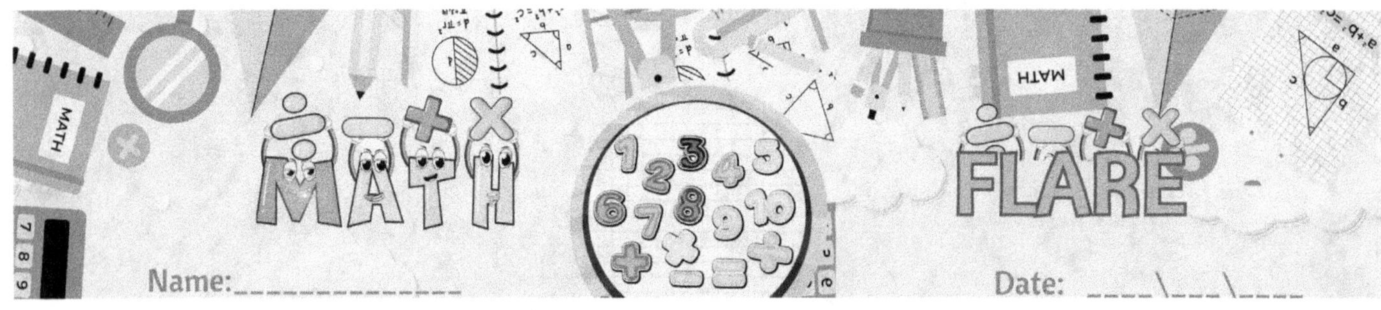

Mixed Numbers: Addition and Subtraction

Calculate.

1) $7\frac{2}{6} + 8\frac{1}{2} =$ $15\frac{5}{6}$

$\frac{44}{6} + \frac{17}{2} = \frac{22\times2 - 17\times3}{3\times2} = \frac{44 - 51}{6} = \frac{95}{6} = 15\frac{5}{6}$

2) $8\frac{1}{3} + 4\frac{6}{9} =$

3) $8\frac{3}{8} + 7\frac{1}{4} =$

4) $1\frac{3}{10} + 7\frac{3}{5} =$

5) $6\frac{1}{2} + 2\frac{1}{3} =$

6) $1\frac{1}{4} + 2\frac{4}{9} =$

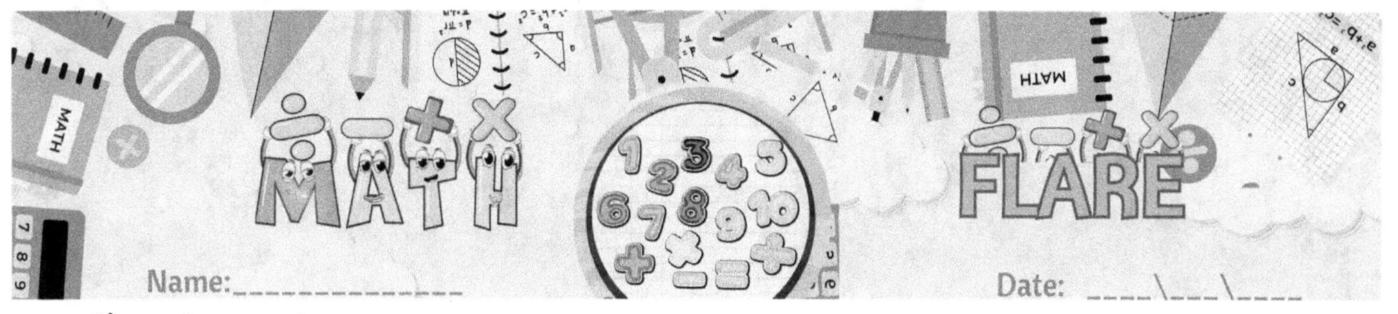

7) $4\frac{6}{8} + 3\frac{1}{6} =$ ___________

8) $9\frac{7}{10} + 7\frac{5}{7} =$ ___________

9) $9\frac{1}{5} - 8\frac{2}{8} =$ ___________

10) $3\frac{1}{3} + 2\frac{3}{7} =$ ___________

11) $9\frac{6}{10} - 6\frac{4}{9} =$ ___________

12) $9\frac{4}{6} + 1\frac{3}{4} =$ ___________

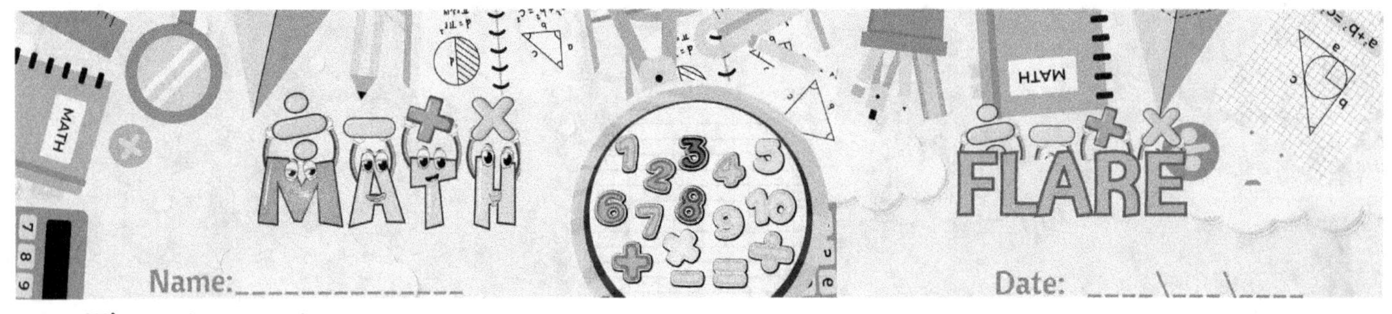

13) $8\frac{1}{2} - 2\frac{1}{3} =$ _______________

14) $8\frac{4}{7} - 4\frac{6}{8} =$ _______________

15) $9\frac{1}{2} + 3\frac{2}{4} =$ _______________

16) $7\frac{1}{5} - 1\frac{9}{10} =$ _______________

17) $6\frac{6}{9} - 6\frac{1}{6} =$ _______________

18) $3\frac{1}{3} + 4\frac{3}{10} =$ _______________

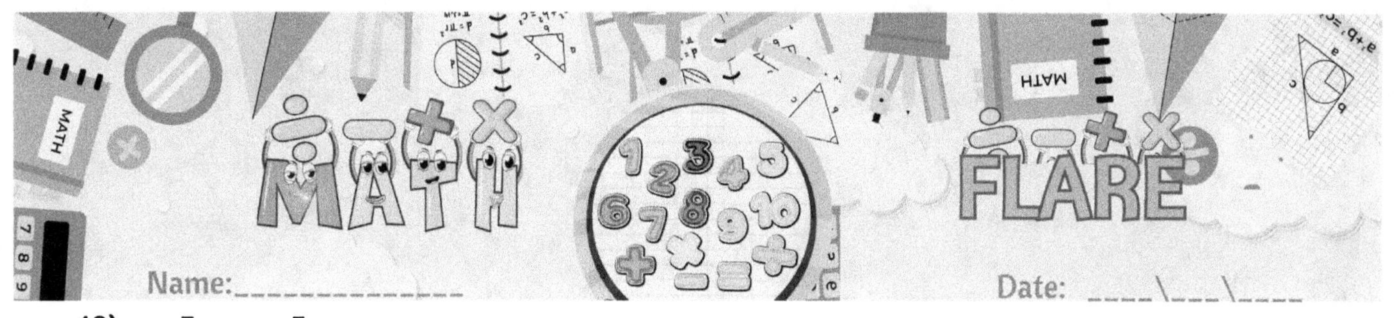

Name:_______________   Date: ____________

19) $3\frac{3}{7} + 2\frac{5}{8} =$ _______________________________

20) $5\frac{3}{5} - 4\frac{1}{6} =$ _______________________________

21) $9\frac{3}{4} + 1\frac{1}{2} =$ _______________________________

22) $3\frac{1}{9} + 8\frac{1}{2} =$ _______________________________

23) $5\frac{5}{6} - 4\frac{2}{5} =$ _______________________________

24) $9\frac{1}{4} + 6\frac{4}{7} =$ _______________________________

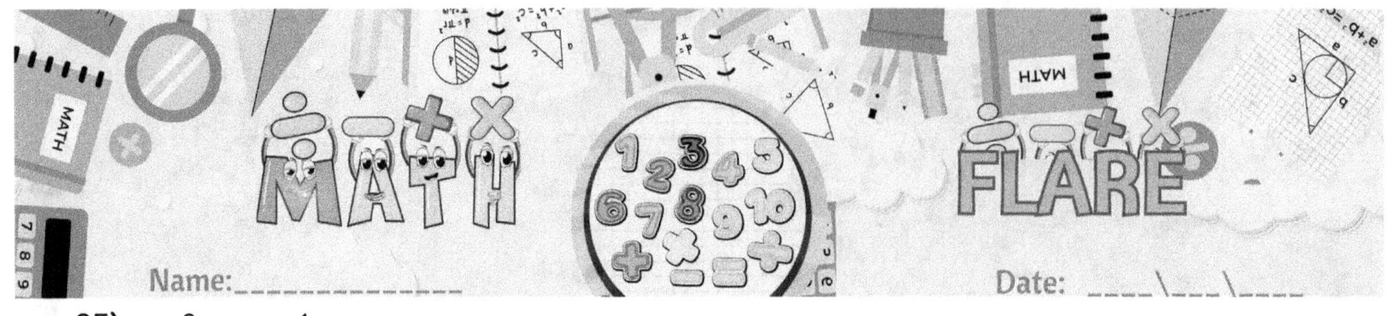

25) $5 \frac{8}{9} - 4 \frac{1}{3} =$ _______________

26) $2 \frac{6}{10} - 1 \frac{3}{8} =$ _______________

27) $3 \frac{3}{4} - 2 \frac{1}{2} =$ _______________

28) $2 \frac{4}{7} + 2 \frac{7}{8} =$ _______________

29) $8 \frac{1}{5} - 7 \frac{2}{3} =$ _______________

30) $2 \frac{4}{10} + 5 \frac{2}{6} =$ _______________

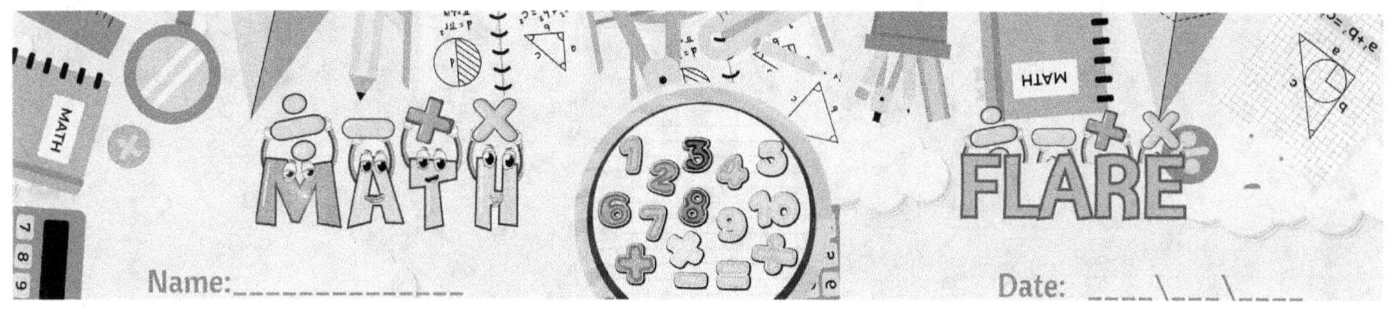

Mixed Numbers: Multiplication and Division

Calculate.

1) $1\frac{7}{10} \times 3\frac{1}{2} =$ $\dfrac{17}{10} \times \dfrac{7}{2} = \dfrac{17 \times 7}{10 \times 2} = \dfrac{119}{20} = 5\frac{19}{20}$

2) $4\frac{2}{6} \times 7\frac{2}{3} =$

3) $1\frac{1}{5} \times 9\frac{2}{10} =$

4) $3\frac{1}{9} \div 3\frac{3}{4} =$

5) $5\frac{2}{8} \div 6\frac{1}{7} =$

6) $1\frac{2}{9} \div 5\frac{3}{10} =$

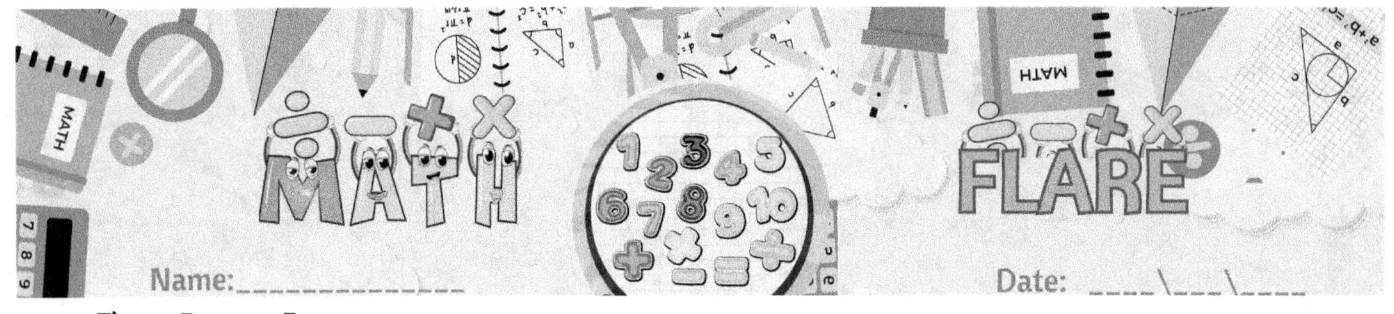

7) $7 \frac{5}{8} \times 1 \frac{3}{7} =$ ___________________

8) $4 \frac{1}{2} \div 5 \frac{3}{4} =$ ___________________

9) $8 \frac{3}{6} \times 7 \frac{2}{3} =$ ___________________

10) $5 \frac{4}{5} \div 6 \frac{3}{6} =$ ___________________

11) $8 \frac{2}{3} \times 1 \frac{3}{9} =$ ___________________

12) $9 \frac{6}{10} \times 4 \frac{5}{8} =$ ___________________

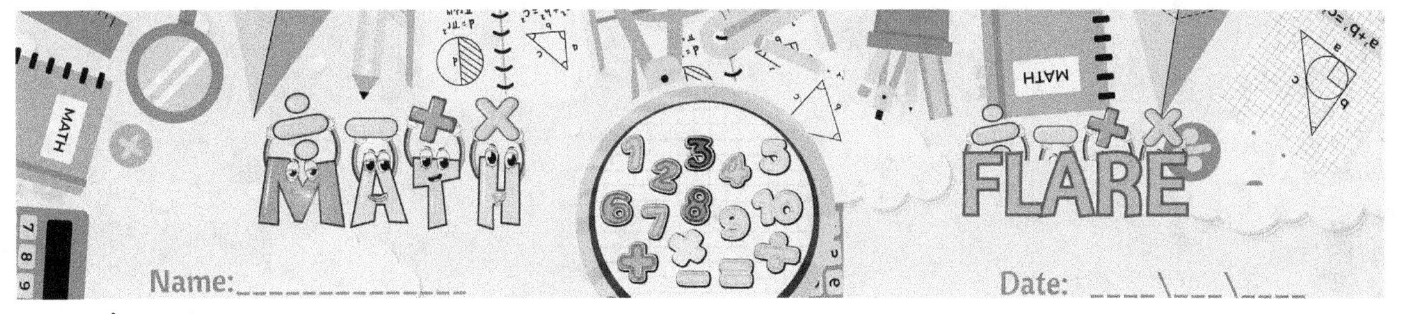

13) $4 \frac{1}{7} \div 5 \frac{3}{5} =$ _______________________________

14) $3 \frac{1}{2} \div 3 \frac{2}{4} =$ _______________________________

15) $1 \frac{3}{9} \div 4 \frac{2}{5} =$ _______________________________

16) $1 \frac{2}{7} \times 8 \frac{1}{2} =$ _______________________________

17) $5 \frac{1}{3} \div 3 \frac{2}{4} =$ _______________________________

18) $7 \frac{2}{6} \div 4 \frac{7}{8} =$ _______________________________

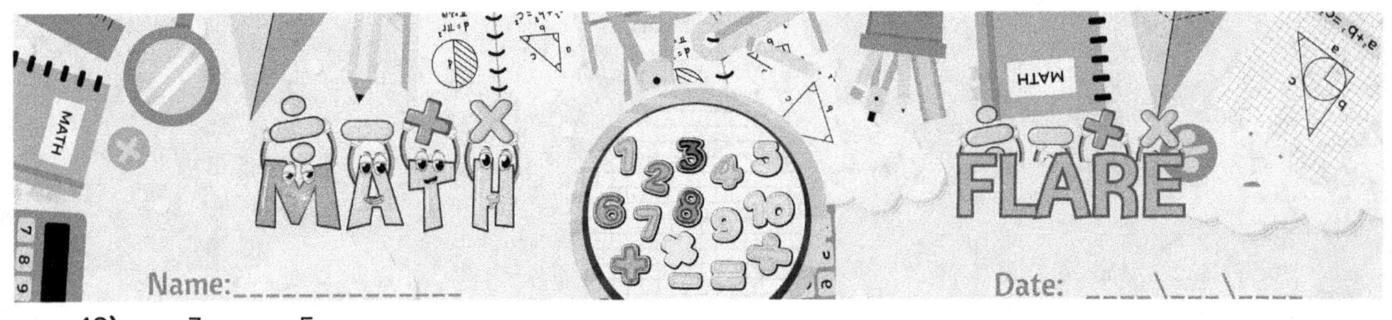

19) $6\frac{3}{10} \times 7\frac{5}{6} =$ ________________________

20) $1\frac{3}{9} \div 9\frac{1}{2} =$ ________________________

21) $4\frac{1}{5} \div 9\frac{2}{3} =$ ________________________

22) $4\frac{4}{8} \times 8\frac{2}{4} =$ ________________________

23) $5\frac{5}{7} \div 9\frac{1}{10} =$ ________________________

24) $3\frac{2}{4} \times 6\frac{6}{7} =$ ________________________

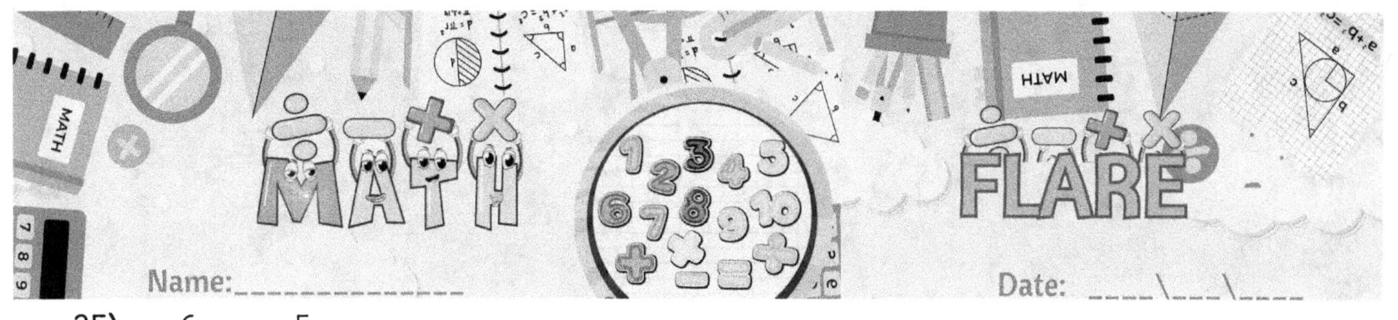

25) $8\frac{6}{8} \div 9\frac{5}{9} =$ _______________

26) $1\frac{5}{6} \div 1\frac{4}{5} =$ _______________

27) $2\frac{9}{10} \times 2\frac{2}{3} =$ _______________

28) $1\frac{1}{2} \times 3\frac{1}{6} =$ _______________

29) $2\frac{1}{2} \times 1\frac{1}{5} =$ _______________

30) $7\frac{1}{4} \div 4\frac{5}{8} =$ _______________

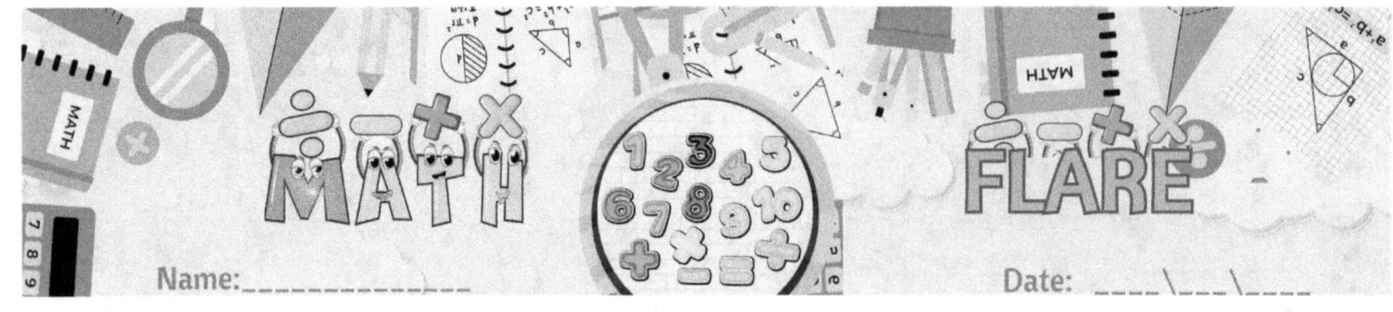

Multiplication with Whole Numbers

1) $1 \times \frac{8}{10} = \frac{1 \times 8}{10} = \frac{8 \div 2}{10 \div 2} = \frac{4}{5}$

2) $3 \times \frac{8}{12} =$ _______________

3) $4 \times \frac{8}{9} =$ _______________

4) $\frac{2}{10}$ of $1 =$ _______________

5) $\frac{10}{15}$ of $2 =$ _______________

6) $\frac{3}{17}$ of $2 =$ _______________

7) $9 \times \frac{1}{4} =$ _______________

8) $2 \times \frac{3}{6} =$ _______________

9) $\frac{4}{7}$ of $9 =$ _______________

10) $\frac{2}{3}$ of $3 =$ _______________

11) $\frac{1}{2}$ of $8 =$ _______________

12) $\frac{9}{11}$ of $2 =$ _______________

13) $4 \times \frac{2}{20} =$ _______________

14) $9 \times \frac{7}{13} =$ _______________

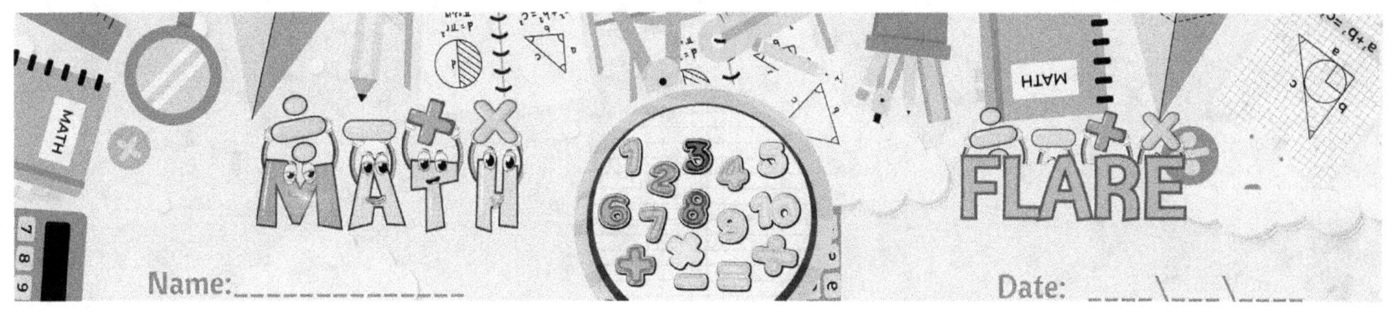

15) $\frac{5}{8}$ of 2 = _______________

16) $\frac{10}{12}$ of 4 = _______________

17) $9 \times \frac{7}{14}$ = _______________

18) $9 \times \frac{11}{19}$ = _______________

19) $4 \times \frac{14}{18}$ = _______________

20) $9 \times \frac{5}{16}$ = _______________

21) $\frac{2}{5}$ of 2 = _______________

22) $\frac{2}{8}$ of 7 = _______________

23) $1 \times \frac{5}{10}$ = _______________

24) $6 \times \frac{15}{19}$ = _______________

25) $\frac{12}{17}$ of 8 = _______________

26) $8 \times \frac{1}{4}$ = _______________

27) $3 \times \frac{1}{3}$ = _______________

28) $\frac{8}{14}$ of 8 = _______________

29) $1 \times \frac{4}{9}$ = _______________

30) $7 \times \frac{1}{5}$ = _______________

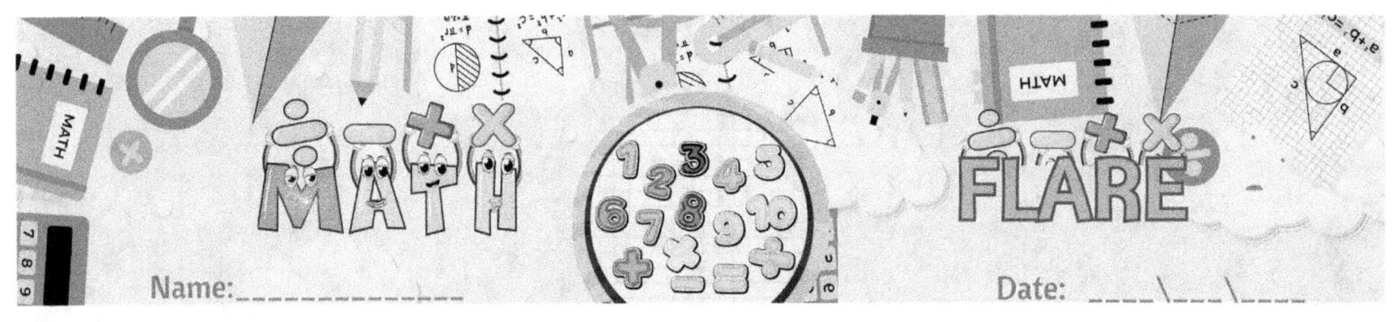

31) $\frac{10}{16}$ of 2 = _______________

32) $5 \times \frac{2}{12}$ = _______________

33) $\frac{2}{11}$ of 7 = _______________

34) $1 \times \frac{17}{20}$ = _______________

35) $8 \times \frac{5}{6}$ = _______________

36) $\frac{11}{18}$ of 1 = _______________

37) $3 \times \frac{11}{13}$ = _______________

38) $\frac{12}{15}$ of 1 = _______________

39) $6 \times \frac{6}{7}$ = _______________

40) $7 \times \frac{5}{12}$ = _______________

41) $5 \times \frac{3}{19}$ = _______________

42) $\frac{3}{7}$ of 2 = _______________

43) $6 \times \frac{6}{18}$ = _______________

44) $\frac{10}{20}$ of 9 = _______________

45) $\frac{15}{17}$ of 5 = _______________

46) $\frac{2}{5}$ of 7 = _______________

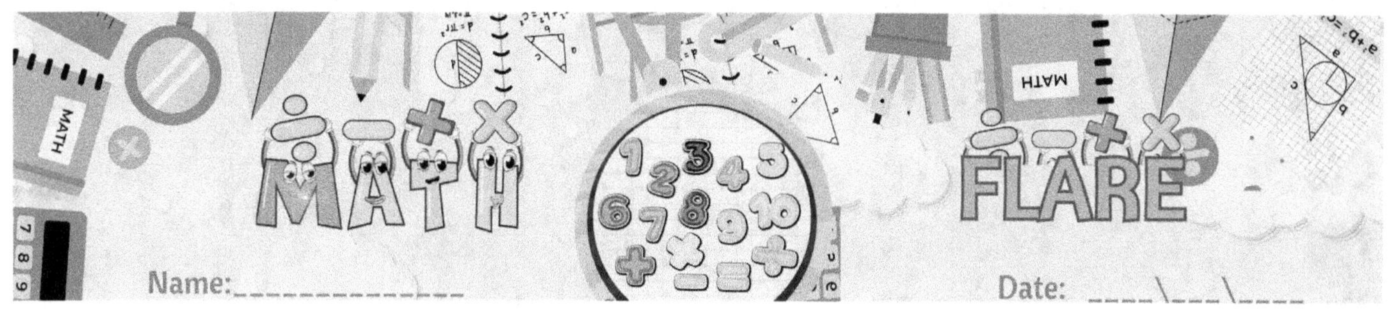

47) $\frac{8}{15}$ of 8 = _________________

48) $\frac{3}{8}$ of 2 = _________________

49) $8 \times \frac{3}{14}$ = _________________

50) $\frac{6}{9}$ of 2 = _________________

51) $7 \times \frac{3}{6}$ = _________________

52) $7 \times \frac{13}{16}$ = _________________

53) $4 \times \frac{2}{4}$ = _________________

54) $3 \times \frac{1}{2}$ = _________________

55) $\frac{2}{11}$ of 4 = _________________

56) $\frac{1}{3}$ of 8 = _________________

57) $5 \times \frac{7}{10}$ = _________________

58) $9 \times \frac{11}{13}$ = _________________

59) $8 \times \frac{12}{18}$ = _________________

60) $\frac{9}{13}$ of 3 = _________________

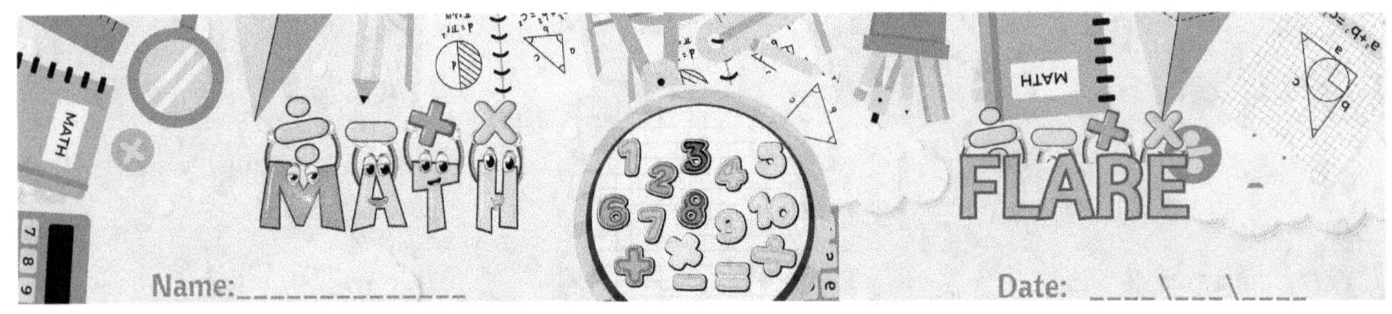

Simplify Fractions: Proper and Improper Fractions

1) $\dfrac{5}{20}$ = $\dfrac{5 \div 5}{20 \div 5} = \dfrac{1}{4}$

2) $\dfrac{180}{30}$ = _______________

3) $\dfrac{105}{27}$ = _______________

4) $\dfrac{399}{56}$ = _______________

5) $\dfrac{267}{57}$ = _______________

6) $\dfrac{270}{35}$ = _______________

7) $\dfrac{63}{21}$ = _______________

8) $\dfrac{30}{6}$ = _______________

9) $\dfrac{637}{70}$ = _______________

10) $\dfrac{272}{136}$ = _______________

11) $\dfrac{9}{18}$ = _______________

12) $\dfrac{378}{117}$ = _______________

13) $\dfrac{128}{16}$ = ___________

14) $\dfrac{623}{105}$ = ___________

15) $\dfrac{1260}{180}$ = ___________

16) $\dfrac{96}{12}$ = ___________

17) $\dfrac{42}{66}$ = ___________

18) $\dfrac{210}{95}$ = ___________

19) $\dfrac{49}{84}$ = ___________

20) $\dfrac{6}{84}$ = ___________

21) $\dfrac{288}{96}$ = ___________

22) $\dfrac{16}{36}$ = ___________

23) $\dfrac{56}{64}$ = ___________

24) $\dfrac{40}{72}$ = ___________

25) $\dfrac{225}{45}$ = ___________

26) $\dfrac{210}{35}$ = ___________

27) $\dfrac{1080}{120}$ = _______________

28) $\dfrac{48}{60}$ = _______________

29) $\dfrac{84}{12}$ = _______________

30) $\dfrac{468}{76}$ = _______________

31) $\dfrac{10}{24}$ = _______________

32) $\dfrac{8}{40}$ = _______________

33) $\dfrac{6}{24}$ = _______________

34) $\dfrac{268}{44}$ = _______________

35) $\dfrac{12}{26}$ = _______________

36) $\dfrac{168}{21}$ = _______________

37) $\dfrac{576}{64}$ = _______________

38) $\dfrac{228}{24}$ = _______________

39) $\dfrac{48}{54}$ = _______________

40) $\dfrac{504}{126}$ = _______________

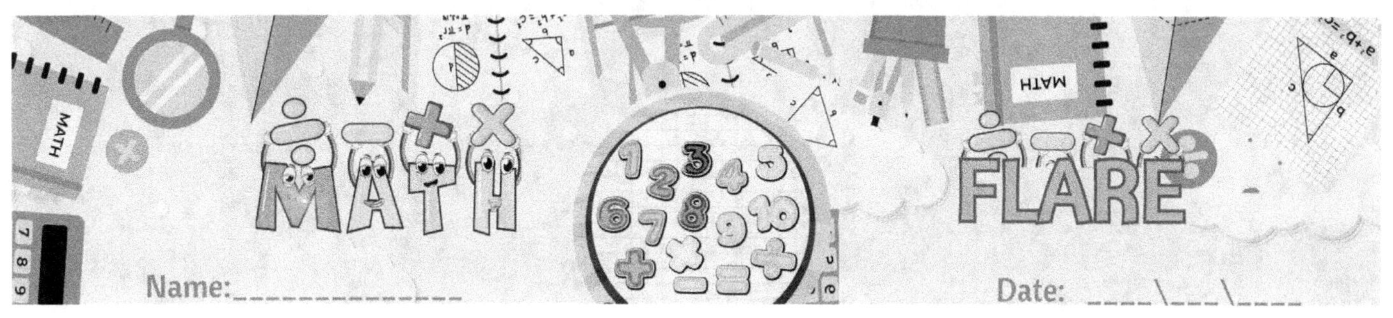

41) $\dfrac{18}{162}$ = ___________________

42) $\dfrac{16}{32}$ = ___________________

43) $\dfrac{86}{16}$ = ___________________

44) $\dfrac{231}{77}$ = ___________________

45) $\dfrac{510}{78}$ = ___________________

46) $\dfrac{504}{102}$ = ___________________

47) $\dfrac{55}{10}$ = ___________________

48) $\dfrac{77}{98}$ = ___________________

49) $\dfrac{760}{80}$ = ___________________

50) $\dfrac{25}{30}$ = ___________________

51) $\dfrac{2}{18}$ = ___________________

52) $\dfrac{252}{36}$ = ___________________

53) $\dfrac{36}{57}$ = ___________________

54) $\dfrac{69}{9}$ = ___________________

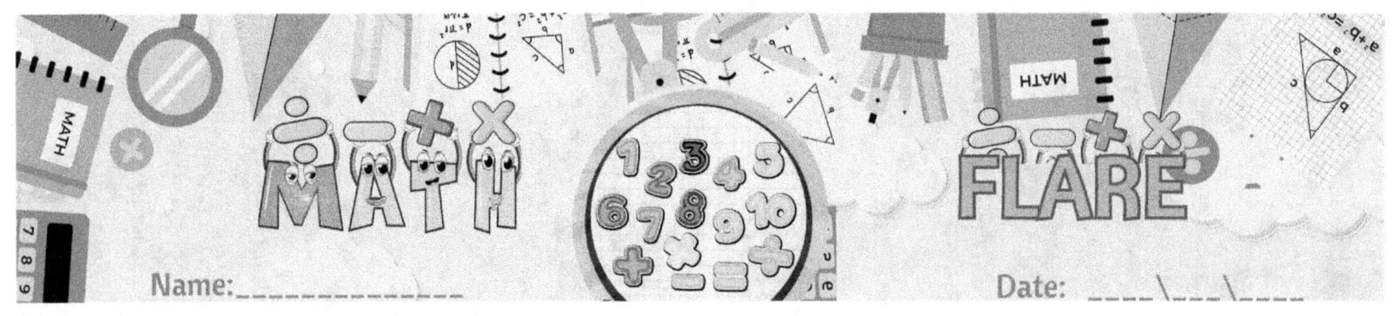

55) $\dfrac{468}{63} =$ _______________

56) $\dfrac{48}{96} =$ _______________

57) $\dfrac{1188}{180} =$ _______________

58) $\dfrac{175}{35} =$ _______________

59) $\dfrac{150}{75} =$ _______________

60) $\dfrac{6}{54} =$ _______________

61) $\dfrac{270}{90} =$ _______________

62) $\dfrac{14}{6} =$ _______________

63) $\dfrac{788}{80} =$ _______________

64) $\dfrac{540}{60} =$ _______________

65) $\dfrac{21}{56} =$ _______________

66) $\dfrac{776}{88} =$ _______________

67) $\dfrac{32}{48} =$ _______________

68) $\dfrac{102}{51} =$ _______________

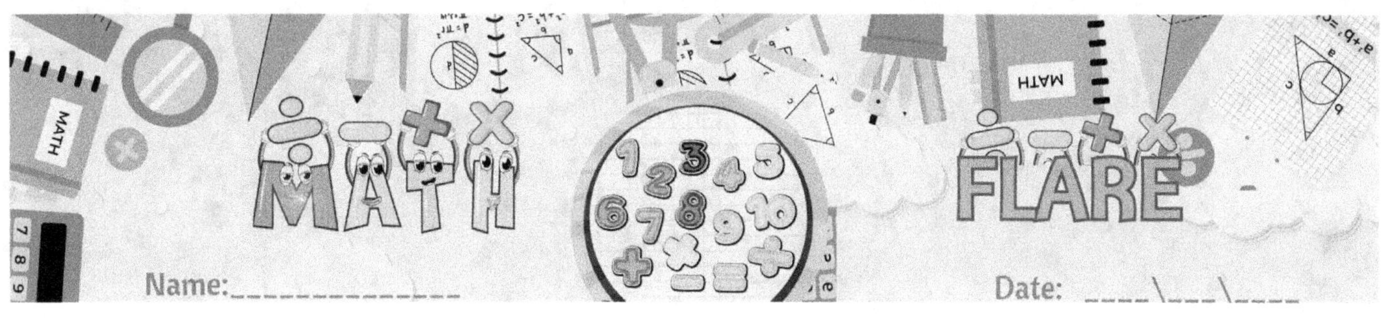

Name:________________ Date: __________

69) $\dfrac{378}{54}$ = _________________

70) $\dfrac{1035}{144}$ = _________________

71) $\dfrac{948}{114}$ = _________________

72) $\dfrac{60}{30}$ = _________________

73) $\dfrac{6}{42}$ = _________________

74) $\dfrac{36}{4}$ = _________________

75) $\dfrac{216}{54}$ = _________________

76) $\dfrac{195}{65}$ = _________________

77) $\dfrac{12}{40}$ = _________________

78) $\dfrac{70}{98}$ = _________________

79) $\dfrac{245}{28}$ = _________________

80) $\dfrac{84}{38}$ = _________________

81) $\dfrac{4}{8}$ = _________________

82) $\dfrac{749}{84}$ = _________________

MathFlare - Math Workbook 5th and 6th Grade

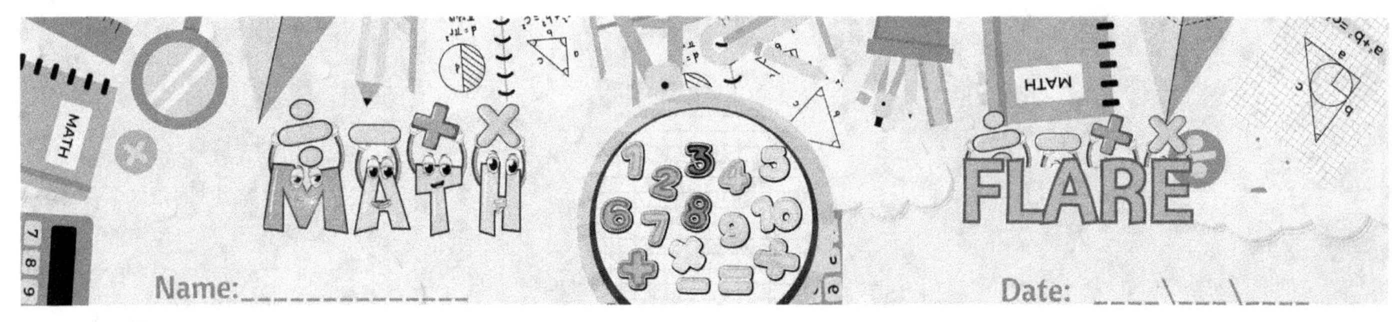

83) $\dfrac{90}{42}$ = _______________

84) $\dfrac{245}{35}$ = _______________

85) $\dfrac{730}{100}$ = _______________

86) $\dfrac{12}{36}$ = _______________

87) $\dfrac{168}{56}$ = _______________

88) $\dfrac{36}{99}$ = _______________

89) $\dfrac{2}{4}$ = _______________

90) $\dfrac{152}{64}$ = _______________

91) $\dfrac{36}{78}$ = _______________

92) $\dfrac{505}{85}$ = _______________

93) $\dfrac{8}{12}$ = _______________

94) $\dfrac{375}{75}$ = _______________

95) $\dfrac{12}{64}$ = _______________

96) $\dfrac{65}{90}$ = _______________

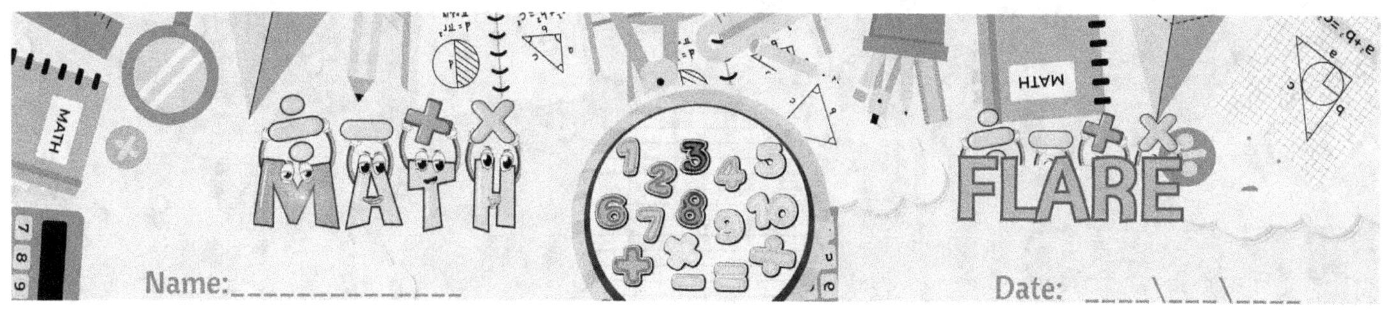

97) $\dfrac{88}{40}$ = _______________

98) $\dfrac{288}{36}$ = _______________

99) $\dfrac{2}{34}$ = _______________

100) $\dfrac{33}{48}$ = _______________

101) $\dfrac{261}{108}$ = _______________

102) $\dfrac{837}{90}$ = _______________

103) $\dfrac{462}{77}$ = _______________

104) $\dfrac{18}{39}$ = _______________

105) $\dfrac{104}{16}$ = _______________

106) $\dfrac{56}{28}$ = _______________

107) $\dfrac{846}{180}$ = _______________

108) $\dfrac{115}{45}$ = _______________

109) $\dfrac{1022}{126}$ = _______________

110) $\dfrac{792}{135}$ = _______________

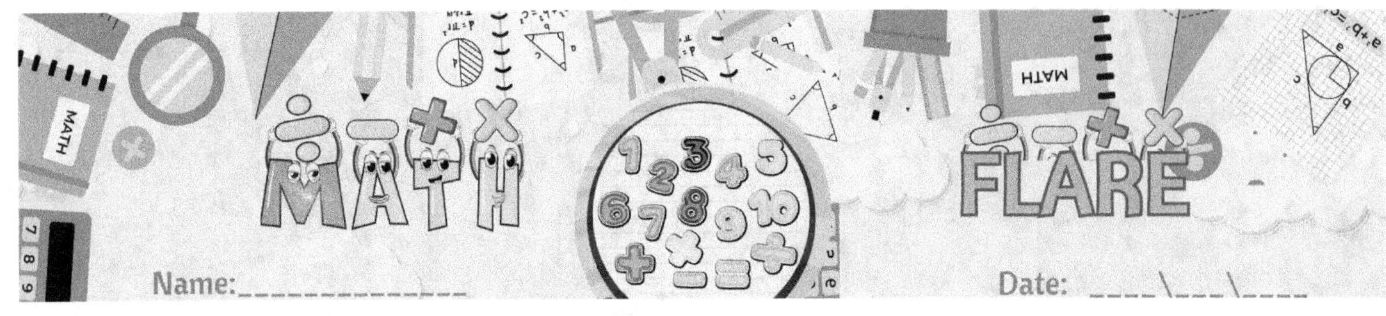

Fractions Addition Word Problems

1) What is the sum of $\frac{1}{3}$ and $\frac{1}{2}$?

$$\frac{1}{3} + \frac{1}{2} = \frac{1\times2 + 3\times2}{3\times2} = \frac{5}{6}$$

2) A recipe calls for $\frac{1}{2}$ cups of sugar and $\frac{1}{3}$ cups of flour. How much of the mixture is needed in total?

3) Avery used $\frac{1}{6}$ of a stick of butter in a recipe and then used another $\frac{2}{7}$ of the stick in a different recipe. How much of the stick did she use in total?

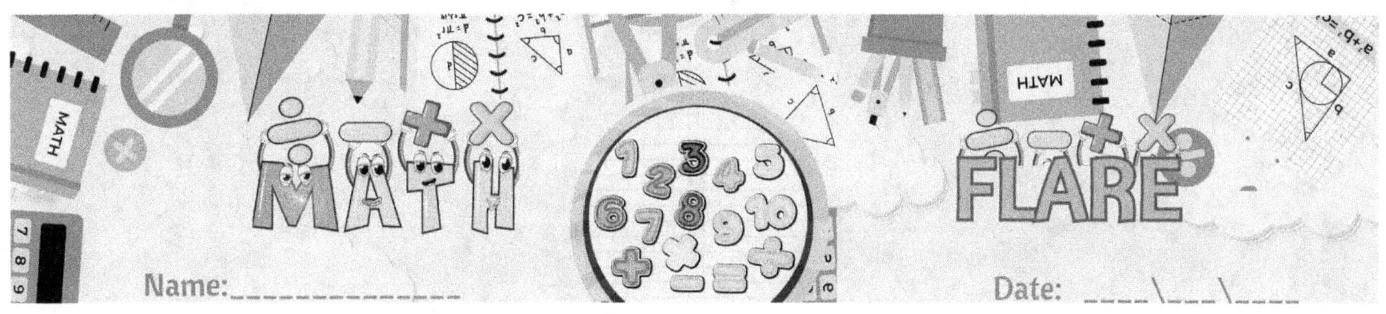

4) Diego practiced math for $\frac{2}{7}$ of an hour and then played video games for another $\frac{1}{3}$ of an hour. How much time did he spend on these activities in total?

5) Charlotte made a salad with $\frac{3}{10}$ of a cup of lettuce and $\frac{6}{9}$ of a cup of spinach. How much salad did she make in total?

6) A juice recipe calls for $\frac{3}{8}$ cups of apple juice and $\frac{3}{7}$ cups of orange juice. How much juice is needed in total?

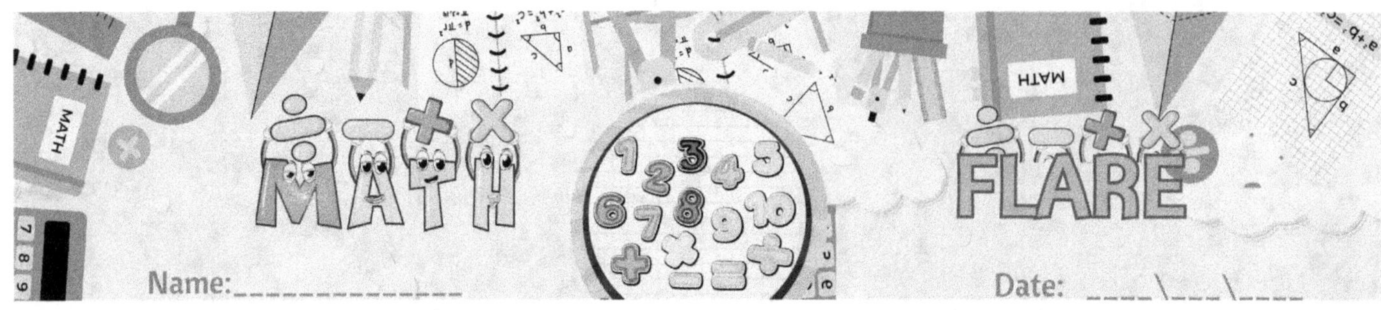

7) Nicholas paints $\frac{1}{4}$ of his paintnig on Monday, and $\frac{3}{10}$ on Tuesday. How much of his painting has he finished in total?

8) Emilia spent $\frac{2}{6}$ of her salary on forks and then $\frac{5}{8}$ of the money on food. How much money did she spend?

9) Sofia bought $\frac{3}{6}$ of a pound of cheese and then added another $\frac{1}{4}$ of a pound to make a sandwich. How much cheese did she use in total?

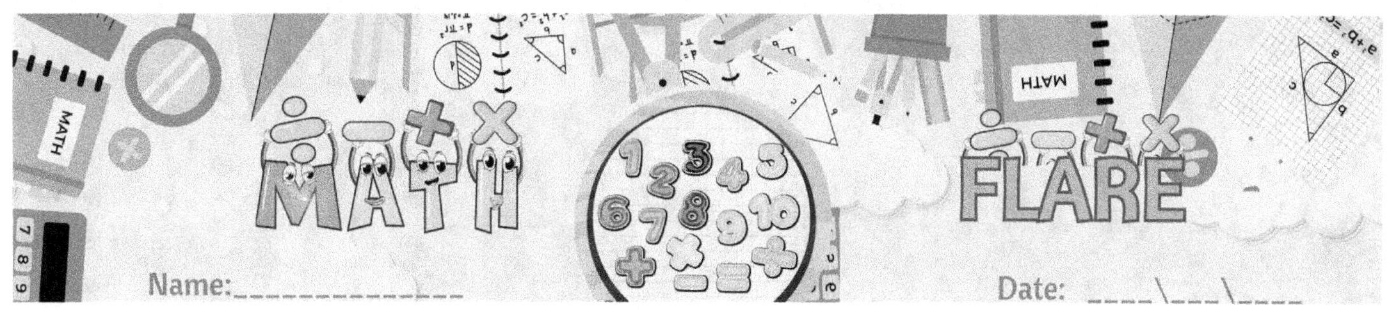

10) Serenity bought $\frac{1}{5}$ of a pound of ground beef and then added another $\frac{3}{10}$ of a pound to make a hamburger patty. How much ground beef did she use in total?

11) A recipe calls for $\frac{3}{9}$ cups of flour and $\frac{2}{7}$ cups of sugar. How much dry ingredient in total is needed for the recipe?

12) Aurora extracts $\frac{2}{3}$ of a glass of orange juice and then added $\frac{1}{6}$ of a glass of apple juice. How much juice is in the glass in total?

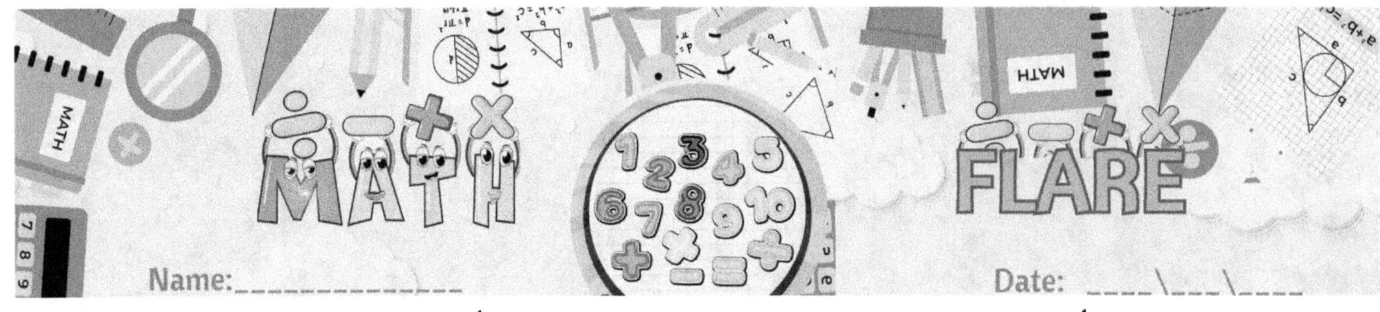

13) Nathaniel walked $\frac{1}{10}$ of a mile and then run another $\frac{1}{6}$ of a mile. How far did he travel in total?

14) Isaac solved $\frac{2}{8}$ of a math quiz and then $\frac{2}{10}$ of the same quiz. How much of the quiz has she solved?

15) Joshua rode $\frac{1}{9}$ of a mile on his bike and then ran $\frac{1}{3}$ of a mile. How far did he travel in total?

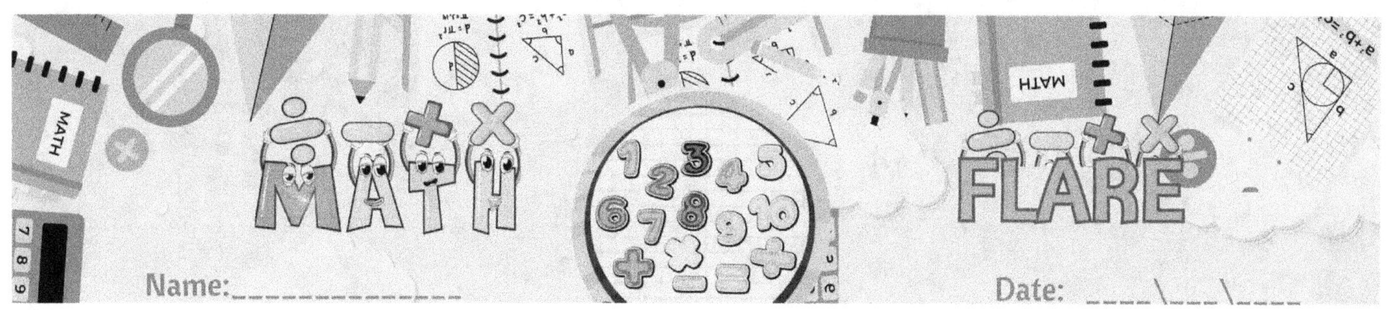

16) A recipe calls for $\frac{1}{4}$ cups of flour and $\frac{1}{2}$ cups of tomato sauce. How much of the ingredients are needed in total for the recipe?

17) Hunter jogged $\frac{1}{5}$ of a mile in the morning and then jogged another $\frac{7}{9}$ of a mile in the evening. How much did he jog in total?

18) Lillian knitted $\frac{4}{6}$ of a scarf and then $\frac{2}{7}$ of the same scarf. How much of the scarf has she knitted so far?

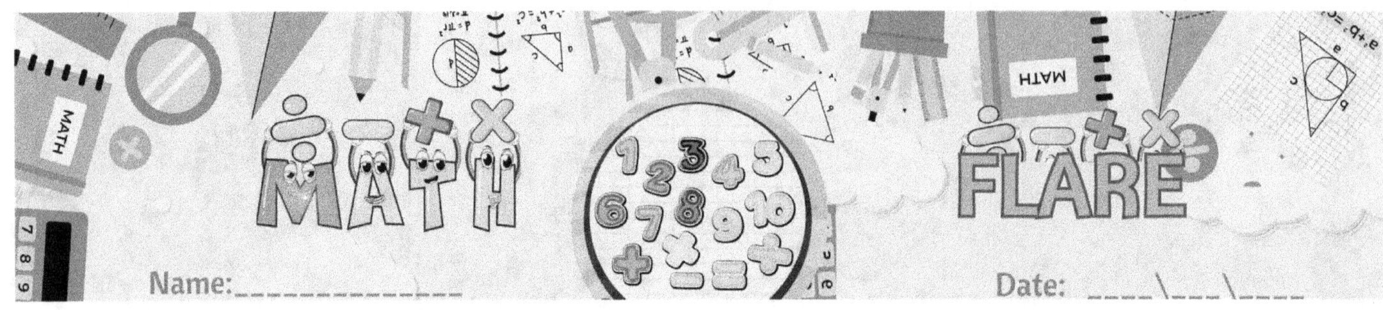

19) Addison baked $\frac{2}{3}$ of a cakes for her friend's birthday. She then baked $\frac{1}{5}$ of cookies. How much did she bake in total?

20) Ellie used $\frac{2}{5}$ of a cup of flour and then $\frac{1}{3}$ of a cup of sugar in her baking. How much of the ingredients did she use in total?

21) Leo completed $\frac{1}{2}$ of his homework and then $\frac{1}{6}$ more. How much of his homework is completed?

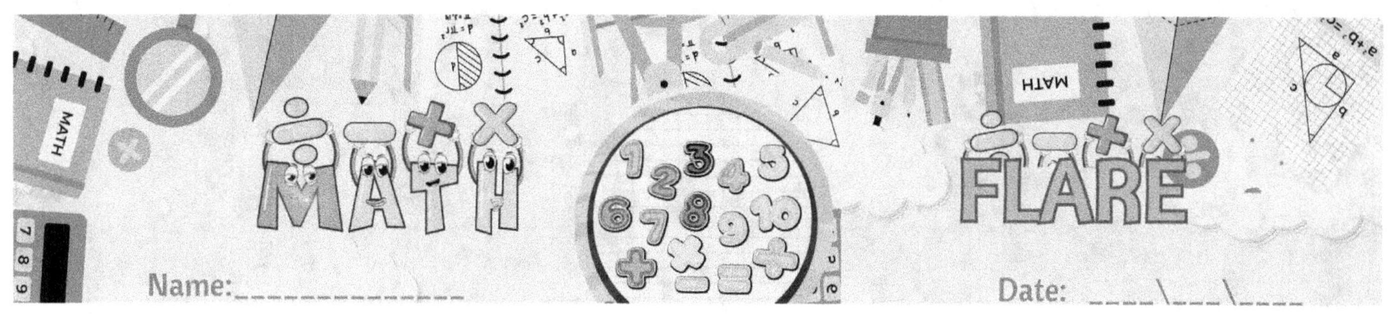

Fractions Subtraction Word Problems

1) Elena has a book that is $\frac{5}{9}$ of an inch thick. She reads $\frac{2}{7}$ of the book. How thick is the remaining portion of the book in inches?

$$\frac{5}{9} - \frac{2}{7} = \frac{5\times7 - 9\times2}{9\times7} = \frac{35 - 18}{63} = \frac{17}{63}$$

2) Colton is making a sandwich that calls for $\frac{5}{8}$ of a pound of beef. He only has $\frac{1}{3}$ of a pound of beef left. How much more beef does he need to make the sandwich?

3) Chloe bought $\frac{3}{5}$ of a pound of peanuts. After sharing $\frac{2}{8}$ of the peanuts with her friend, how many pounds of peanuts did Chloe have left?

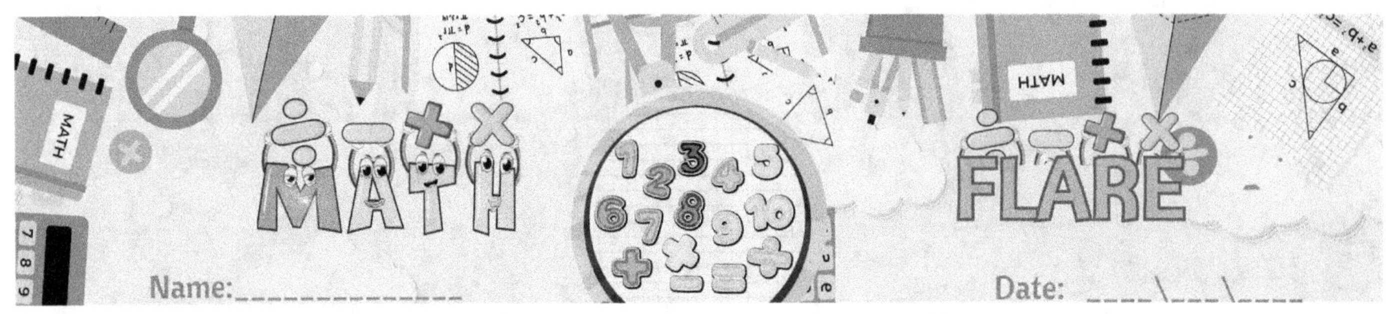

4) Reagan wants to make a dish that calls for $\frac{9}{10}$ of a cup of yogurt. She only has $\frac{5}{7}$ of a cup of yogurt left. How much more yogurt does she need to make the dish?

5) Maverick has a rope that is $\frac{2}{5}$ of a meter long. He needs to cut off $\frac{1}{4}$ of a meter to tie a knot. How long is the rope after the knot is tied?

6) Josiah has $\frac{4}{5}$ of a pound of cheese. He uses $\frac{1}{3}$ of the cheese to make a sandwich. How much cheese is left in pounds?

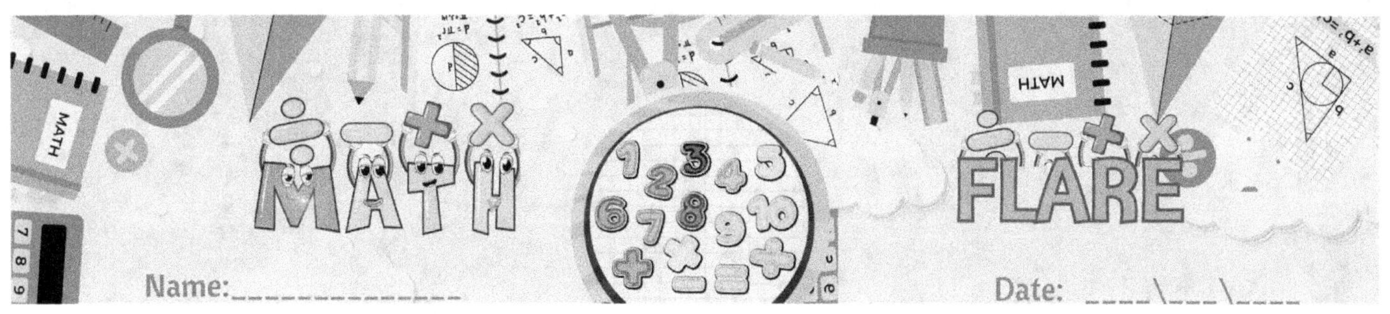

7) Paisley is knitting a scarf that needs $\frac{2}{8}$ of the yarn. If she has already used $\frac{3}{9}$ yards of yarn, how much does she have left?

8) Ellie is painting a room with a can of paint that has $\frac{2}{3}$ gallons in it. She has used $\frac{2}{7}$ of the paint so far. How much paint is left in the can?

9) A recipe calls for $\frac{9}{10}$ of a cup of milk. If $\frac{8}{9}$ of the milk is already used, how much milk is left in cups?

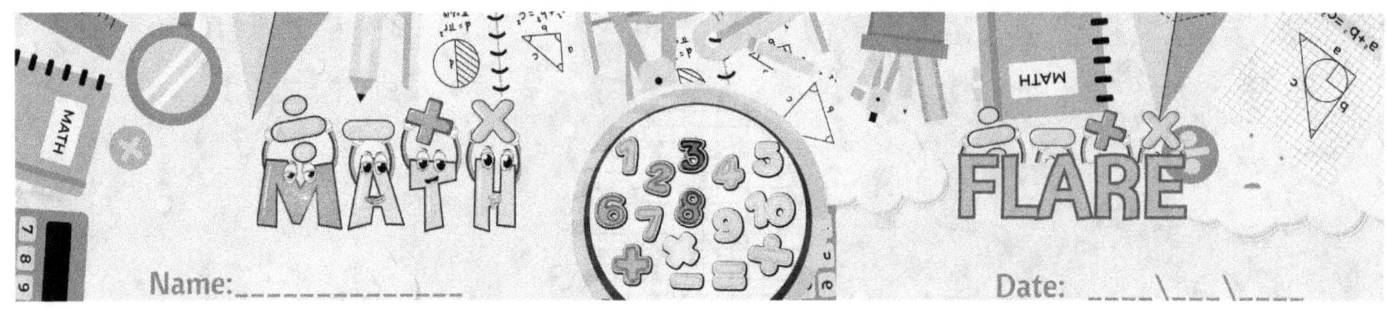

10) Addison has $\frac{5}{8}$ of a pound of flour. She uses $\frac{2}{9}$ of the flour to make a pencake. How much flour is left in pounds?

11) Victoria has $\frac{3}{4}$ of a pound of beef. She cooks $\frac{2}{5}$ of the beef. How much beef is left in pounds?

12) Ella needs $\frac{1}{2}$ of a cup of sugar to make lemonade. She only has $\frac{1}{3}$ of a cup of sugar. How much more sugar does she need to make the lemonade?

13) Sofia has $\frac{8}{10}$ of a container of coins. She gives $\frac{3}{8}$ of the coins to her sister. How much coins does she have left?

14) Ian and Isabella are cooking dinner and need $\frac{4}{10}$ of a cup of oil. Ian accidentally spills $\frac{1}{4}$ of a cup of oil. How much oil do they have left?

15) Carter has $\frac{6}{8}$ of a pizza left over from last night. He eats $\frac{3}{6}$ of the pizza for lunch. How much pizza does he have left?

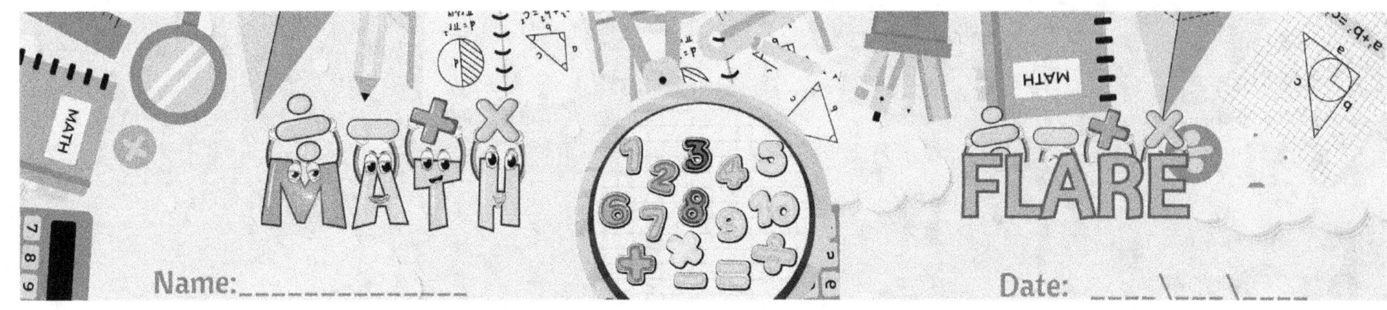

16) Jose has a rope that is $\frac{1}{3}$ of a yard long. He cuts off $\frac{1}{9}$ of the rope. How long is the remaining rope in yards?

17) A recipe calls for $\frac{1}{2}$ of a cup of sugar. If $\frac{4}{10}$ of the sugar is already used, how much sugar is left in cups?

18) Micah has a length of ribbon that is $\frac{8}{10}$ meters long. He wants to cut off $\frac{2}{3}$ of the ribbon to use for a gift. How long will the remaining ribbon be?

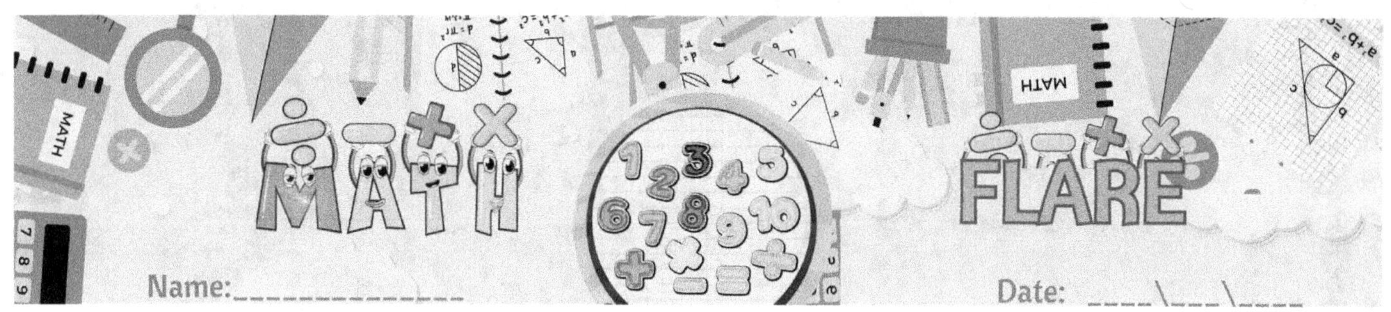

19) Leo has a collection of Spoons that weighs $\frac{3}{7}$ of a pound. If he loses $\frac{2}{6}$ of the weight, how much does the collection now weigh in pounds?

20) Ava is running on a track that is $\frac{6}{9}$ of a mile long. She has already run $\frac{3}{9}$ of the mile. How much further does she have to run?

21) Hannah has $\frac{2}{4}$ of a pound of ground chicken. She uses $\frac{1}{4}$ of the chicken to make a burger. How much chicken is left in pounds?

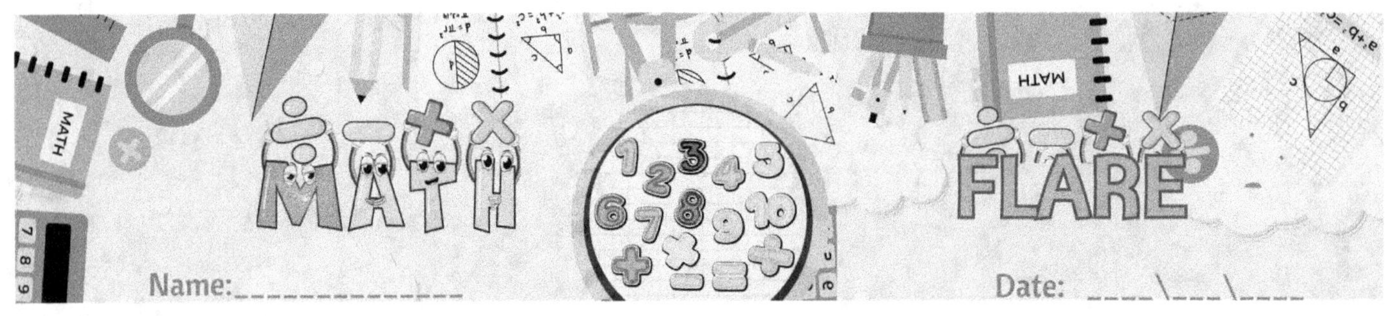

Fractions Multiplication Word Problems

1) If a recipe calls for $\frac{1}{2}$ cup of sugar to make 1 dozen cookies, how much sugar is needed to make 4 dozen cookies?

$$\frac{1 \times 4}{2 \times 1} = \frac{4}{2} = 2$$

2) If a recipe calls for $\frac{2}{6}$ cup of butter and you want to make $\frac{1}{3}$ as much, how much butter do you need?

3) Ethan spent $\frac{1}{5}$ of his money to buy Bottles. His friend Andrew spent 3 times more to buy the Bottles. How much did Andrew spend?

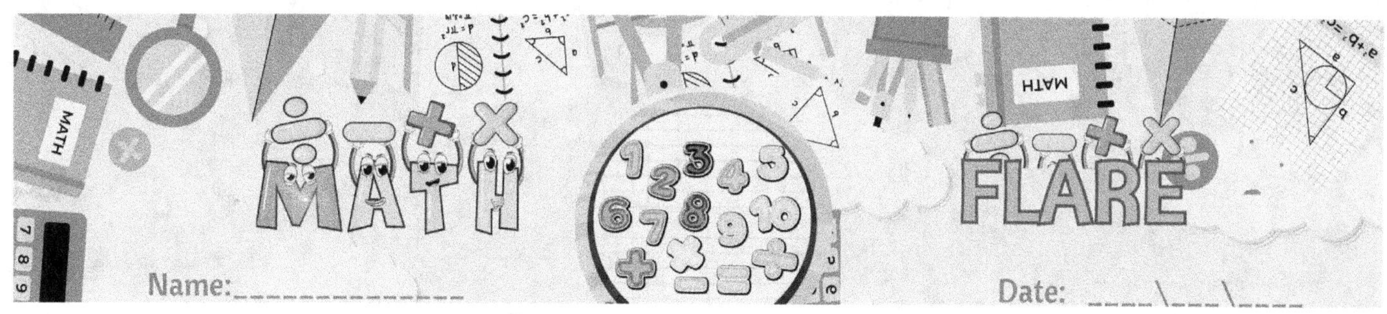

4) If a container holds $\frac{3}{4}$ of a gallon of water and you need 3 gallons of water, how many containers do you need?

5) Emily ran $\frac{1}{3}$ miles every day for 10 days. How many miles did she run in total?

6) A bike tire has a radius of $\frac{1}{2}$ foot. If the tire rolls 6 times, how far does the bike travel?

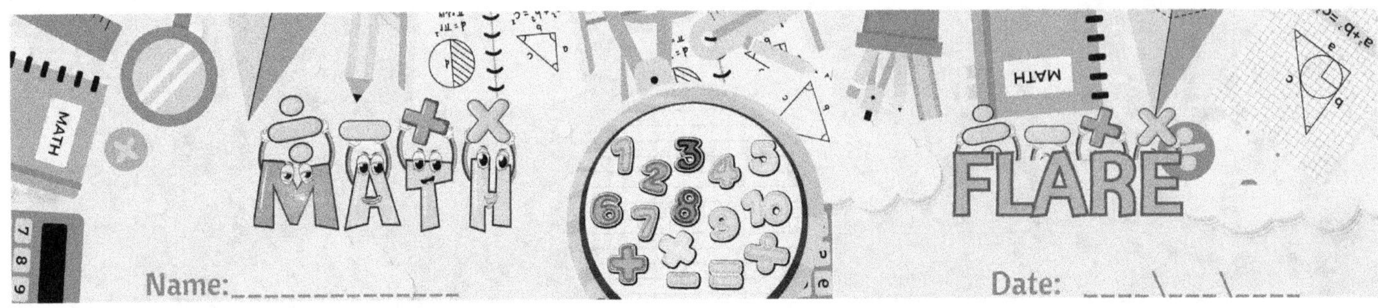

7) A factory can produce $\frac{2}{6}$ of a car in one hour. How many cars can the factory produce in 8 hours?

8) If a bag of flour weighs $\frac{2}{3}$ of a pound and you need $\frac{5}{6}$ bags, how many pounds of flour do you need in total?

9) A store sells $\frac{6}{8}$ of wallets in one day, how many days will it take to sell 4 wallets?

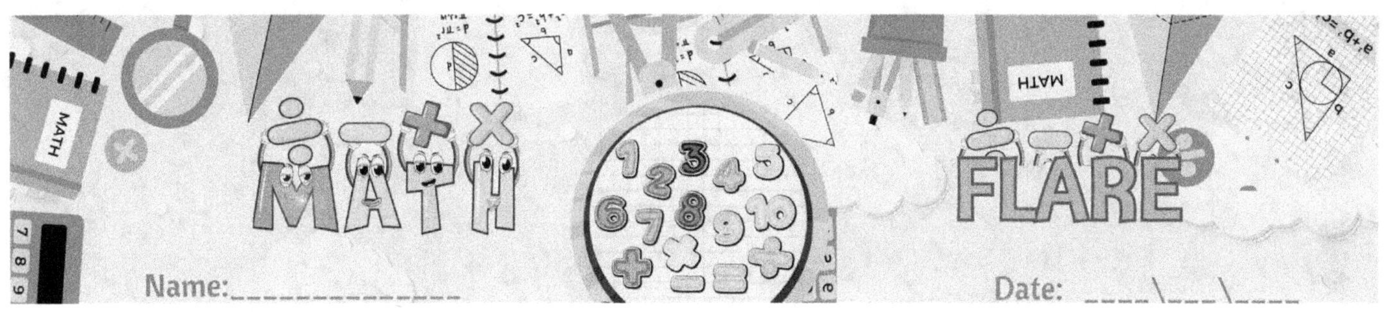

10) If a recipe calls for $\frac{4}{5}$ cup of flour and you want to make it 5, how much flour do you need?

11) Elizabeth needs $\frac{4}{5}$ cup of milk to make 1 cup of coffee, how much milk is needed to make 4 cups of coffee?

12) If a garden has an area of $\frac{7}{9}$ square feet and you want to increase it by a factor of 2, what will be the new area of the garden?

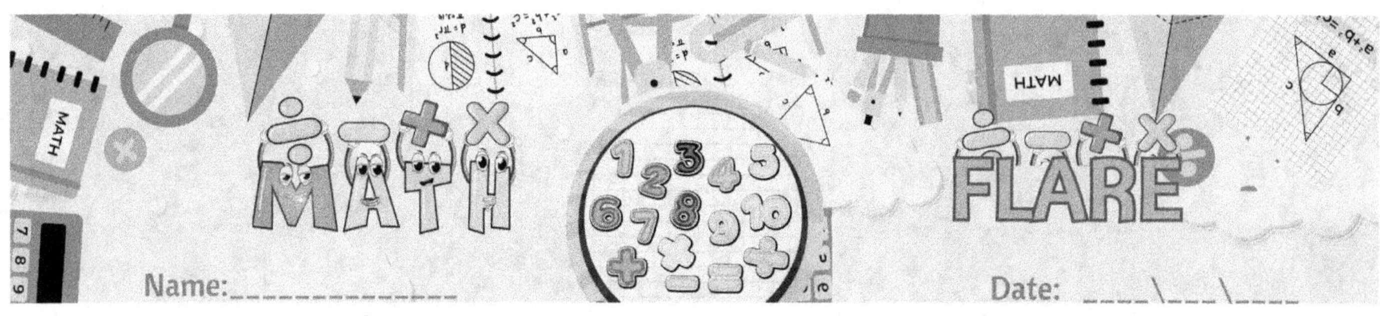

13) Piper drove $\frac{6}{7}$ of the distance to the mall. If the distance to the mall is $\frac{1}{2}$ miles, how far did Piper drive?

14) If a person can run at a speed of $\frac{1}{3}$ miles per hour, how long will it take him to run 4 miles?

15) Matthew needs $\frac{1}{2}$ cup of flour for a recipe and he wants to make $\frac{1}{10}$ batches of the recipe, how much flour will he need in total?

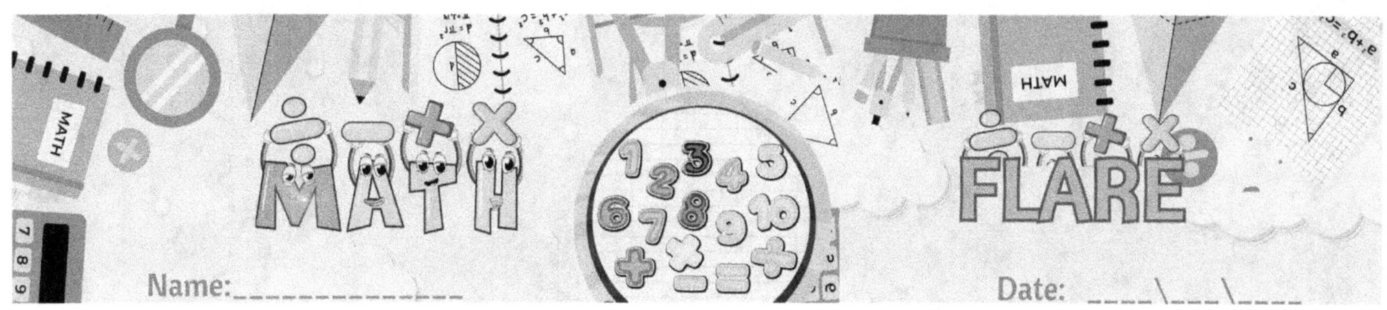

16) A cake recipe calls for $\frac{2}{5}$ cups of sugar to make one cake. If Zara wants to make 6 cakes, how many cups of sugar will she need?

17) Brandon is making a dish that calls for $\frac{1}{2}$ cup of cooking oil. If he wants to make 2 dishes of the same recipe, how much cooking oil does he need?

18) If a recipe calls for $\frac{5}{10}$ cup of milk and you want to make $\frac{6}{9}$ times as much, how much milk do you need?

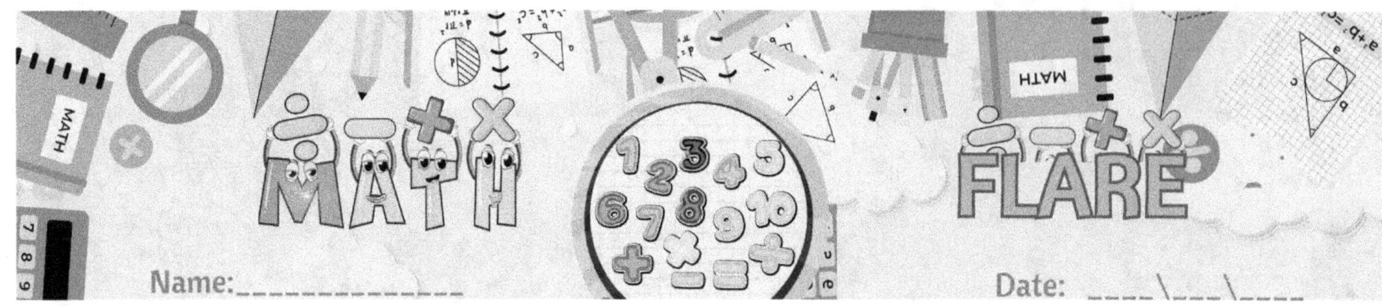

19) If a container holds $\frac{2}{6}$ of a bags of Cakes and you need 3 bags of Cakes, how many containers do you need?

20) If you need to make 5 batches of cookies, and each batch requires $\frac{5}{7}$ cup of chocolate chips, how many cups of chocolate chips do you need in total?

21) A school needs to make 100 cupcakes for a fundraiser. If a batch of cupcakes requires $\frac{2}{4}$ cups of sugar, how many cups of sugar will they need in total?

Chapter. 05

Geometry

Area and Perimeter

The area of a shape represents the amount of space it occupies. The perimeter of a shape is the total distance around its outer edge.

Area of Rectangle

For a square, since all four sides are equal, we only need to know the length of one side to find its area. We can calculate the area of a square by multiplying the length of one side by itself (squared). So, if the length of one side of the square is 's', then the area (A) is given by:

$$A = s \times s$$

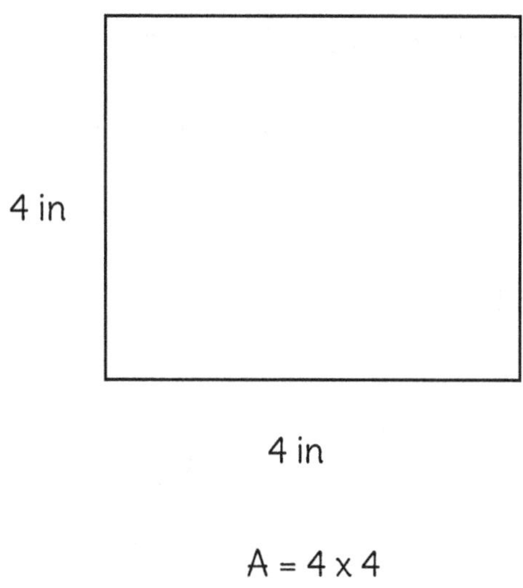

$$A = 4 \times 4$$
$$A = 16$$

Perimeter of Rectangle

For a square, since all four sides are equal, we can find the perimeter by adding up the lengths of all four sides. If 's' represents the length of one side, then the perimeter (P) is given by:

$$P = 4 \times s$$

$$P = 4 \times 4$$

$$P = 16$$

Area of Triangle:

The area of a triangle represents the amount of space enclosed within its three sides. The formula for calculating the area of a triangle depends on the type of triangle. For a general triangle, we use the formula:

$$A = \frac{1}{2} \times \text{base} \times \text{height}$$

Where:

- *A* represents the area of the triangle.

- The base is the length of any one side of the triangle.

- The height is the perpendicular distance from the base to the opposite vertex.

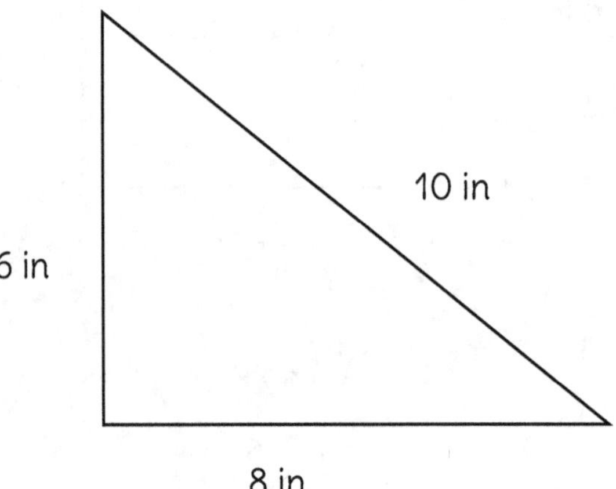

$$A = \frac{1}{2} \times \text{base} \times \text{height}$$

$$A = \frac{1}{2} \times 6 \times 8$$

$$A = \frac{1}{2} \times 48$$

$$A = 24$$

Perimeter of Triangle:

The perimeter of a triangle is the total length of its three sides. To find the perimeter, we simply add the lengths of all three sides together:

$$P = \text{side1} + \text{side2} + \text{side3}$$

$$P = 6 + 8 + 10$$

$$P = 24$$

Equilateral Triangle

An equilateral triangle is a triangle in which all three sides are equal in length. To find the area and perimeter of an equilateral triangle, we can use the following formulas:

- Area (A): $\frac{\sqrt{3}}{4} \times a^2$ where a is the length of one side of the equilateral triangle.

- Perimeter (P): $P = 3a$ where a is the length of one side of the equilateral triangle.

Let's solve a problem:

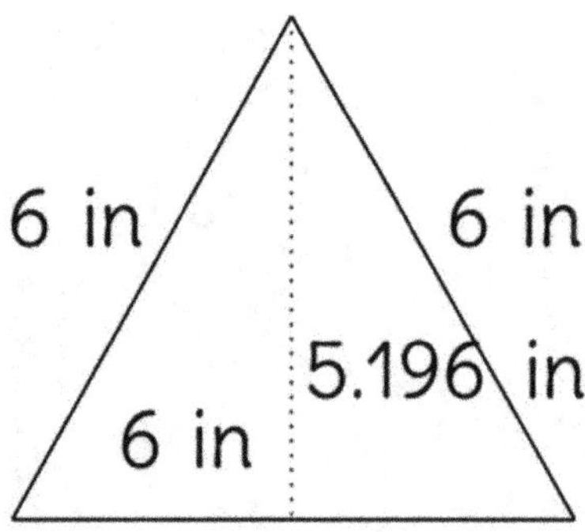

Area of Equilateral Triangle:

$$\text{Area (A): } \frac{\sqrt{3}}{4} \times (6)^2$$

$$\text{Area (A): } \frac{\sqrt{3}}{4} \times 36$$

$$\text{Area (A): } \frac{36\sqrt{3}}{4}$$

$$\text{Area (A): } \frac{36(1.73)}{4}$$

$$\text{Area (A): } \frac{62.35}{4}$$

$$\text{Area (A): } 15.59 \text{ in}^2$$

Perimeter of Equilateral Triangle:

$$P = 3a$$

$$P = 3(6) = 18$$

MathFlare - Math Workbook 5th and 6th Grade

Isosceles Triangle

An isosceles triangle is a triangle with at least two sides of equal length. The angles opposite the equal sides are also equal.

Area of Isosceles Triangle

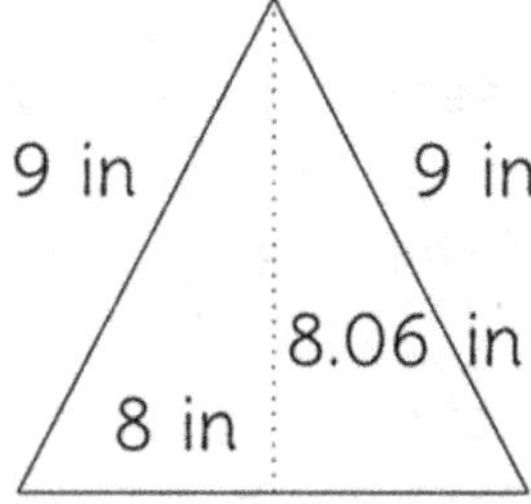

$$A = \frac{1}{2} \times base \times height$$

$$A = \frac{1}{2} \times 8 \times 8$$

$$A = \frac{1}{2} \times 64$$

$$A = 32$$

Perimeter of Isosceles Triangle

The perimeter of a triangle is the total length of its three sides. To find the perimeter, we simply add the lengths of all three sides together:

$$P = side1 + side2 + side3$$

$$P = 9 + 9 + 8$$

$$P = 26$$

Scalene Triangle

A scalene triangle is a triangle with no equal sides and no equal angles. The formula for finding various properties of a scalene triangle is as follows:

Area (A): The area of a scalene triangle can be calculated using Heron's formula, which is given by:

$$A = \sqrt{s(s-a)(s-b)(s-c)}$$

where s is the semi-perimeter of the triangle,

and a, b, and c are the lengths of its three sides.

Perimeter (P): The perimeter of a scalene triangle is the sum of the lengths of its three sides.

$$P = side1 + side2 + side3$$

Let's find the Area and Perimeter of a Scalene Triangle:

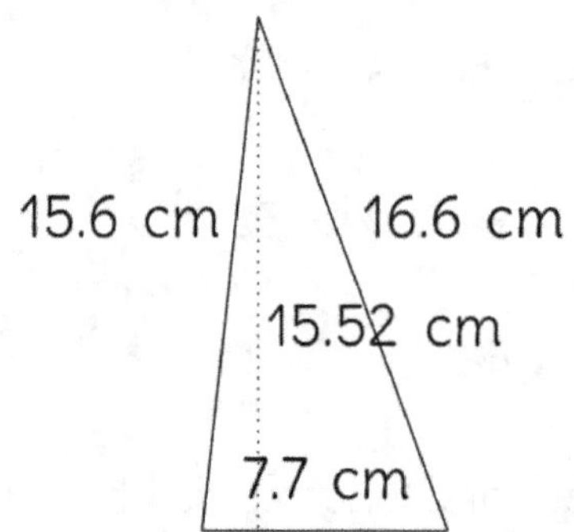

Area (A): First, we calculate the semi-perimeter (s):

$$S = \frac{a+b+c}{2} = \frac{15.6 + 16.6 + 7.7}{2} = \frac{39.8}{2} = 19.9 \text{ cm}$$

MathFlare - Math Workbook 5th and 6th Grade

Heron's formula to find the area:

$$A = \sqrt{s(s-a)(s-b)(s-c)}$$

$$A = \sqrt{19.9\,(19.9 - 15.6)(19.9 - 16.6)(19.9 - 7.7)}$$

$$A = \sqrt{19.9 \times 4.3 \times 3.3 \times 12.2}$$

$$A = \sqrt{3445} \approx 59$$

Perimeter (P):

$$P = side1 + side2 + side3$$

$$P = 15.6 + 16.6 + 7.7$$

$$P = 39.8$$

Area and Perimeter of an L-shape

The L-shaped figure typically consists of two rectangles joined together to form an L-shape. To find the area and perimeter of an L-shaped figure, we will need to calculate the areas and perimeters of each rectangle and then combine them.

Area=Area of Rectangle 1 + Area of Rectangle 2

Perimeter=Perimeter of Rectangle 1 + Perimeter of Rectangle 2

Let's find the Area and Perimeter of an L-shape:

Area of L-Shape

$$\text{Area 1} = 4.38 \times 4.5 = 19.7 \text{ cm}^2$$

$$\text{Area 2} = 11.28 \times 6.54 = 73.7 \text{ cm}^2$$

$$\text{Area} = 19.7 + 73.7$$

$$\text{Area} = 93.481 \text{ cm}^2$$

Perimeter of L-Shape

$$P = 11.28 + 6.54 + 6.78 + 4.38 + 4.5 + 10.92$$

$$P = 44.4 \text{ cm}$$

Area and Circumference of circles

To find the area (A) and circumference (C) of a circle, we use the following formulas:

1. Area of a Circle (A) = $\pi \times (radius)^2$

   - where π (pi) is a constant with value of (3.14). It is a ratio of the circumference of a circle to its diameter,
   - the radius (r) is the distance from the center of the circle.

2. Circumference of a Circle (C) = $2 \times \pi \times radius$

Let's solve an example: suppose a swimming pool has a radius of 11 meters, we are required to calculate its Area and Circumference:

$$\text{Area } (A) = \pi \times (radius)^2$$

$$A = 3.14 \times 11^2$$

$$A = 3.14 \times 121$$

$$A = 379.94 \text{ square meters}$$

$$\text{Circumference } (C) = 2 \times \pi \times radius$$

$$C = 2 \times 3.14 \times 11$$

$$C = 69.08 \text{ square meters}$$

Angles

Types of Angles: Angles can be classified based on their measures:

- **Acute Angle:** An angle less than 90°.

- **Right Angle:** An angle exactly equal to 90°.

- **Obtuse Angle:** An angle greater than 90° and less than 180°.

- **Straight Angle:** An angle exactly equal to 180°.

- **Reflex Angle:** An angle greater than 180° and less than 360°.

- **Full Angle:** An angle equal to 360°.

Measure angles with a protractor. It looks like a semicircle or a half-disc with degree markings from 0° to 180°.To measure an angle using a protractor, we place the center of the protractor at the vertex of the angle, align one side of the angle with the zero mark on the protractor, and read the degree measure where the other side intersects the protractor.

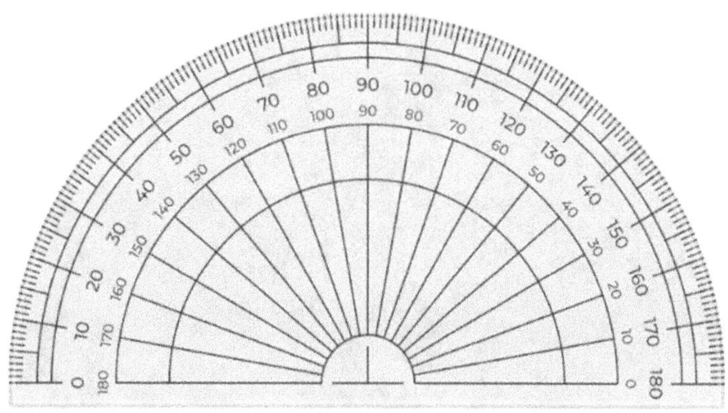

Image: Protector

For example, let's measure the following angle.

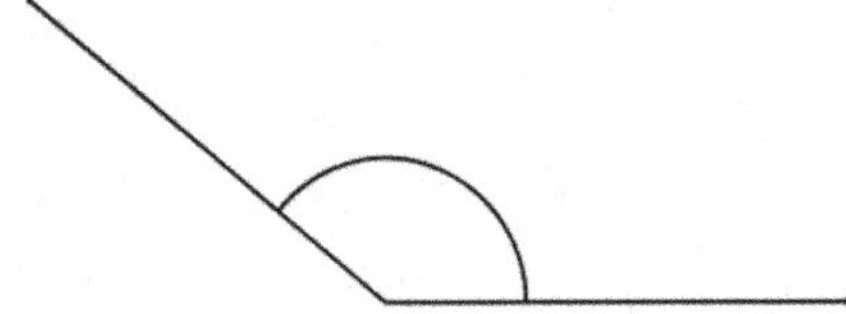

The angle is 140°.

We also know that the angle is greater than 90° and less than 180°, so this is an Obtuse angle.

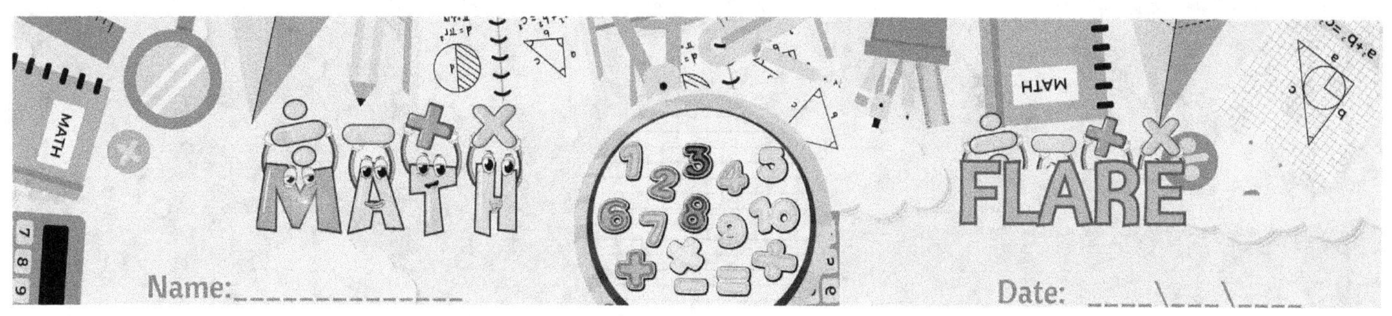

Area and Perimeter: Rectangles and Triangles

1)

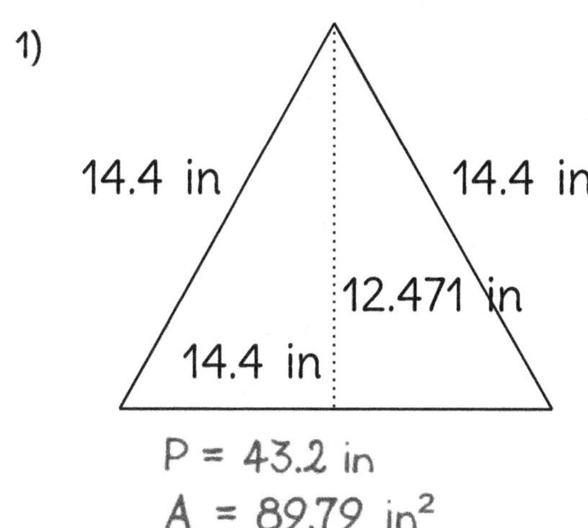

P = 43.2 in
A = 89.79 in²

2)

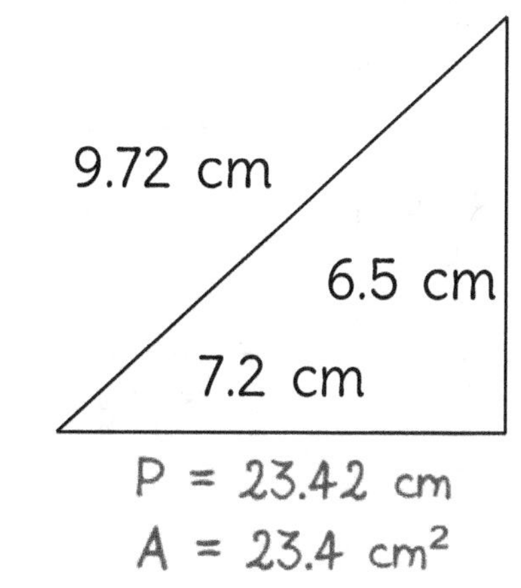

P = 23.42 cm
A = 23.4 cm²

3)

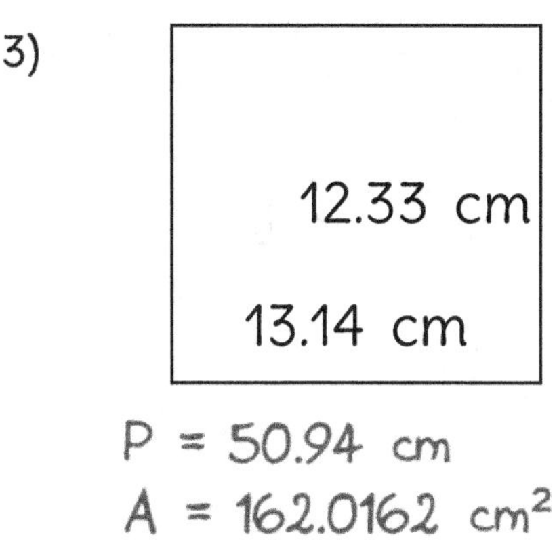

P = 50.94 cm
A = 162.0162 cm²

4)

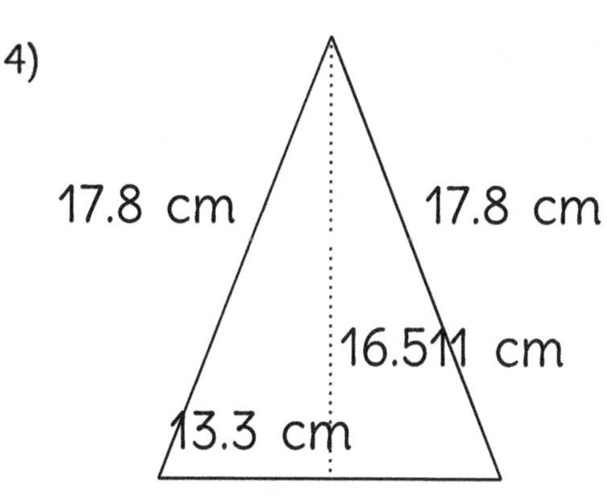

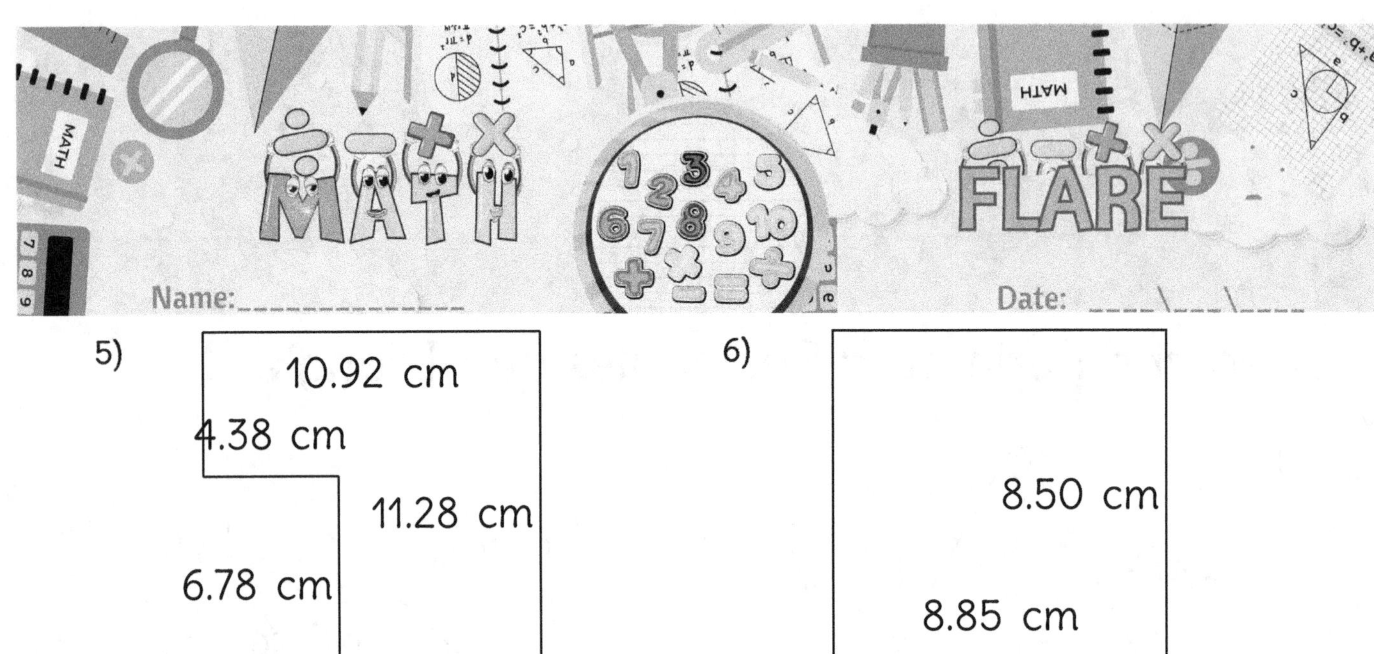

5)

P = 44.40 cm   A = 93.4812 cm²

6)

7)

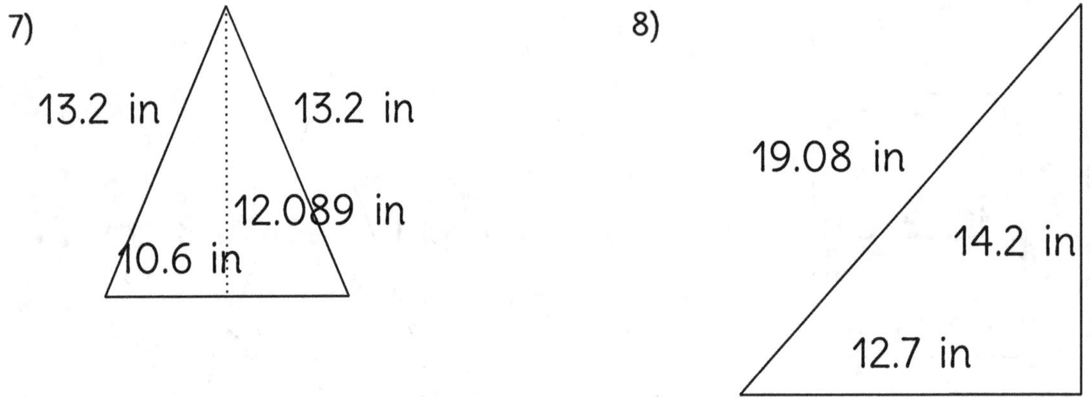

8)

Name:
Date:

9)

10.08 cm
7.1 cm
7.2 cm

10)

7.92 in
5.84 in

11)

6.28 in
7.88 in

12)

14.7 cm
14.7 cm
13.084 cm
13.4 cm

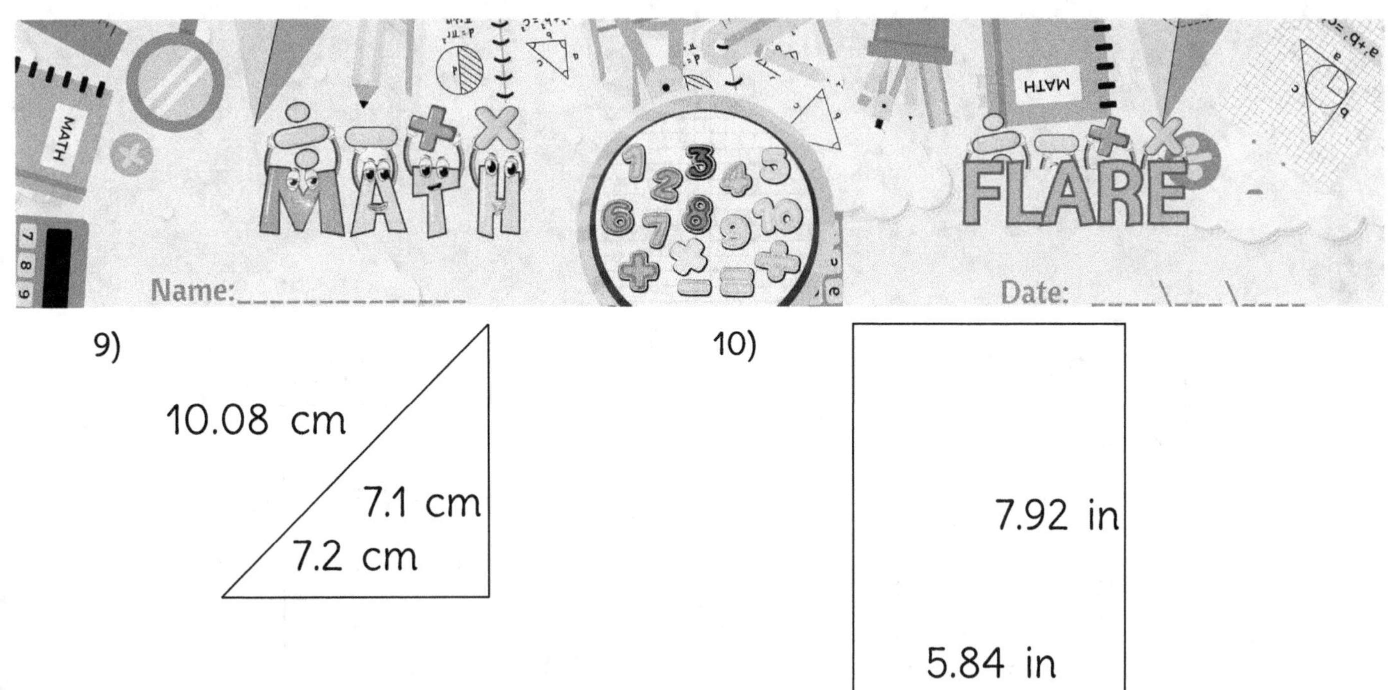

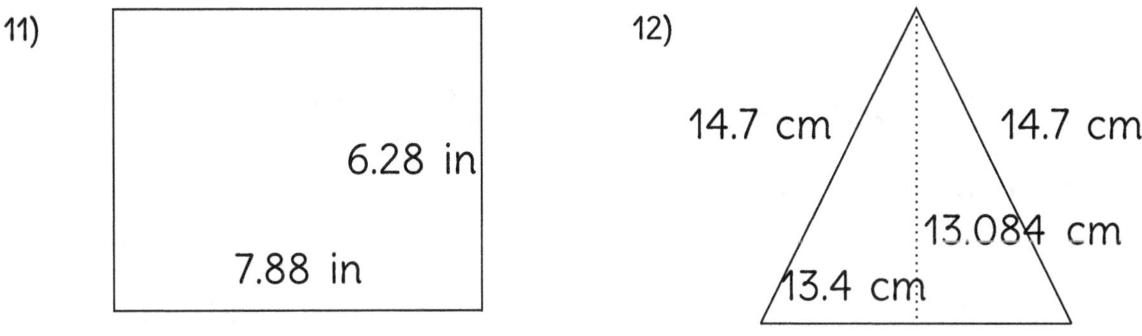

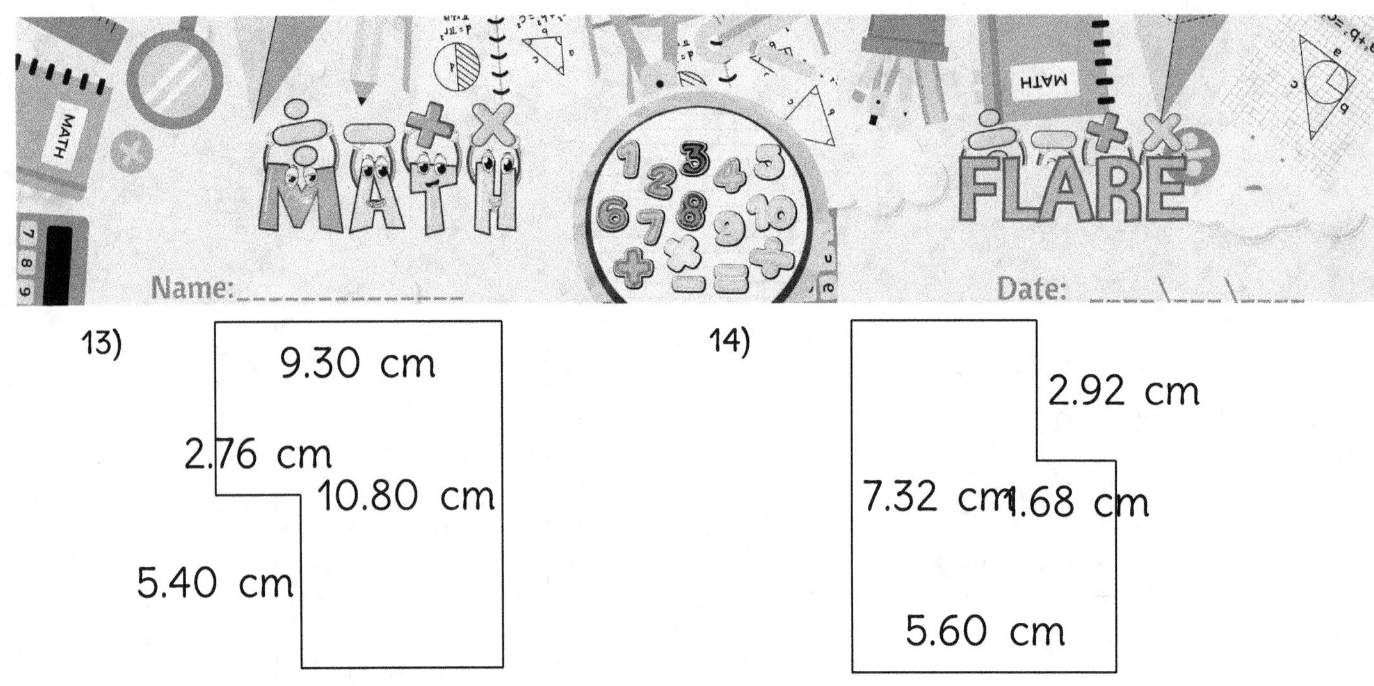
13)
9.30 cm
2.76 cm
10.80 cm
5.40 cm
14)
2.92 cm
7.32 cm 1.68 cm
5.60 cm

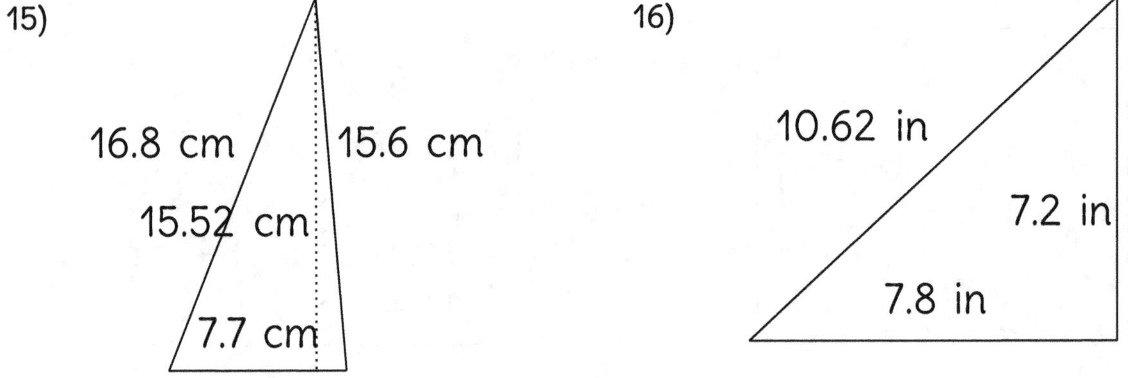
15)
16.8 cm
15.6 cm
15.52 cm
7.7 cm
16)
10.62 in
7.2 in
7.8 in

Name:
Date:
MATH
FLARE

17)

16.83 cm
10.08 cm
16.74 cm
10.08 cm

18)
13.9 cm
13.3 cm
13.30 cm
5.0 cm

19)

19.62 in
11.1 in
16.2 in

20)
16.71 cm
11.0 cm
12.5 cm

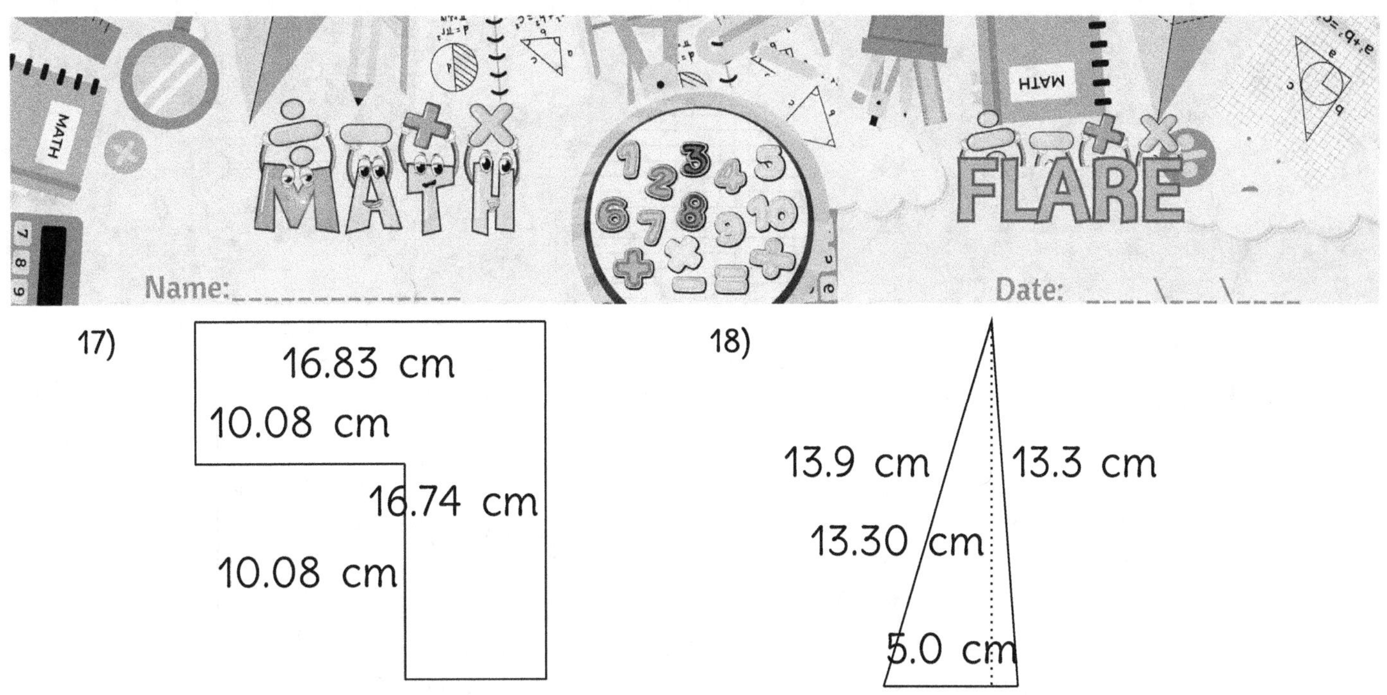

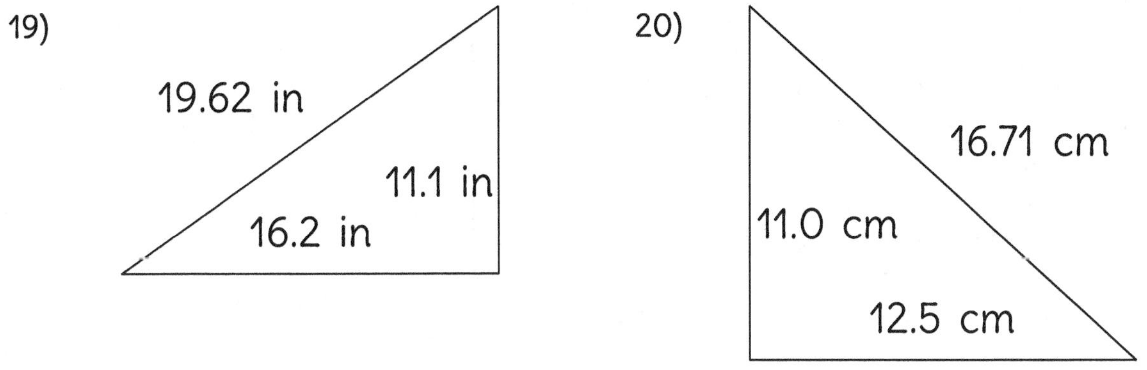

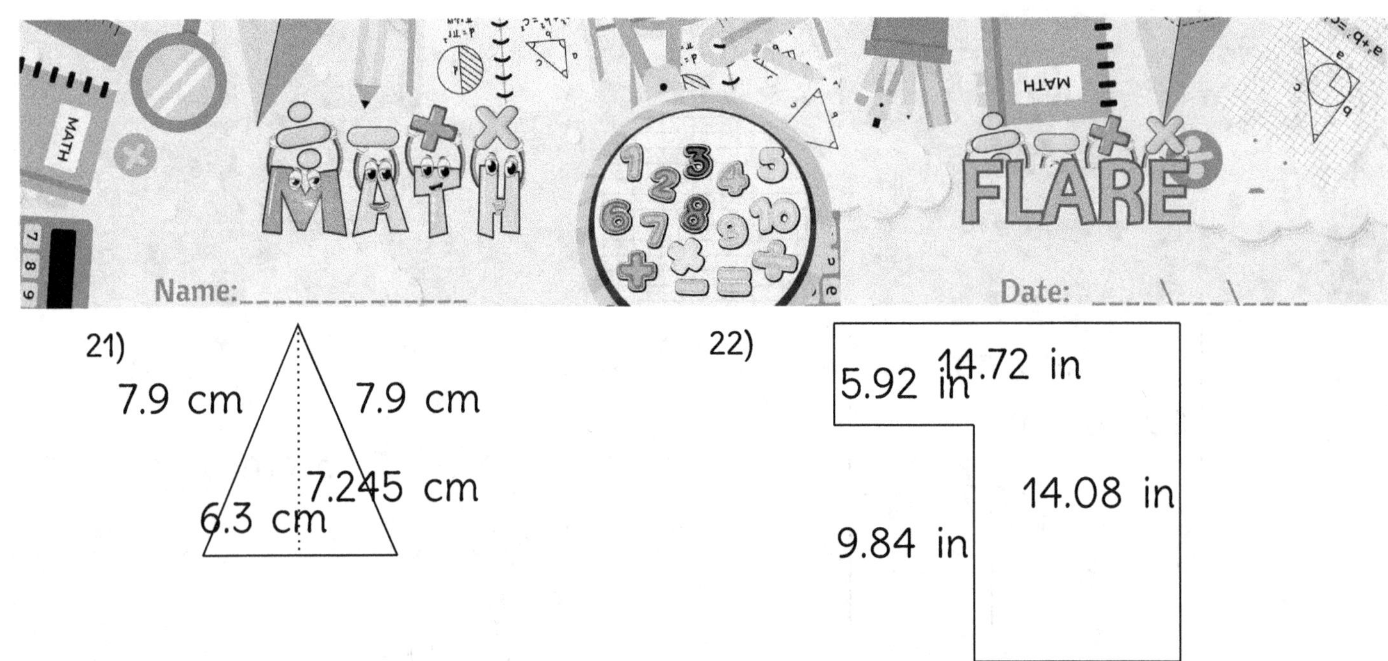

21)

7.9 cm   7.9 cm
7.245 cm
6.3 cm

22)

5.92 in   14.72 in
14.08 in
9.84 in

23)

14.69 in
9.1 in
11.5 in

24)

11.60 cm
9.2 cm
7 cm

MATH
FLARE
Name:
Date:

25)

3.68 in
7.40 in
3.24 in
6.48 in

26)

16.61 in
11.1 in
12.4 in

27)

14.40 in
16.47 in

28)

23.13 in
15.6 in
17.1 in

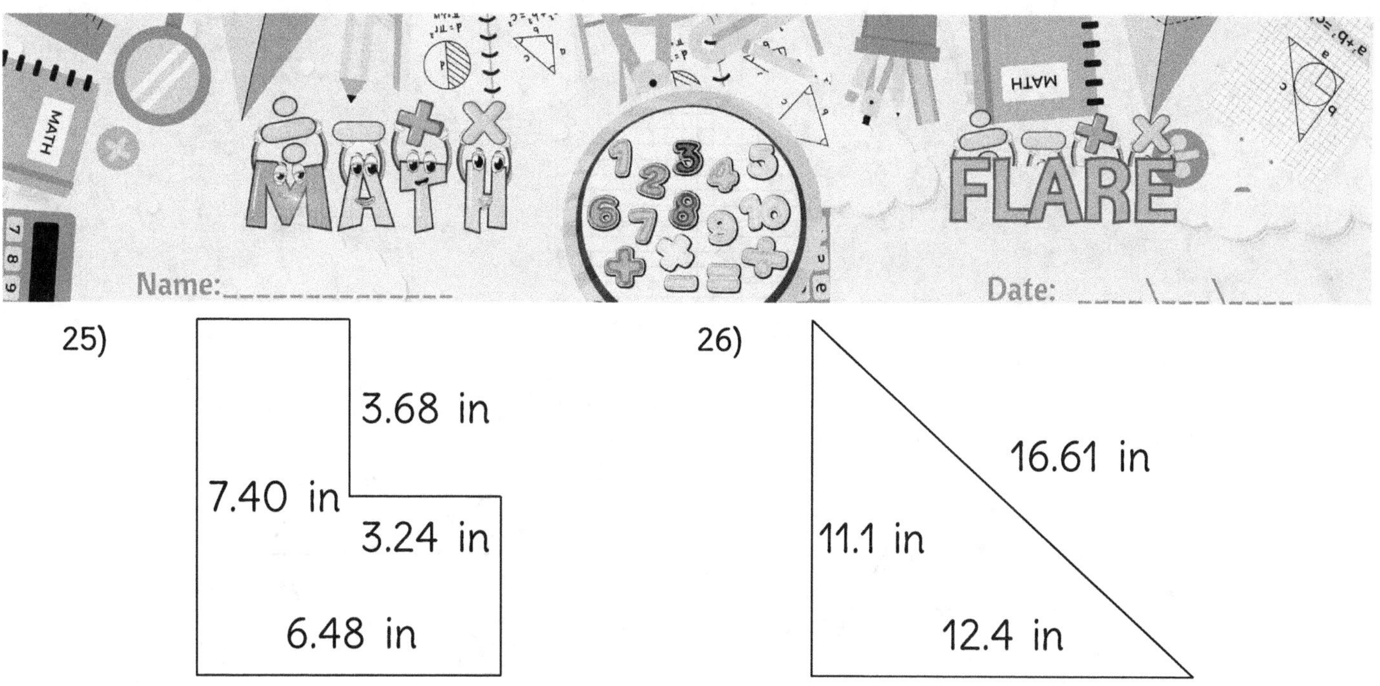

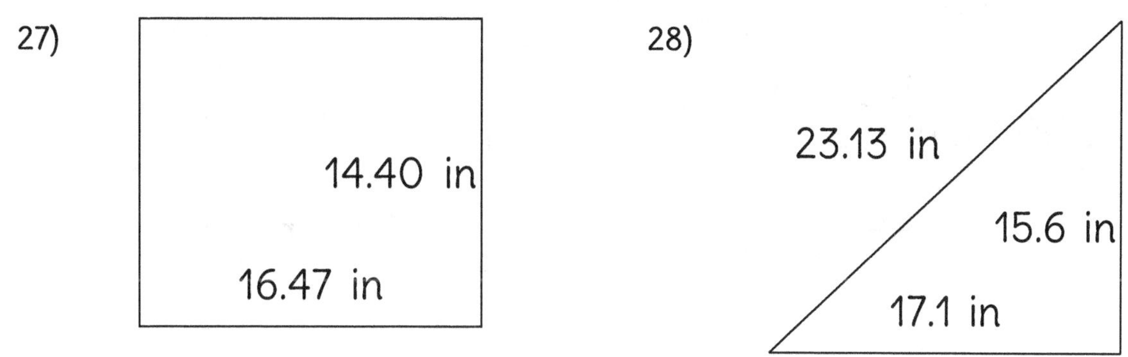

Name:
Date:

29)

10.6 in
10.6 in
9.180 in
10.6 in

30)

12.9 in
12.9 in
11.172 in
12.9 in

31)

10.32 cm
17.20 cm
11.52 cm
8.08 cm

32)

11.62 in
10.57 in

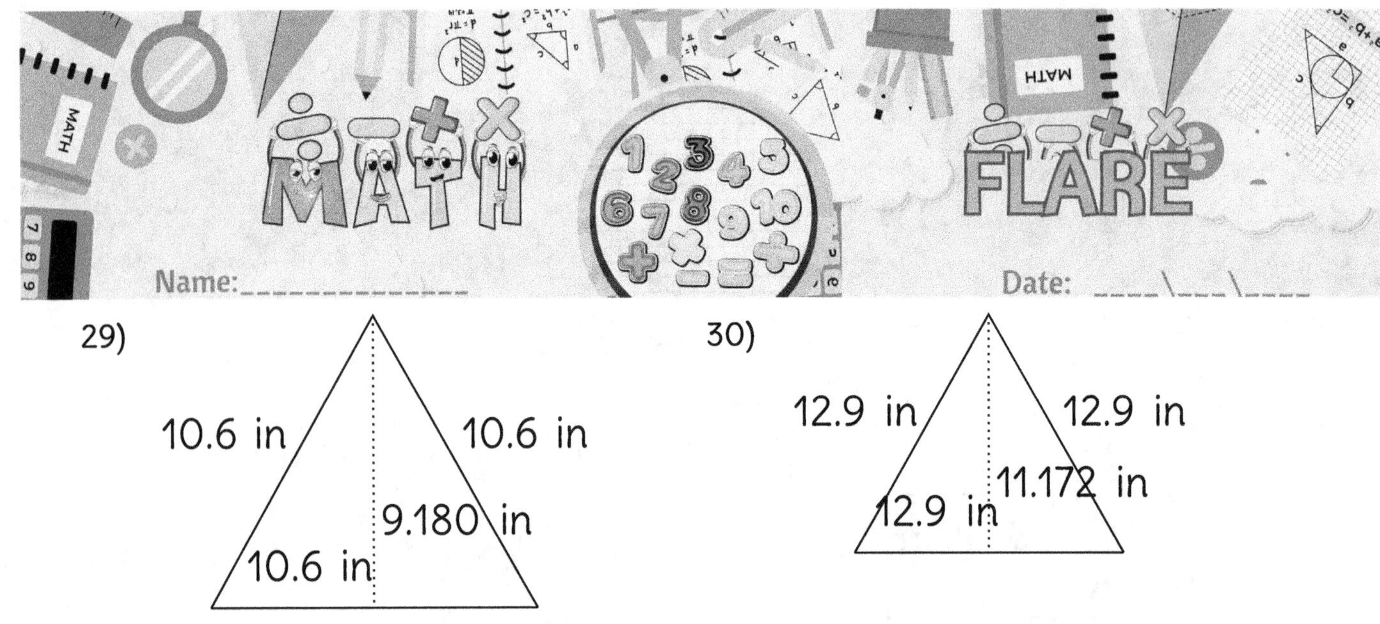

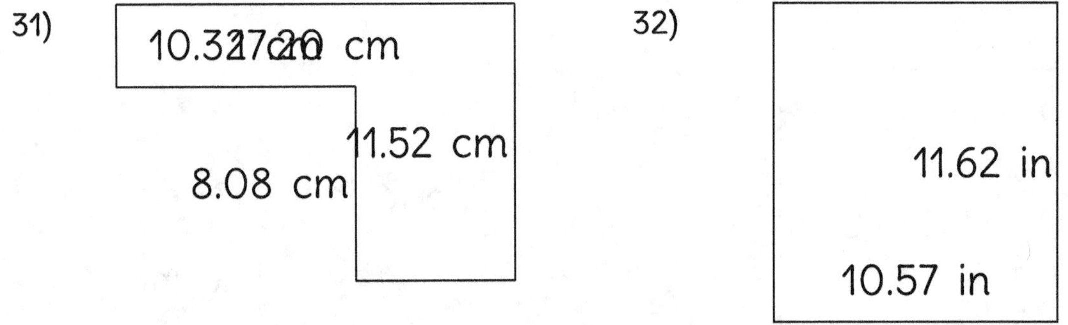

Name:
Date:
MATH FLARE

33)

6.7 cm
6.9 cm
6.64 cm
3.0 cm

34)

8.28 in
16.56 in
7.74 in
15.57 in

35)

5.4 in
3.2 in
2.64 in
6.6 in

36)

10.72 cm
8.2 cm
6.8 cm

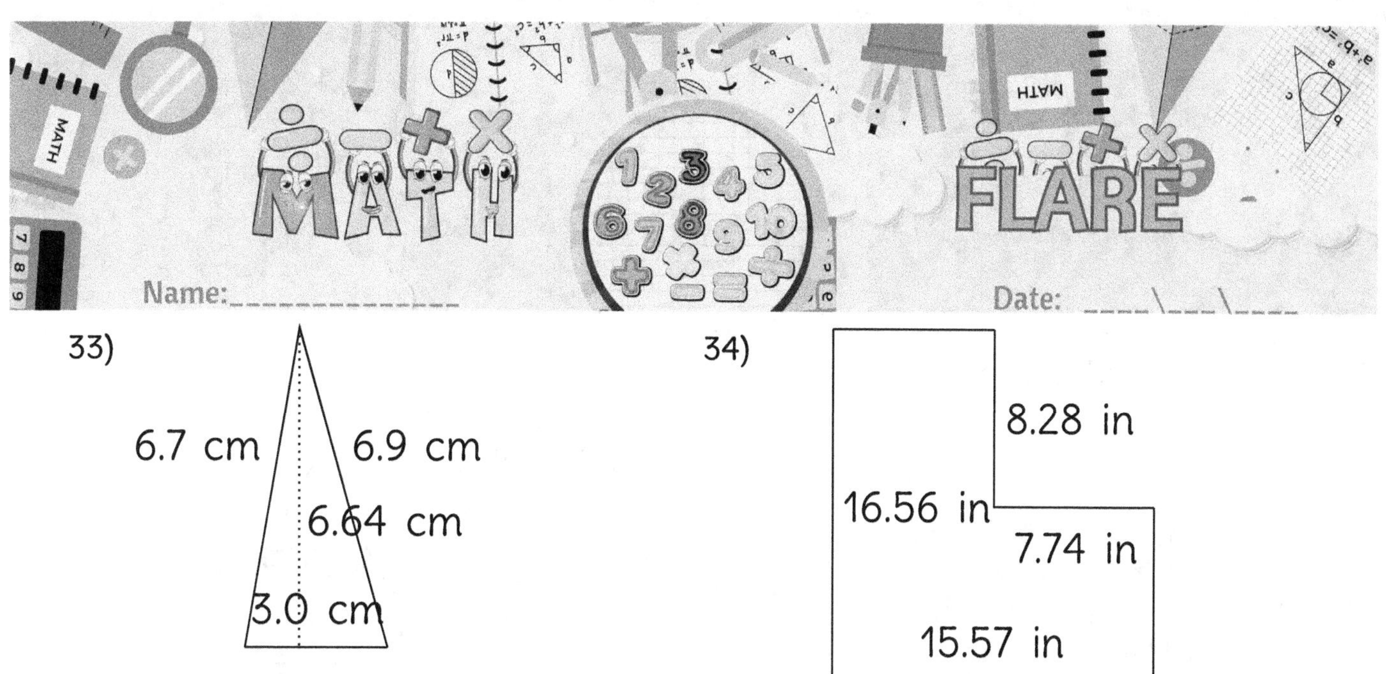

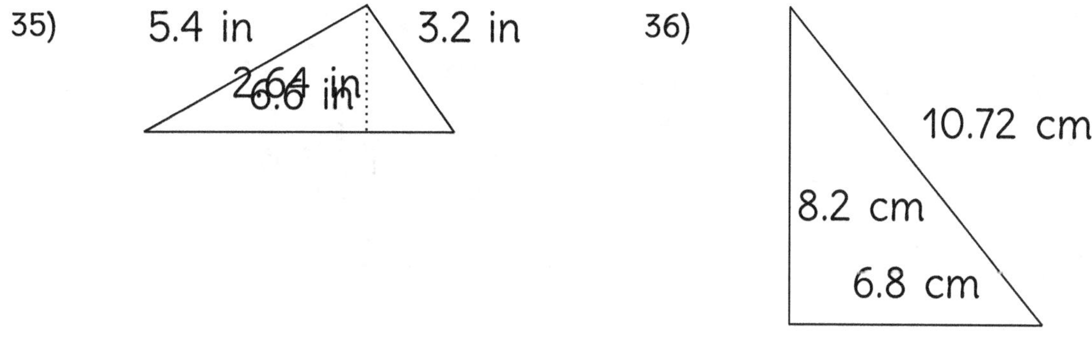

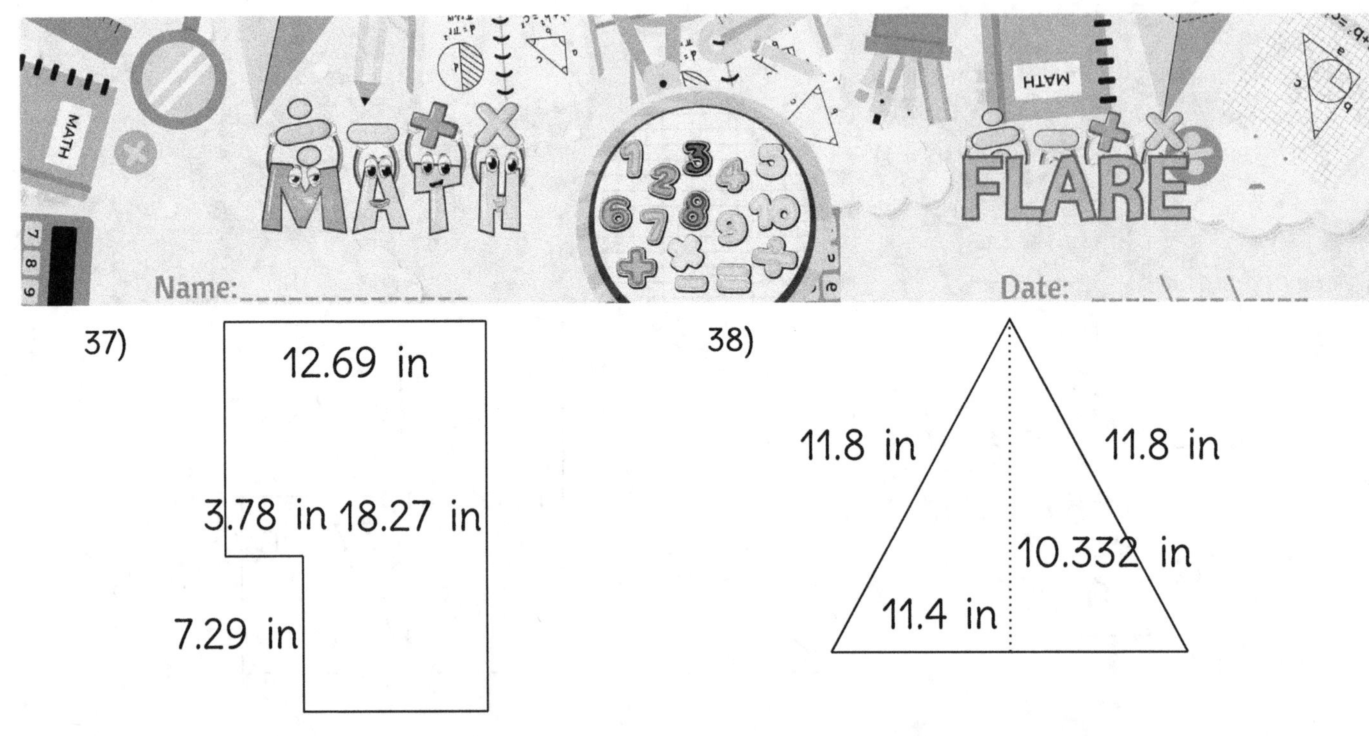
37)
12.69 in
3.78 in 18.27 in
7.29 in
38)
11.8 in
11.8 in
10.332 in
11.4 in

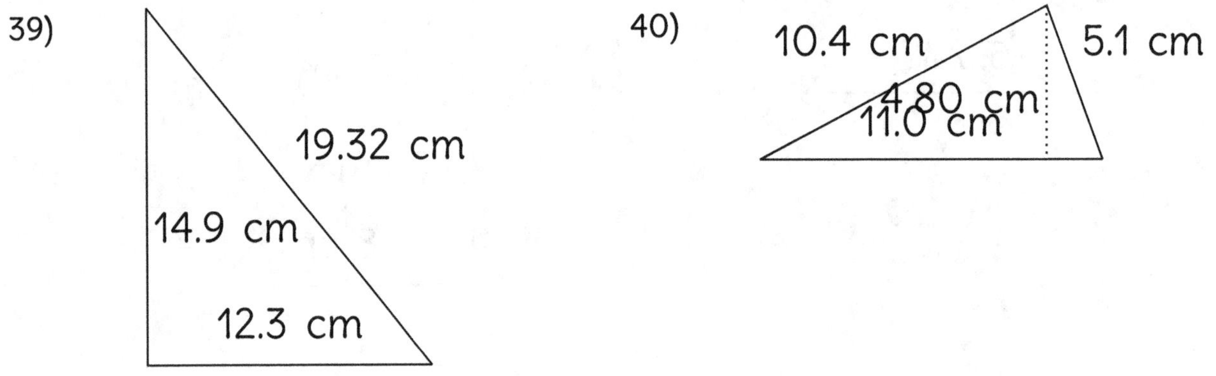
39)
19.32 cm
14.9 cm
12.3 cm
40)
10.4 cm
5.1 cm
4.80 cm
11.0 cm

Name:
Date:
MATH
FLARE

41)

5.7 in
5.7 in
5.215 in
4.6 in

42)

11.25 in
8.4 in
7.5 in

43)

10.61 in
6.6 in
8.3 in

44)

11.58 in
4.62 in
9.18 in
4.56 in

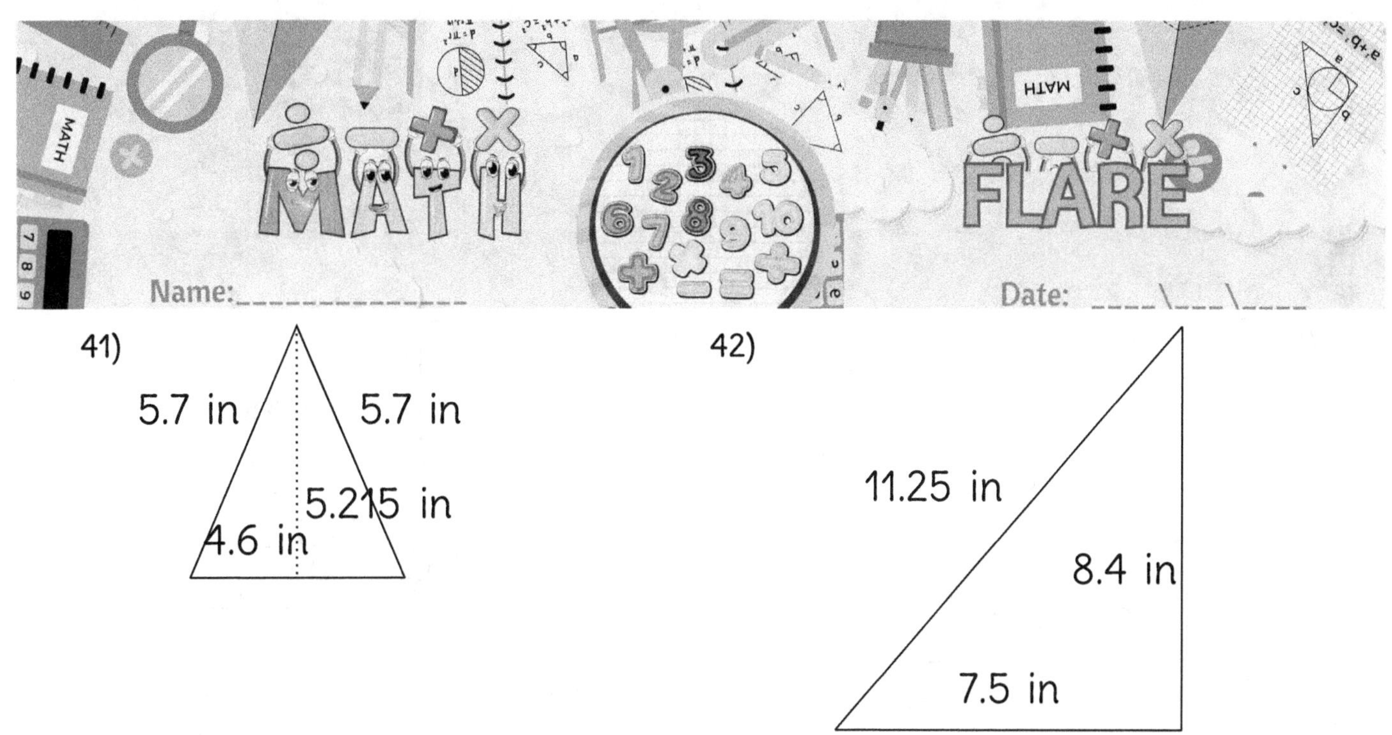

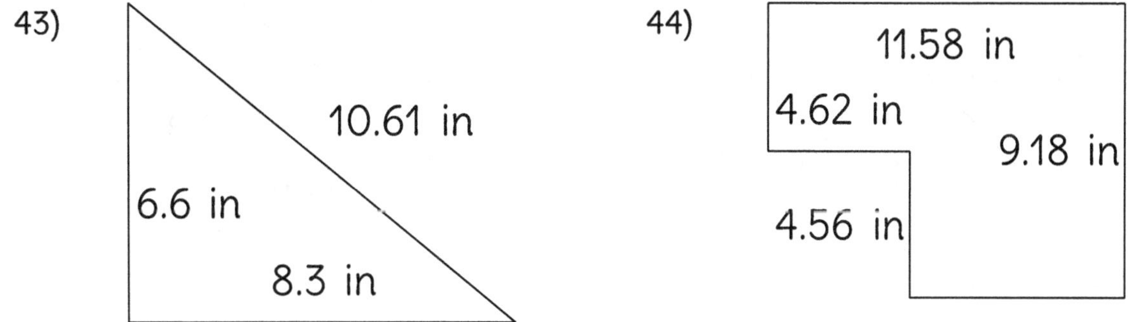

Name:
Date:
45)
11.90 in
8.8 in
8.0 in
46)
4.45 cm
7.45 cm
6.45 cm
10.75 cm

47)

18.17 in
12.8 in
12.9 in

48)

11.91 cm
7.5 cm
9.2 cm

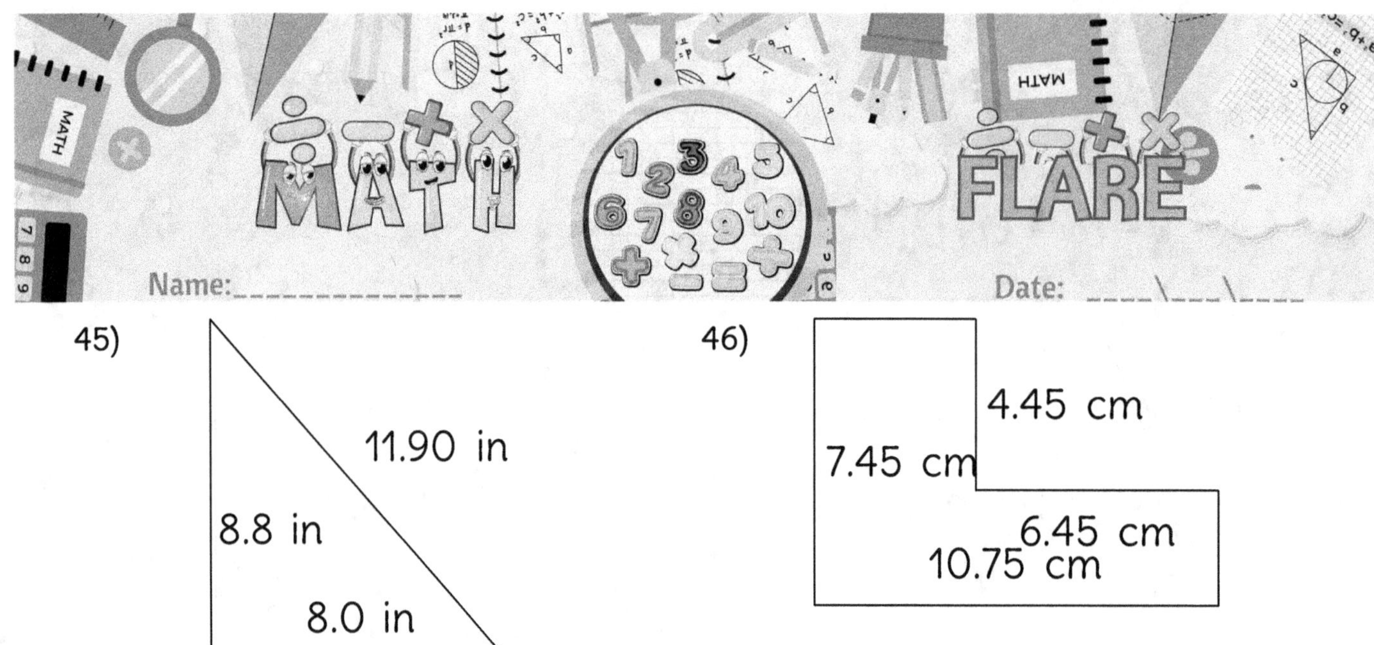

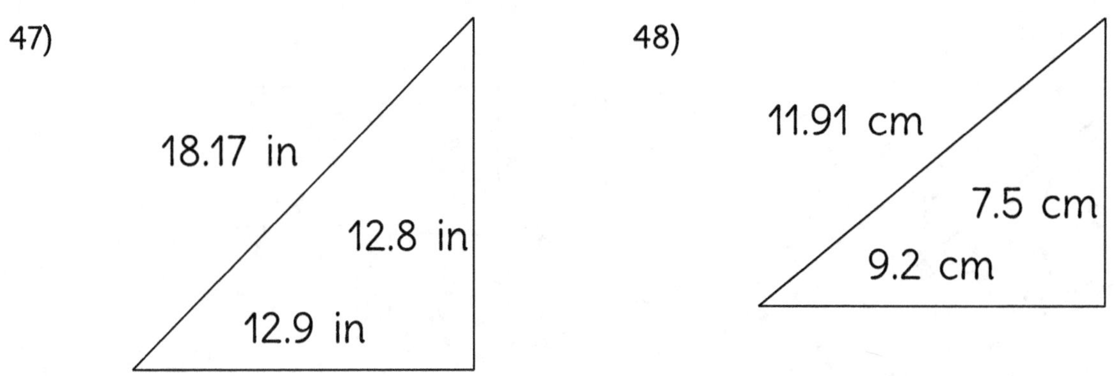

Area and Circumference

Calculate the circumference of each circle. Pi Value = 3.14

1) 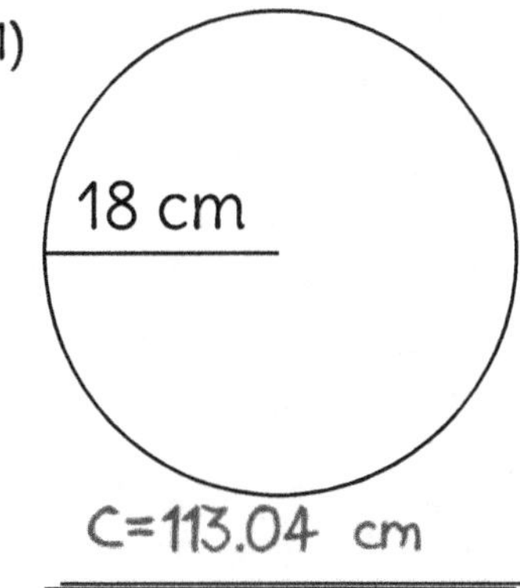

C=113.04 cm

A=1,017.36 cm²

2) 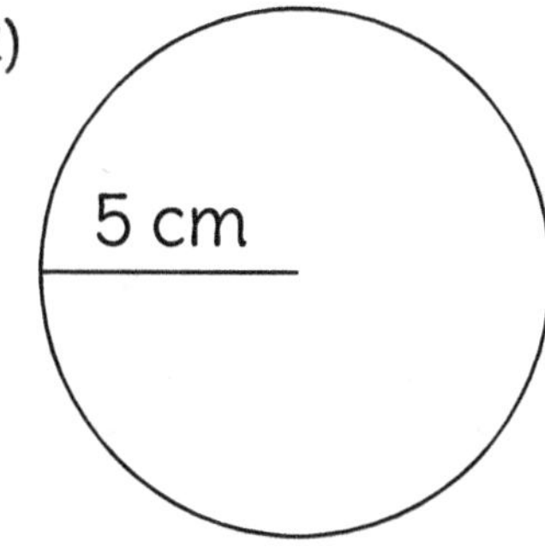

3) 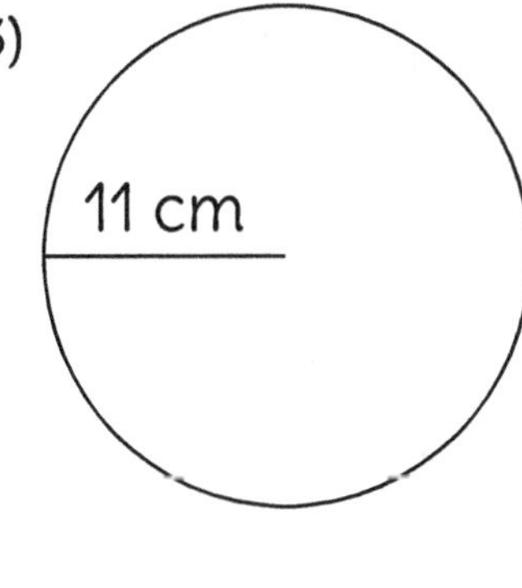

4) 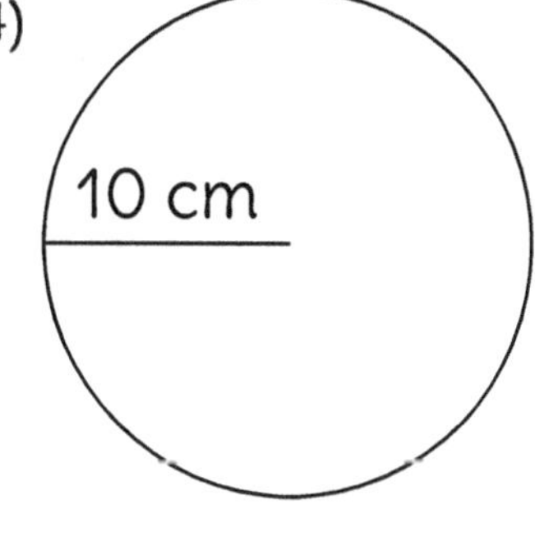

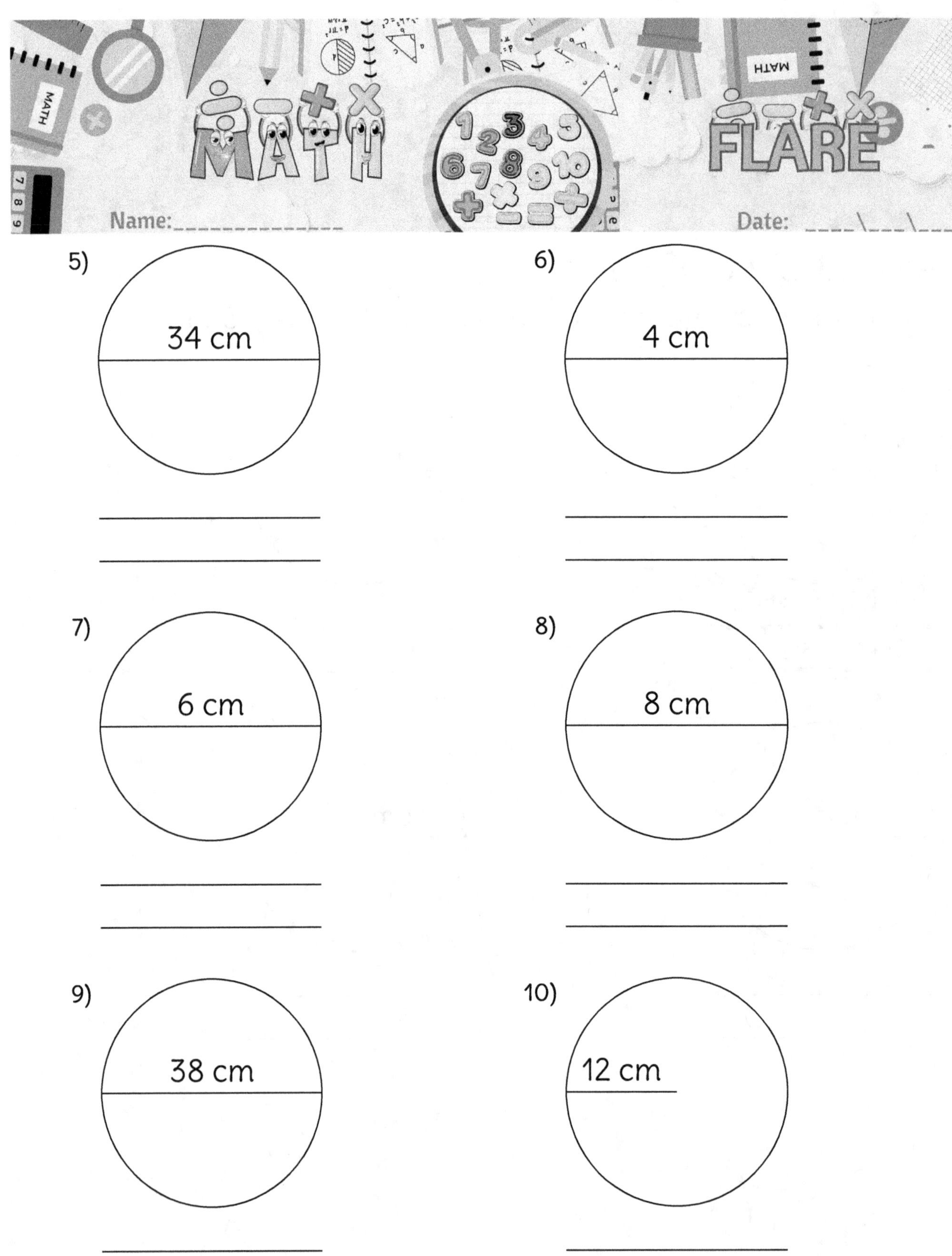

5)
34 cm

6)
4 cm

7)
6 cm

8)
8 cm

9)
38 cm

10)
12 cm

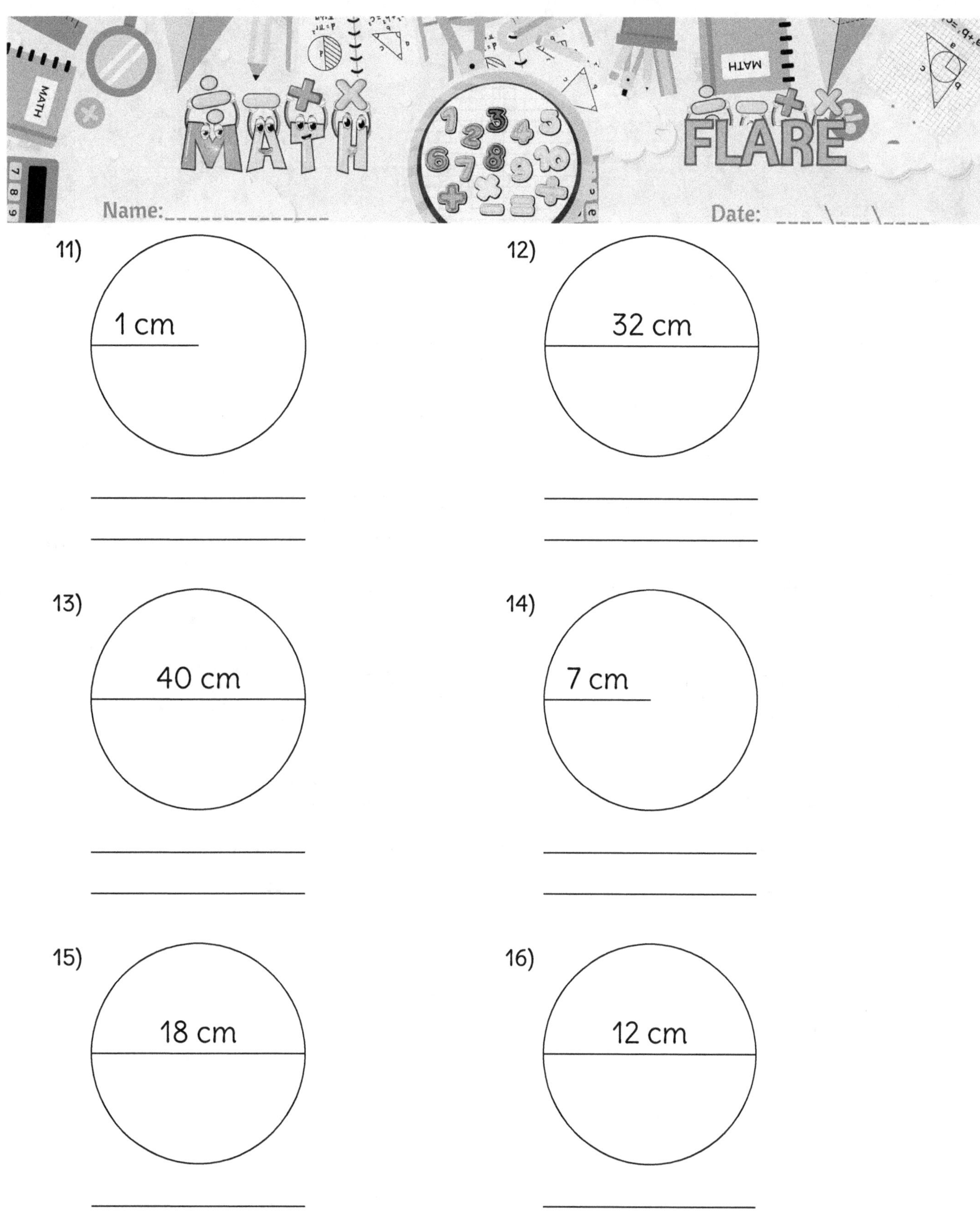
11)
1 cm

12)
32 cm

13)
40 cm

14)
7 cm

15)
18 cm

16)
12 cm

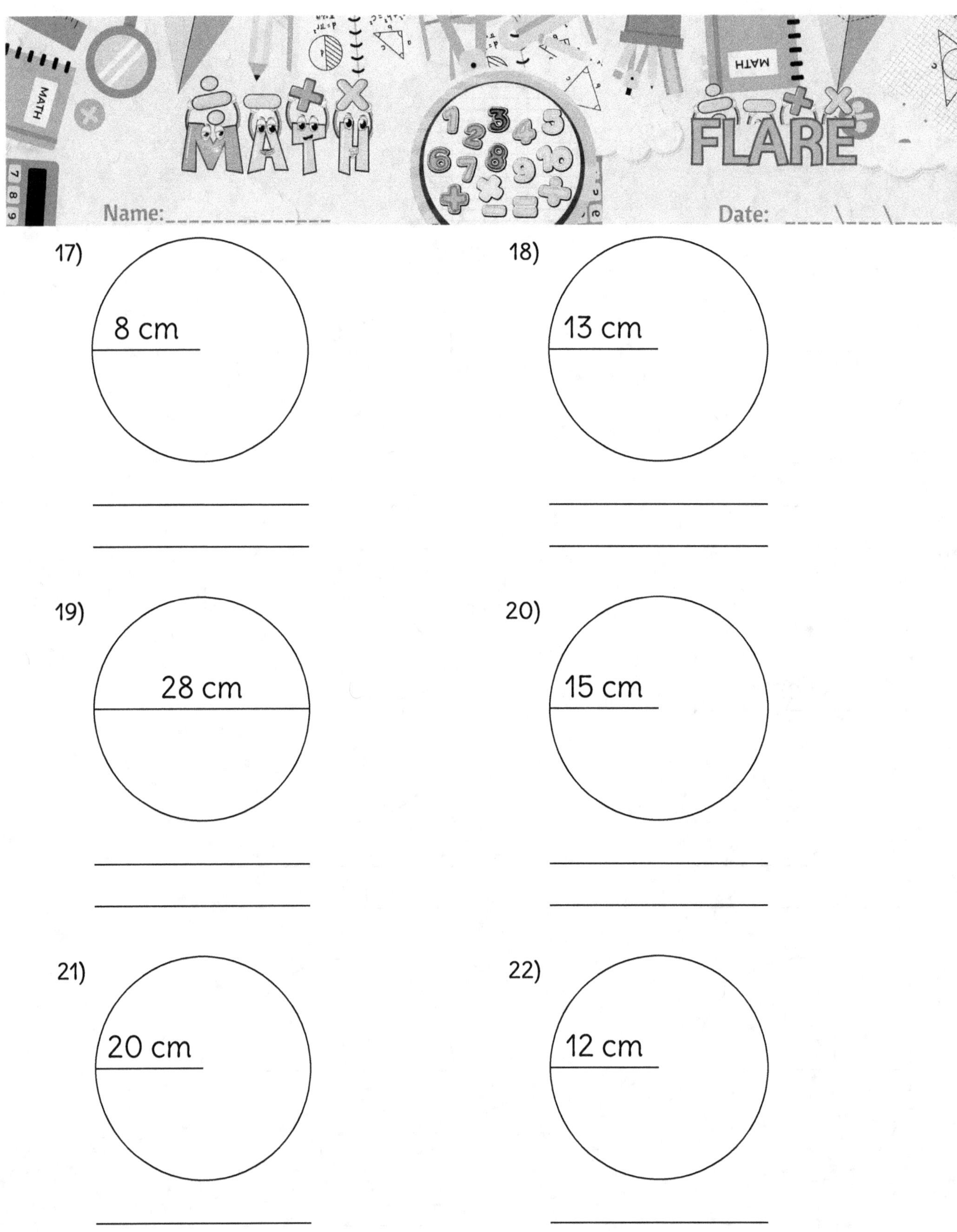

MATH
FLARE
Name:
Date:
17)
8 cm
18)
13 cm
19)
28 cm
20)
15 cm
21)
20 cm
22)
12 cm

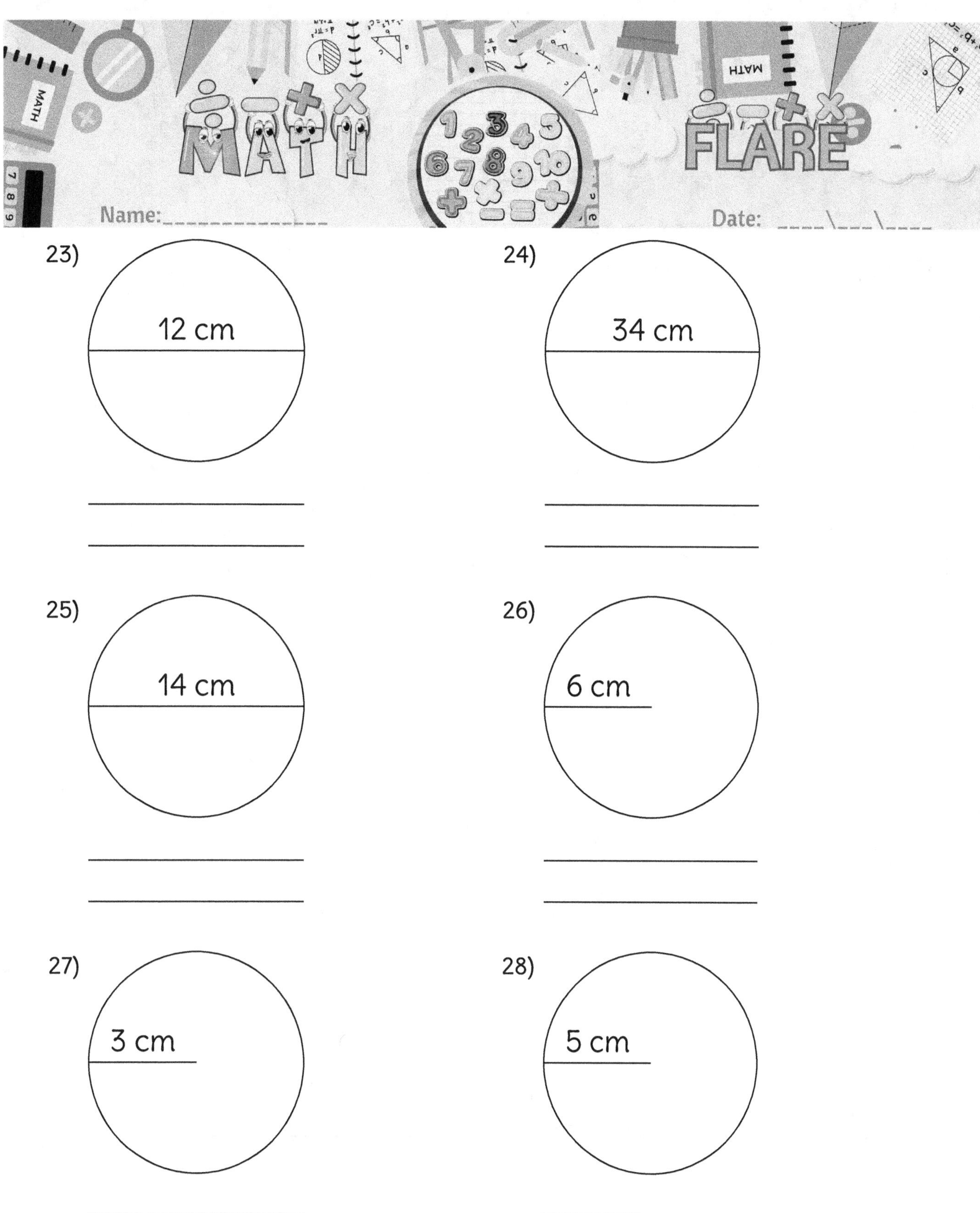

23)

____

____

24)

____

____

25)

____

____

26)

____

____

27)

____

____

28)

____

____

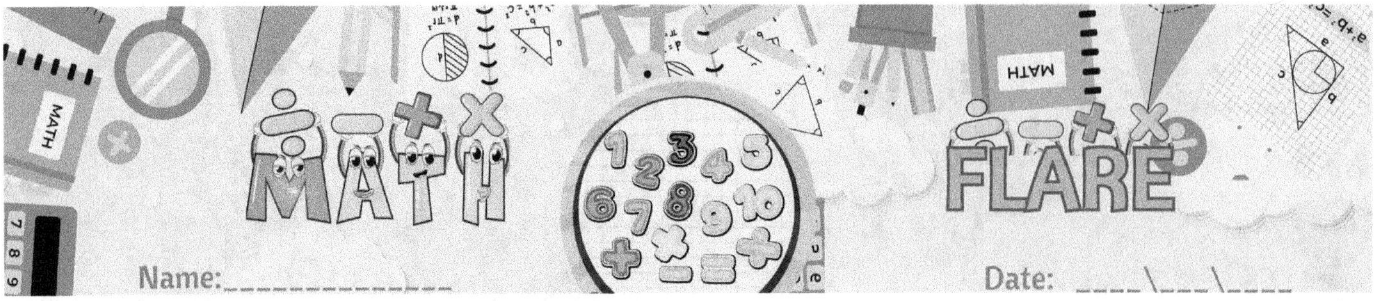

Measuring Angles

1)

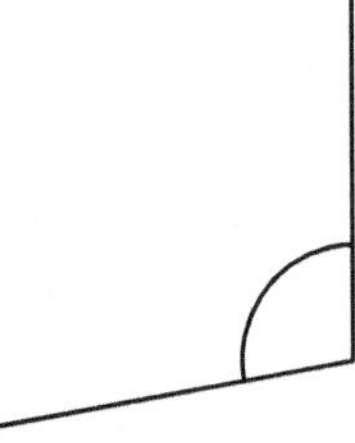

100o Obtuse

2)

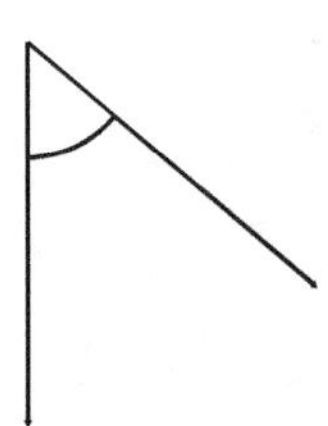

3)

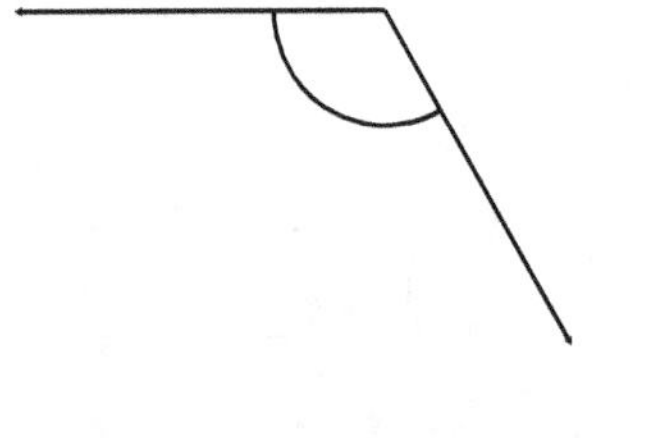

4)

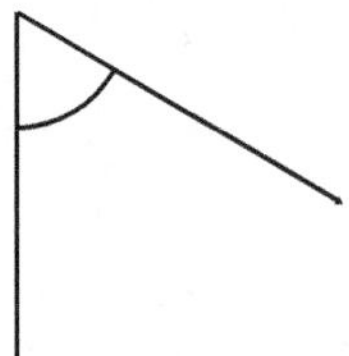

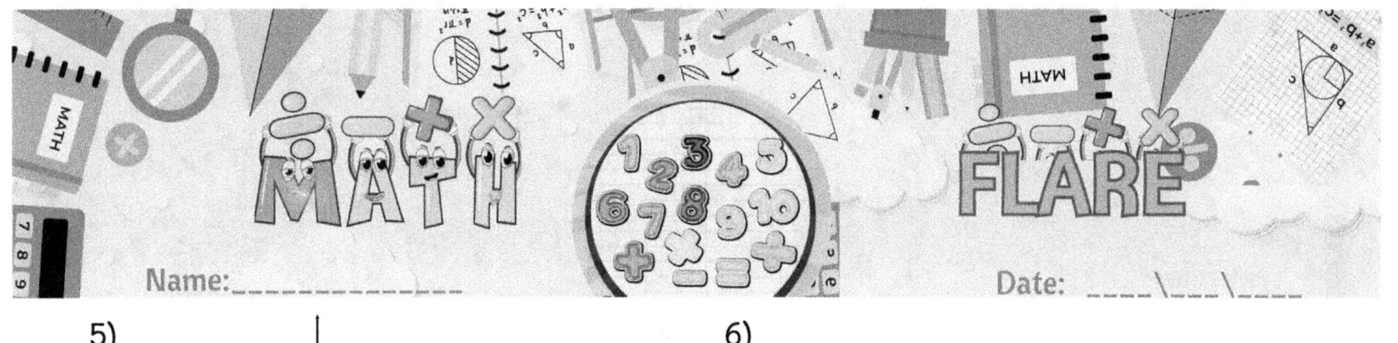

5)

6)

7)

8)

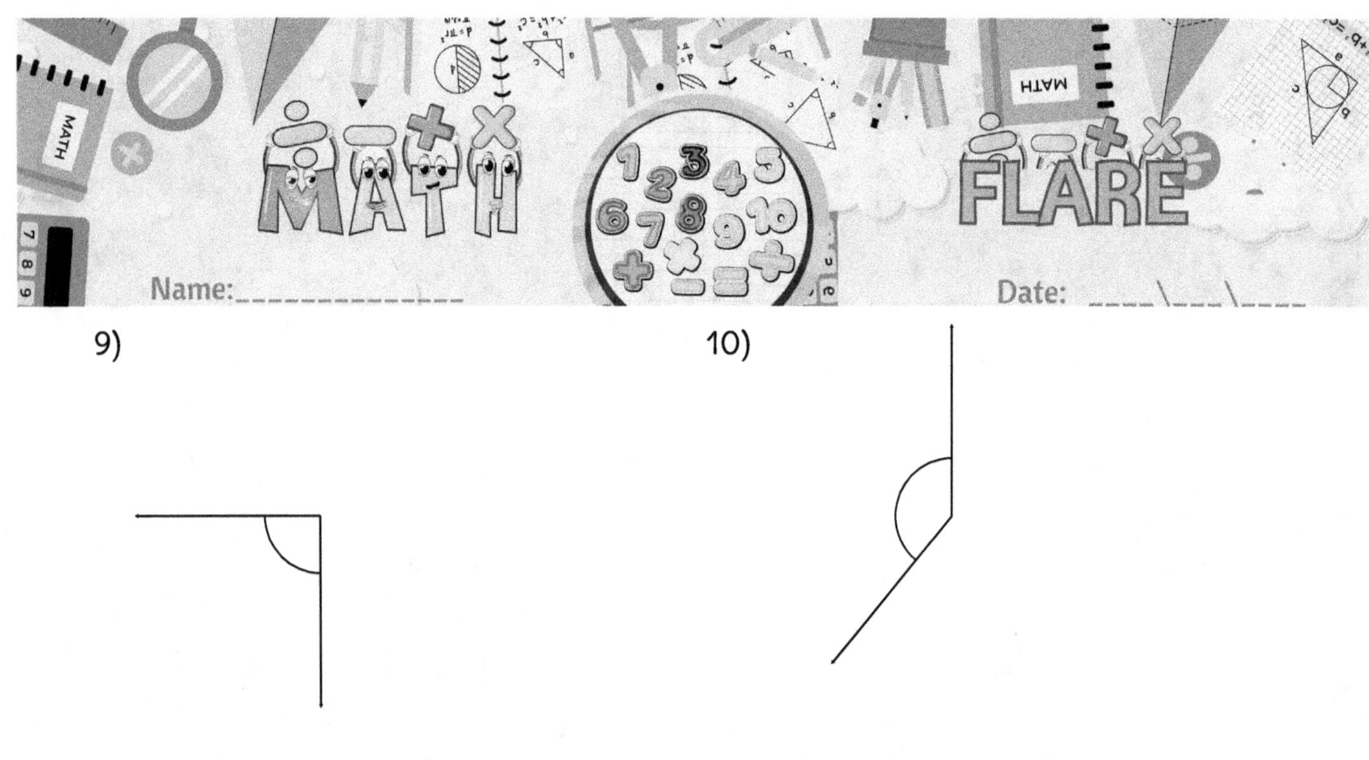

9)

10)

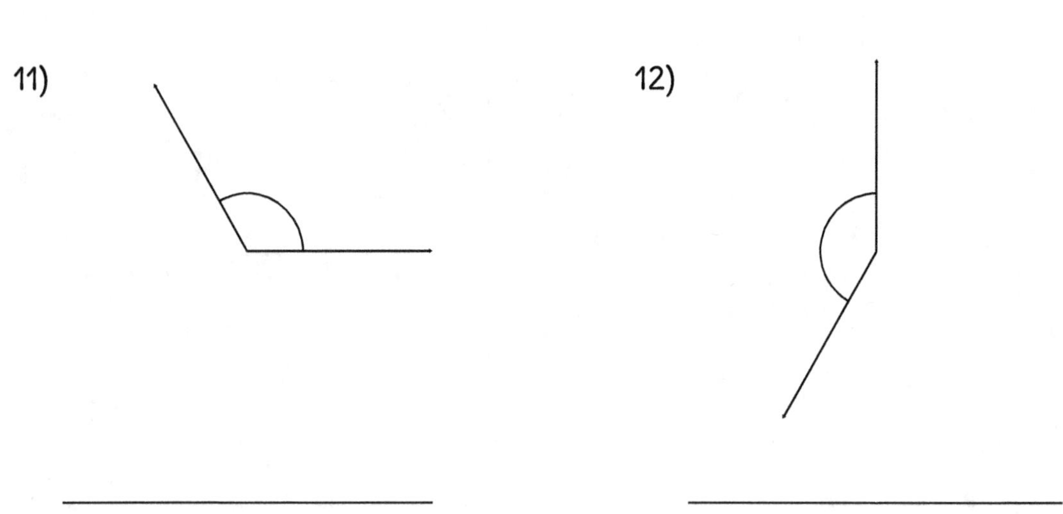

11)

12)

13)

14)

15)

16)

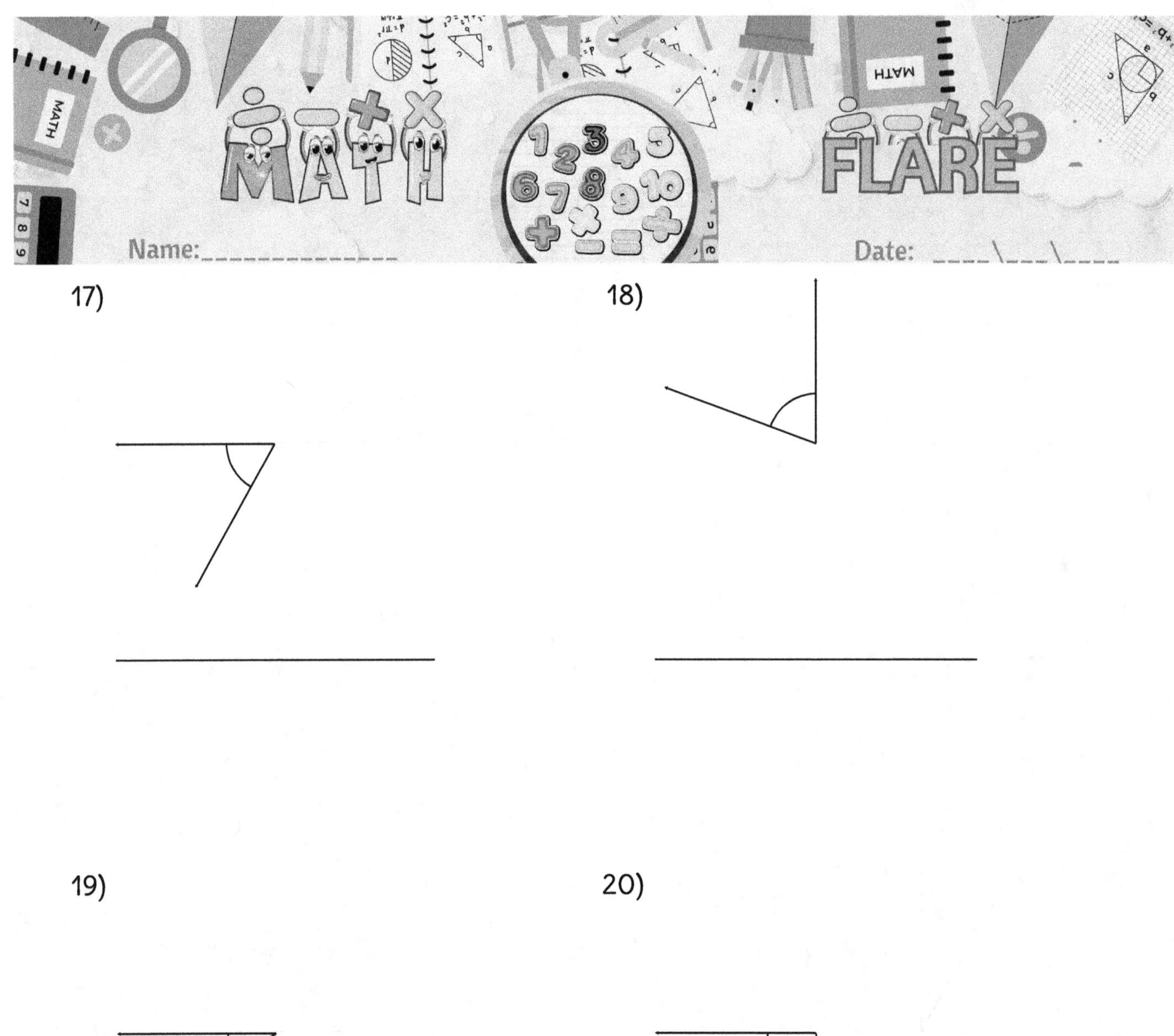

17)

18)

19)

20)

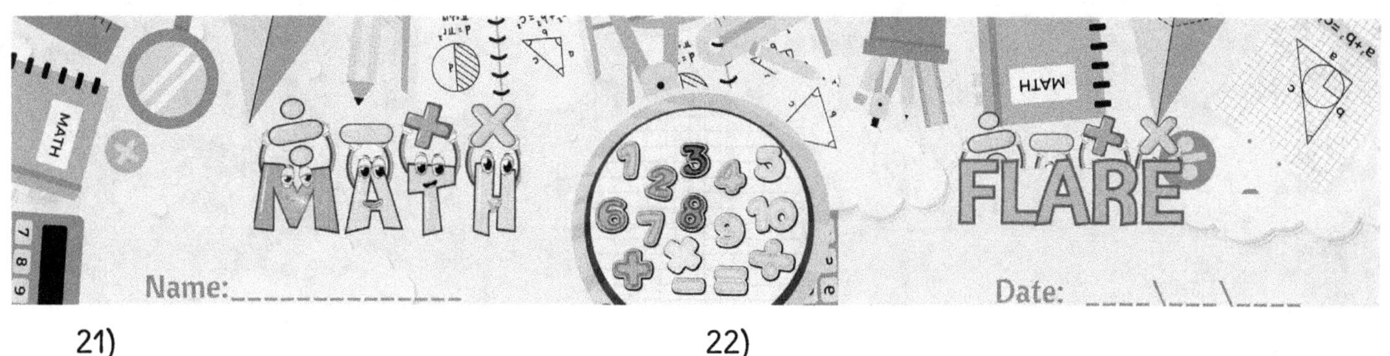

21)

22)

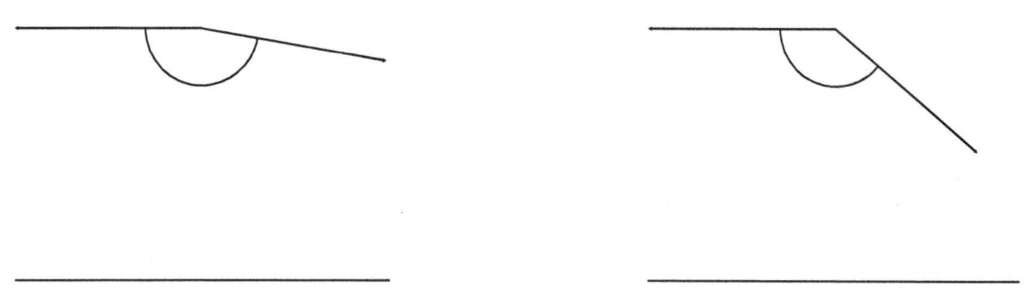

23)

24)

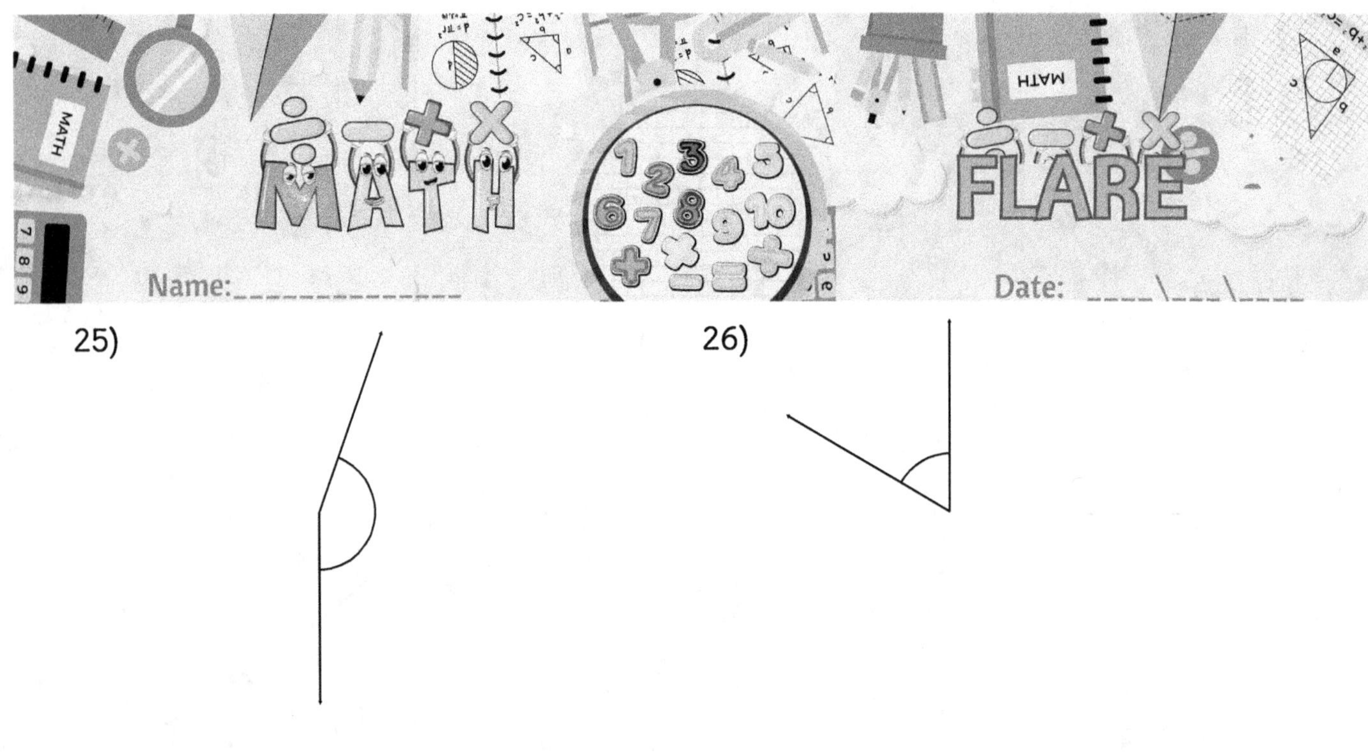

25)

26)

27)

28)

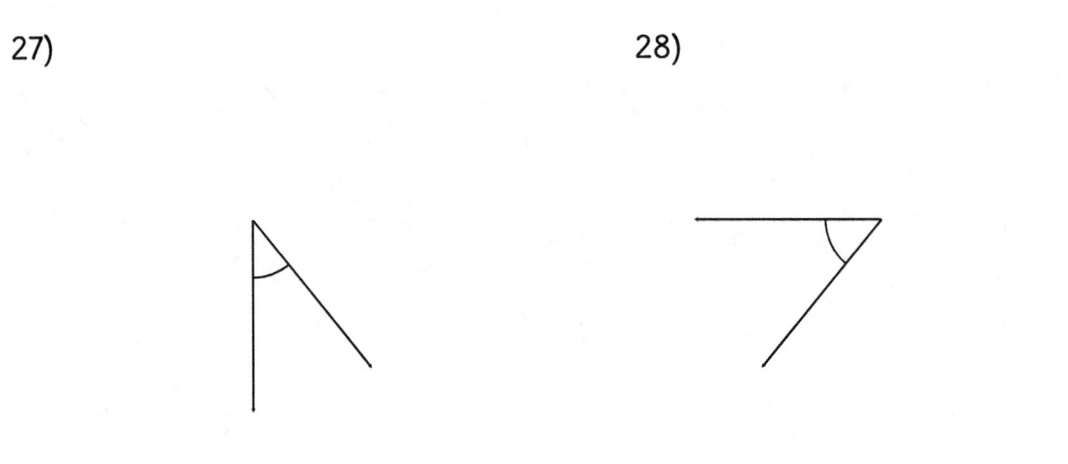

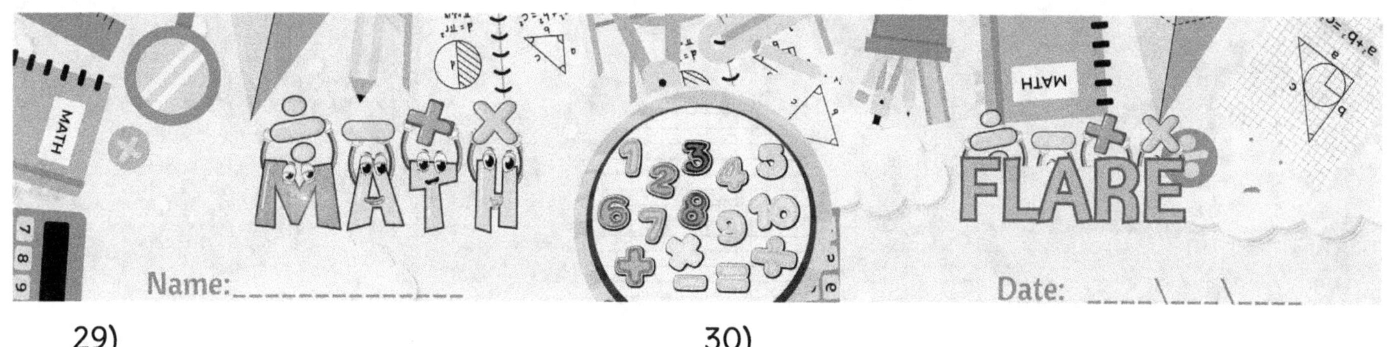

29)

30)

31)

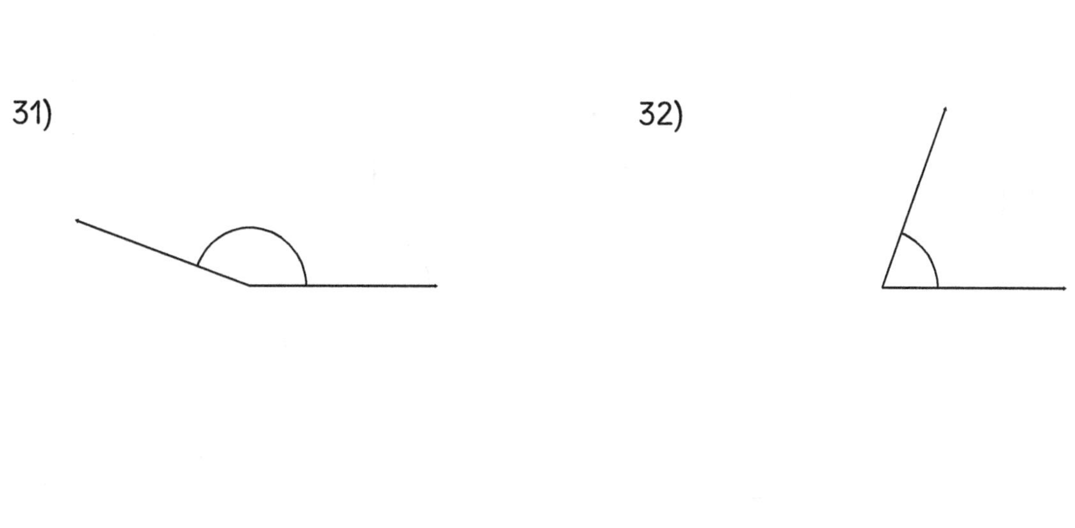

32)

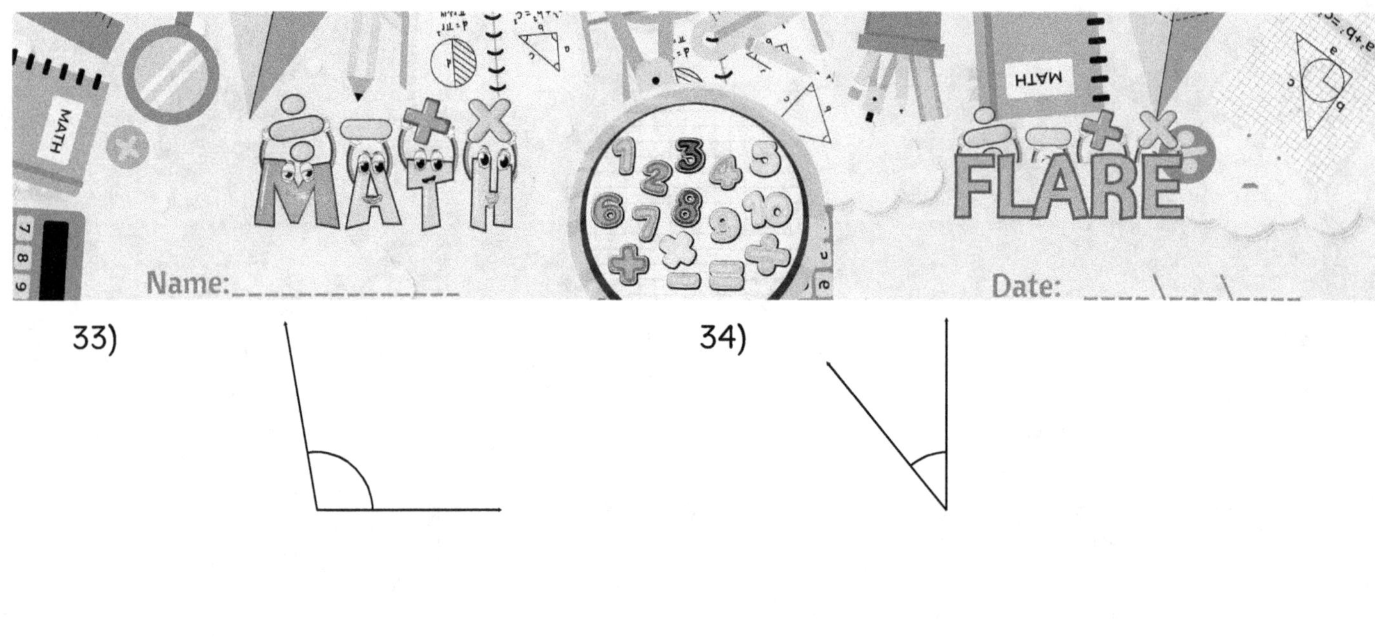

33)

34)

___________________   ___________________

35)

36)

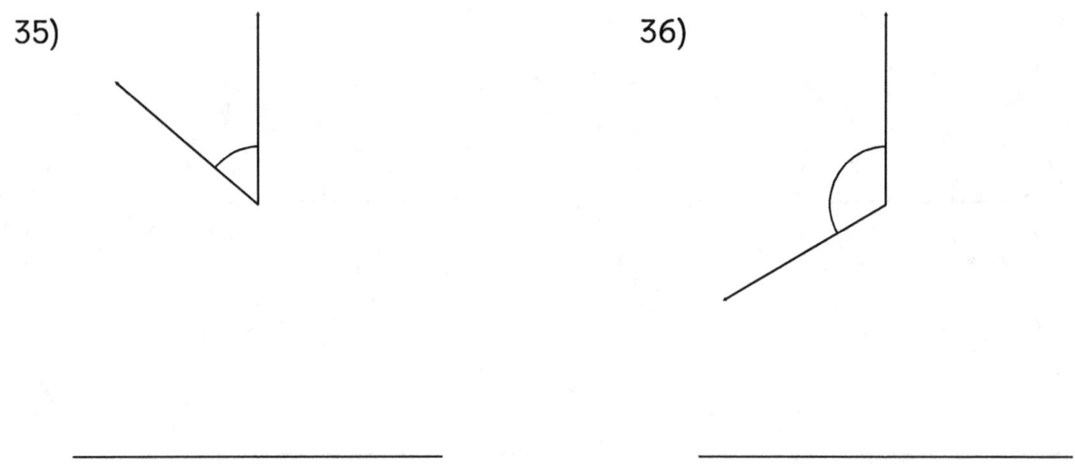

___________________   ___________________

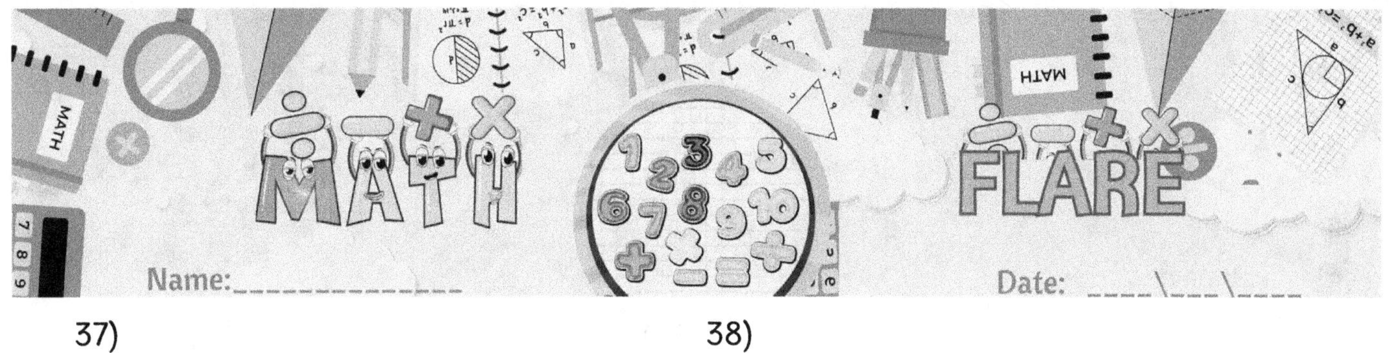

37)

38)

39)

40)

41)

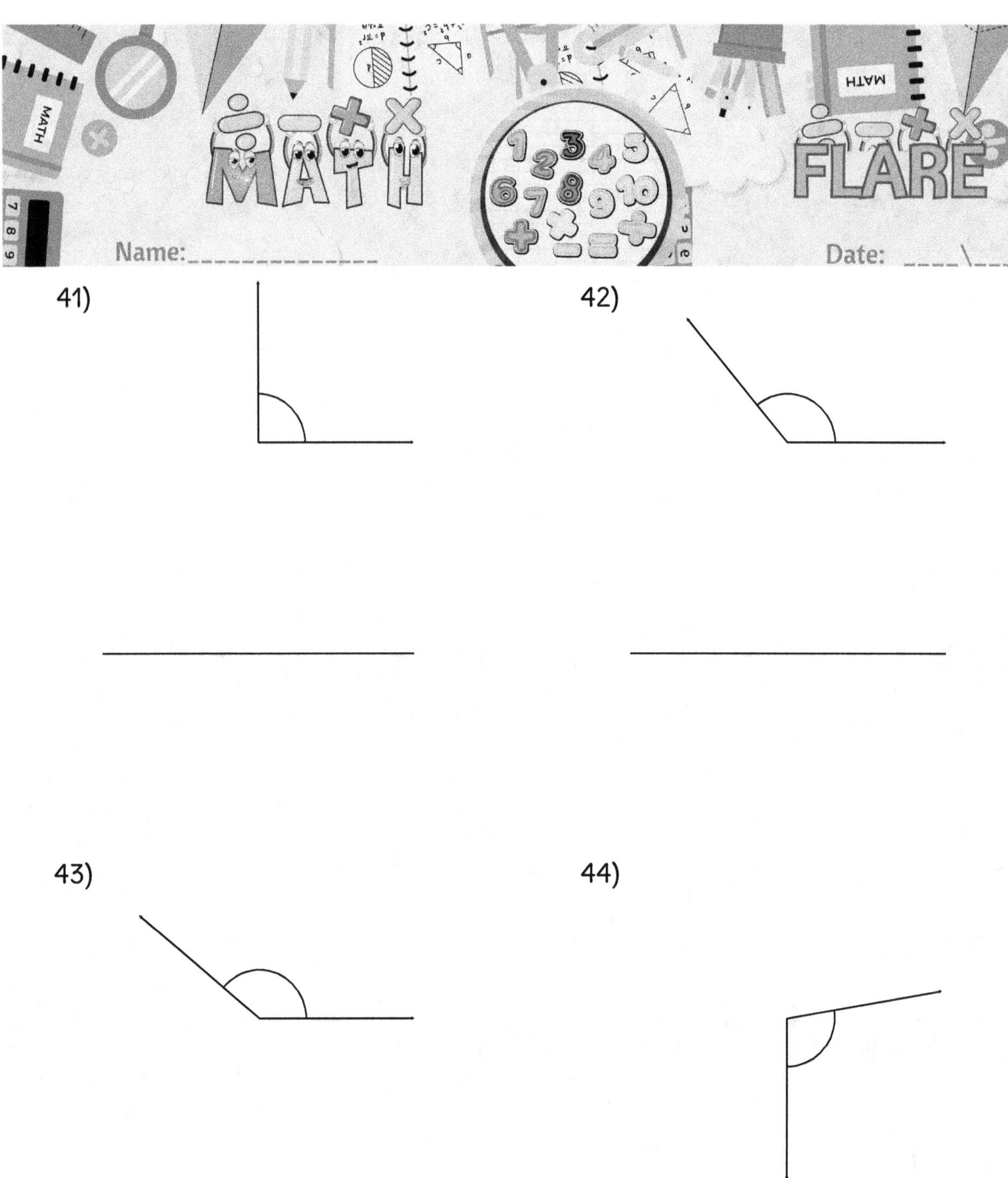

42)

43) ______________________

44) ______________________

Chapter. 06

Unit Conversion

Metric Conversion
1 meter (m) = 100 centimeters (cm)
1 meter (m) = 1000 millimeters (mm)
1 kilometer (km) = 1000 meters (m)
1 hectare (ha) = 10000 square meters (m^2)
1 square meter (m^2) = 10000 square centimeters (cm^2)
1 cubic meter (m^3) = 1000 liters (L)

Weights and Measures
1 kilogram (kg) = 1000 grams (g)
1 liter (L) = 1000 milliliters (mL)
1 tonne (t) = 1000 kilograms (kg)
1 centimeter (cm) = 10 millimeters (mm)
1 gram (g) = 1000 milligrams (mg)
1 kilometer (km) = 100000 centimeters (cm)

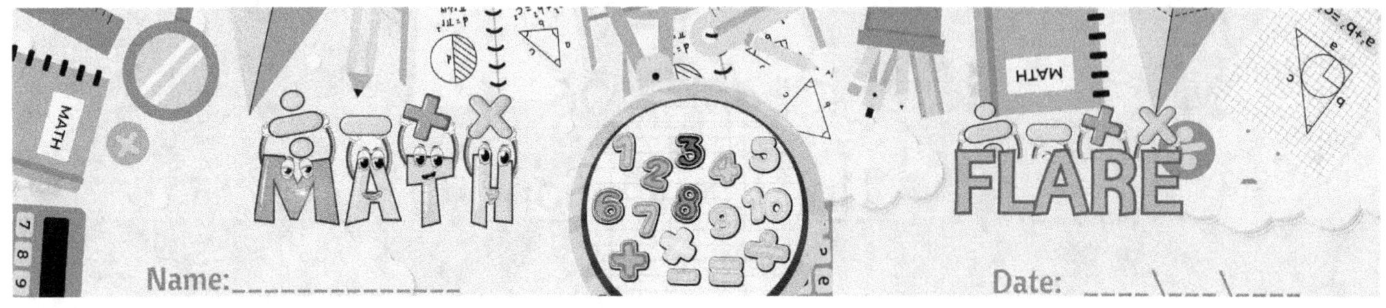

Metric Conversion

Convert the given measures.

1) 5 kl = _______1,320.860_______ gal

2) 5 g = _______________ t

3) 2 l = _______________ gal

4) 4 kl = _______________ gal

5) 4 km = _______________ mi

6) 5 m = _______________ mi

7) 7 g = _______________ lb

8) 4 kg = _______________ lb

9) 4 m = _______________ mi

10) 3 km = _______________ mi

11) 2 kl = _______________ gal

12) 1 km = _______________ mi

13) 6 kg = _______________ t

14) 7 kl = _______________ gal

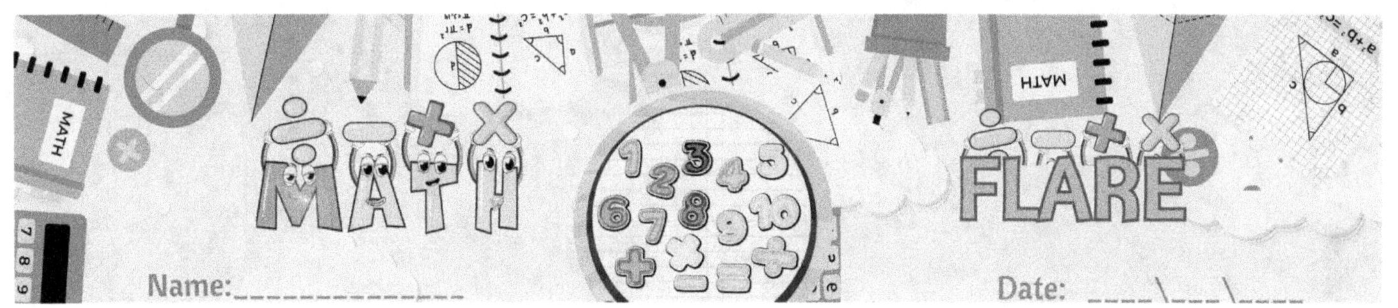

15) 8 kg = _________________ t

16) 7 g = _________________ lb

17) 7 l = _________________ gal

18) 5 kg = _________________ t

19) 8 km = _________________ mi

20) 3 g = _________________ lb

21) 7 kg = _________________ t

22) 4 m = _________________ mi

23) 4 kg = _________________ lb

24) 8 kg = _________________ t

25) 2 l = _________________ gal

26) 7 g = _________________ lb

27) 4 kg = _________________ t

28) 7 m = _________________ mi

29) 4 g = _________________ lb

30) 4 g = _________________ t

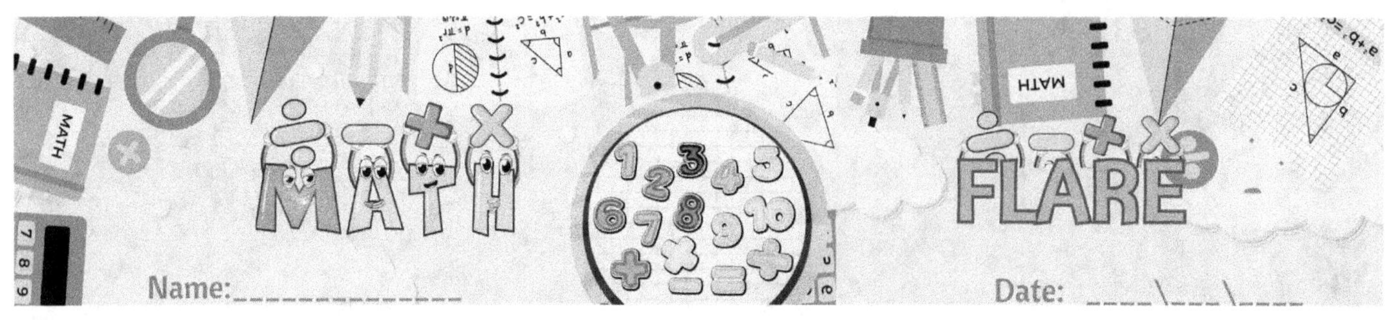

Name:_________________   Date: _______________

31) 7 kg = _________________ t   32) 9 kg = _________________ t

33) 4 g = _________________ t   34) 3 m = _________________ mi

35) 6 km = _________________ mi   36) 5 g = _________________ lb

37) 3 km = _________________ mi   38) 9 m = _________________ mi

39) 9 m = _________________ mi   40) 8 km = _________________ mi

41) 1 m = _________________ mi   42) 3 g = _________________ lb

43) 7 g = _________________ lb   44) 6 m = _________________ mi

45) 1 kg = _________________ lb   46) 3 kg = _________________ lb

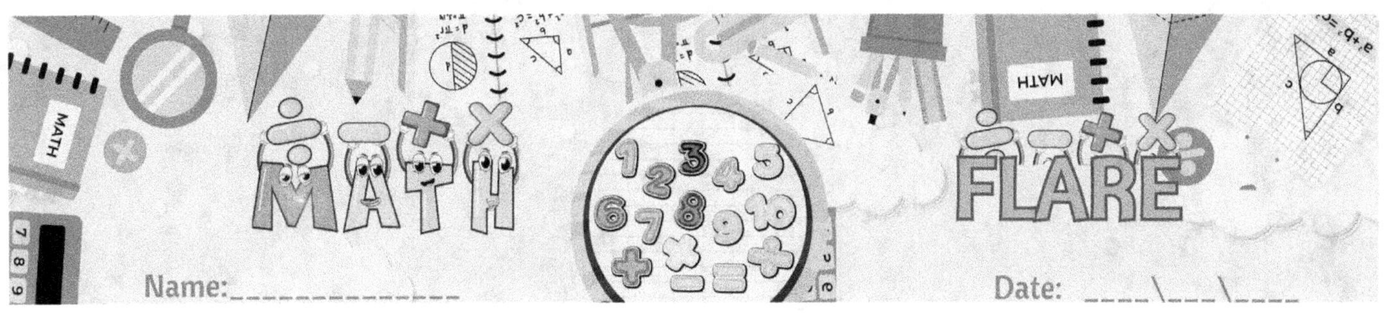

47) 8 kl = _________________ gal

48) 2 g = _________________ t

49) 7 km = _________________ mi

50) 6 kl = _________________ gal

51) 4 kl = _________________ gal

52) 5 kg = _________________ lb

53) 2 kl = _________________ gal

54) 1 kg = _________________ lb

55) 7 km = _________________ mi

56) 2 l = _________________ gal

57) 1 km = _________________ mi

58) 3 kg = _________________ lb

59) 4 km = _________________ mi

60) 6 g = _________________ t

61) 2 g = _________________ lb

62) 1 g = _________________ t

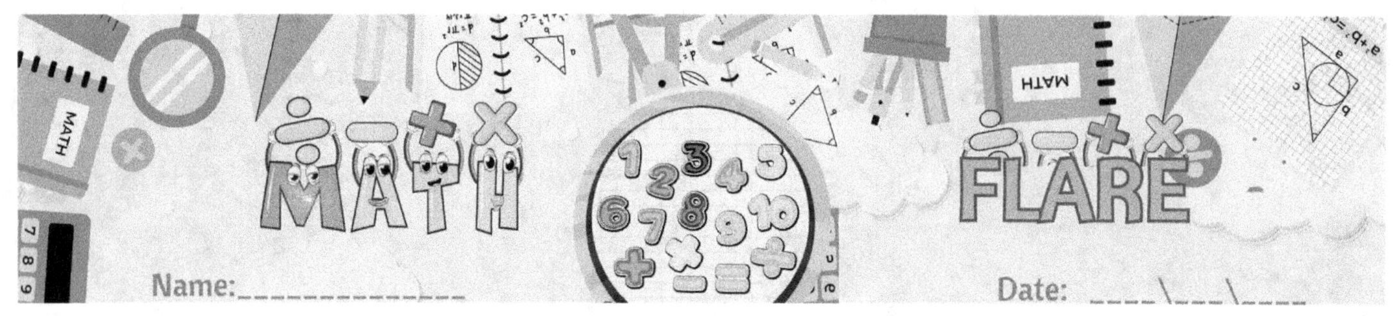

63) 2 l = _______________ gal 64) 1 g = _______________ t

65) 5 l = _______________ gal 66) 3 g = _______________ lb

67) 6 g = _______________ lb 68) 4 kg = _______________ t

69) 2 l = _______________ gal 70) 5 g = _______________ lb

71) 5 kg = _______________ lb 72) 7 g = _______________ lb

73) 5 km = _______________ mi 74) 2 m = _______________ mi

75) 3 g = _______________ t 76) 6 g = _______________ t

77) 7 kg = _______________ lb 78) 7 kg = _______________ lb

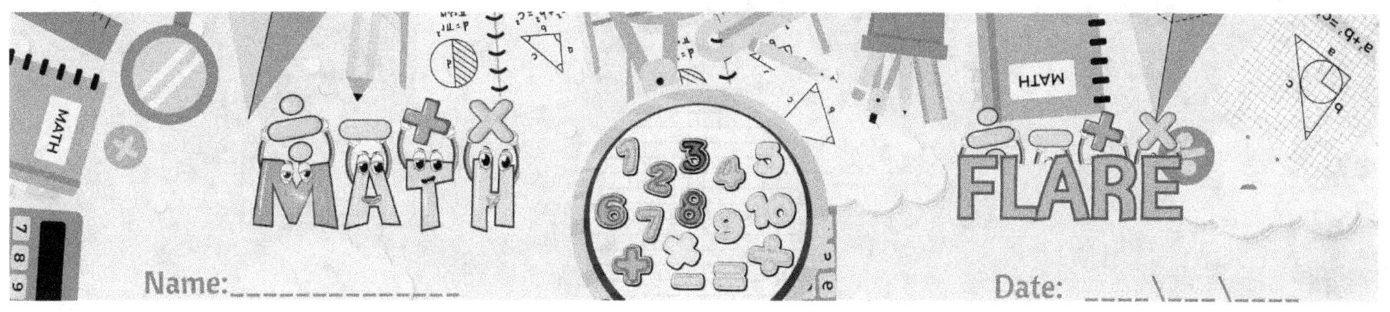

Metric Weights and Measures

Convert the given measures to new units.

1) 88 kL = _____88,000_____ L

2) 82 kg = _____________ t

3) 84 km = _____________ m

4) 28 kg = _____________ t

5) 98 t = _____________ kg

6) 72 km = _____________ m

7) 96 kL = _____________ L

8) 34 kg = _____________ t

9) 79 m = _____________ km

10) 41 kg = _____________ t

11) 62 m = _____________ km

12) 57 kL = _____________ L

13) 47 m = _____________ km

14) 17 km = _____________ m

15) 69 kg = _______________ t   16) 40 km = _______________ m

17) 72 m = _______________ km   18) 12 L = _______________ kL

19) 22 km = _______________ m   20) 24 m = _______________ km

21) 85 t = _______________ kg   22) 64 kL = _______________ L

23) 63 m = _______________ km   24) 20 km = _______________ m

25) 41 L = _______________ kL   26) 26 kg = _______________ t

27) 67 L = _______________ kL   28) 91 km = _______________ m

29) 19 kg = _______________ t   30) 76 t = _______________ kg

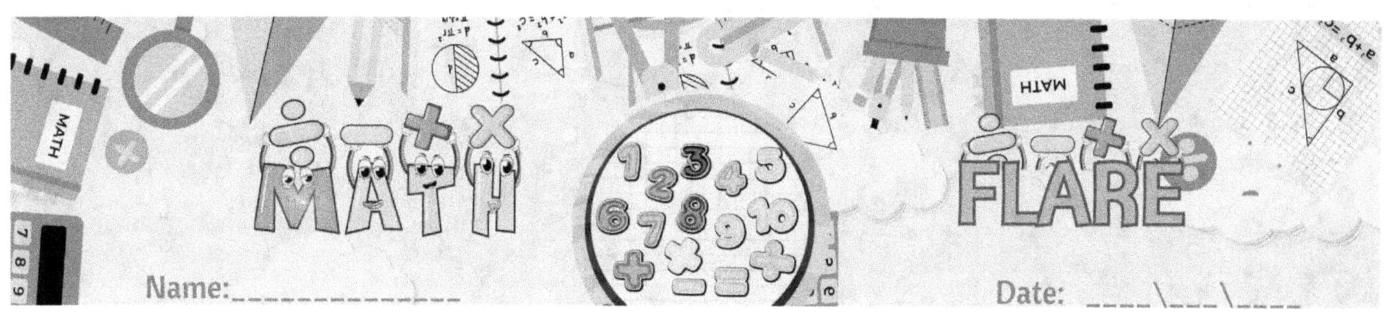

31) 38 t = _____________ kg   32) 39 L = _____________ kL

33) 56 t = _____________ kg   34) 82 km = _____________ m

35) 92 kL = _____________ L   36) 11 kL = _____________ L

37) 45 kg = _____________ t   38) 16 L = _____________ kL

39) 32 kL = _____________ L   40) 47 kg = _____________ t

41) 40 kg = _____________ t   42) 76 kL = _____________ L

43) 59 L = _____________ kL   44) 14 kL = _____________ L

45) 45 m = _____________ km   46) 20 kg = _____________ t

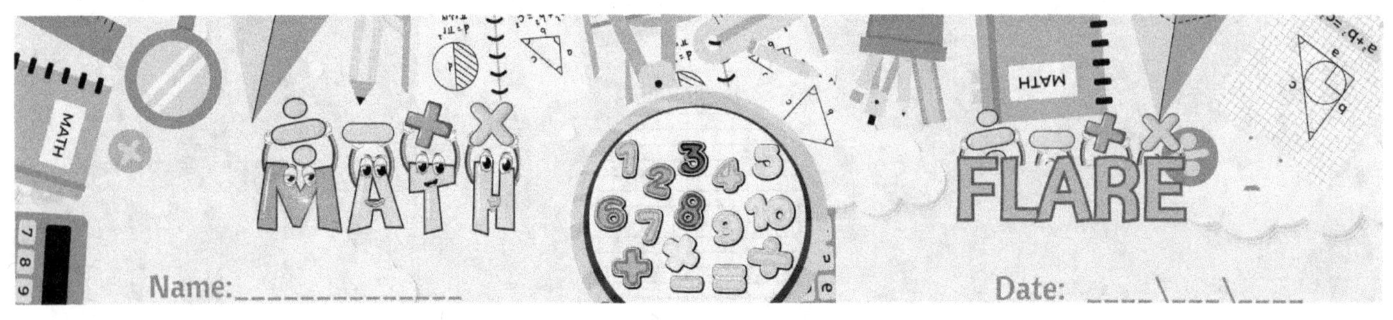

47) 29 m = ________________ km

48) 44 L = ________________ kL

49) 32 kg = ________________ t

50) 49 m = ________________ km

51) 17 m = ________________ km

52) 60 kL = ________________ L

53) 13 kL = ________________ L

54) 28 kL = ________________ L

55) 31 m = ________________ km

56) 18 kg = ________________ t

57) 67 kL = ________________ L

58) 57 m = ________________ km

59) 41 kL = ________________ L

60) 70 kg = ________________ t

61) 64 m = ________________ km

62) 50 L = ________________ kL

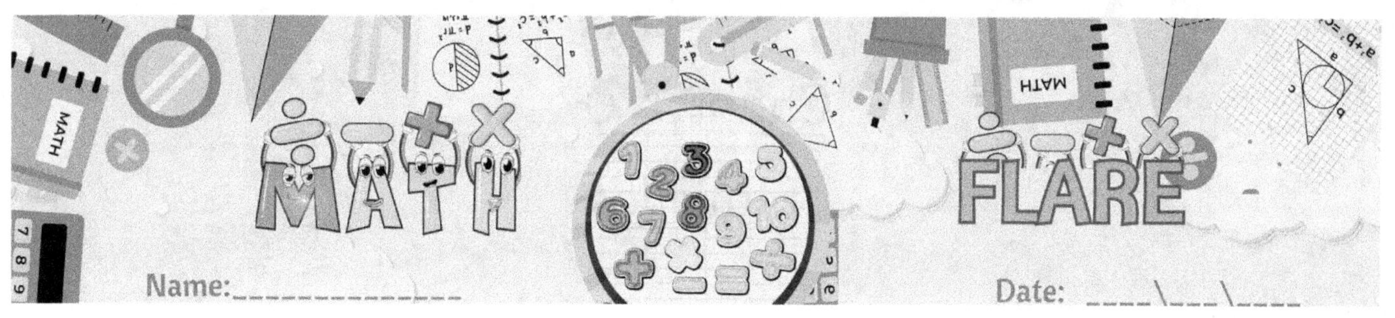

63) 27 m = ___________ km   64) 18 km = ___________ m

65) 23 kL = ___________ L   66) 57 km = ___________ m

67) 79 L = ___________ kL   68) 10 L = ___________ kL

69) 76 L = ___________ kL   70) 63 L = ___________ kL

71) 91 m = ___________ km   72) 49 kL = ___________ L

73) 34 L = ___________ kL   74) 86 kg = ___________ t

75) 60 kg = ___________ t   76) 37 kL = ___________ L

77) 80 L = ___________ kL   78) 57 t = ___________ kg

Chapter. 07
Statistics

Mean

The mean, also known as the average, is a measure of central tendency.

To find the mean of a set of numbers:

- Add up all the numbers in the set.
- Divide the sum by the total count of numbers in the set.

For example: consider the set of numbers: 70, 72, 49, 69, 27, 76.

$$\text{Mean} = \frac{70 + 72 + 49 + 69 + 27 + 76}{6}$$

$$= \frac{363}{6} = 60.5$$

Median

The median is a measure of central tendency that represents the middle value of a dataset when the values are arranged in ascending or descending order.

To find the median of a set of numbers:

- Arrange the numbers in ascending or descending order.
- If the total count of numbers is odd, the median is the middle value.
- If the total count of numbers is even, the median is the average of the two middle values.

For example: consider the set of numbers: 70, 72, 49, 69, 27, 76.

$$27, 49, 69, 70, 72, 76$$

$$\text{Median} = \frac{69 + 70}{2} = \frac{139}{2} = 69.5$$

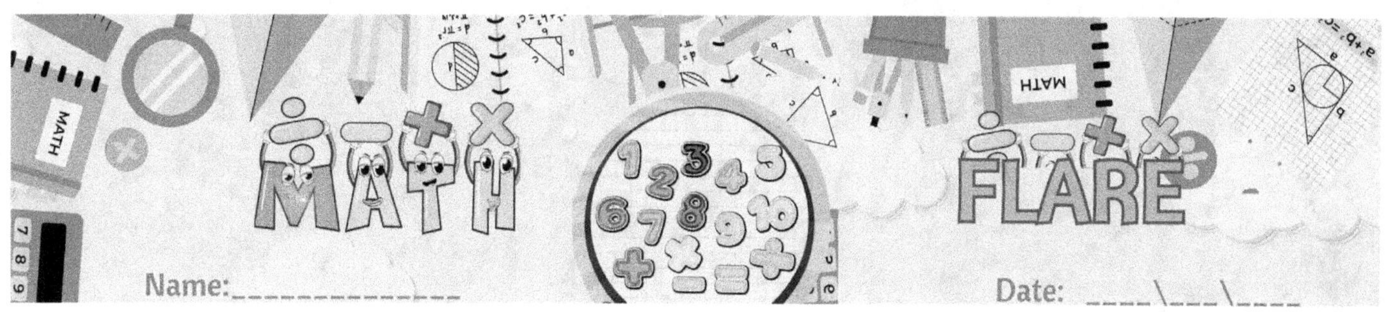

Mean and Median

Find the Mean, Median of the following sets of data.

1) 70, 72, 49, 69, 27, 76

   Mean = 60.5   Median = 69.5

$$\text{Mean} = \frac{70,\ 72,\ 49,\ 69,\ 27,\ 76}{6}$$

$$\text{Mean} = \frac{363}{6} \quad 60.5$$

27, 49, 69, 70, 72, 76

$$\text{Median} = \frac{69 + 70}{2} = 69.5$$

2) 30, 31, 57, 83, 37, 86

   Mean = ___   Median = ___

3) 74, 89, 73, 72, 29, 36

   Mean = ___   Median = ___

4) 95, 65, 96, 68, 61, 24

   Mean = ___   Median = ___

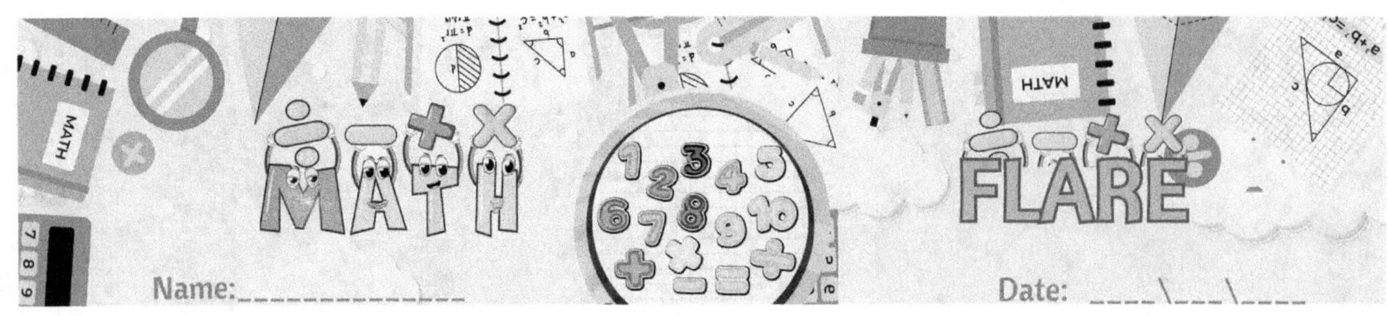

5) 69, 48, 64, 60, 93, 39

Mean = _______   Median = _____

6) 53, 35, 74, 79, 65, 95

Mean = _______   Median = _____

7) 12, 76, 92, 33, 44, 83

Mean = _______   Median = _____

8) 96, 94, 63, 88, 84, 3

Mean = _______   Median = _____

9) 70, 54, 56, 20, 34, 14

Mean = _______   Median = _____

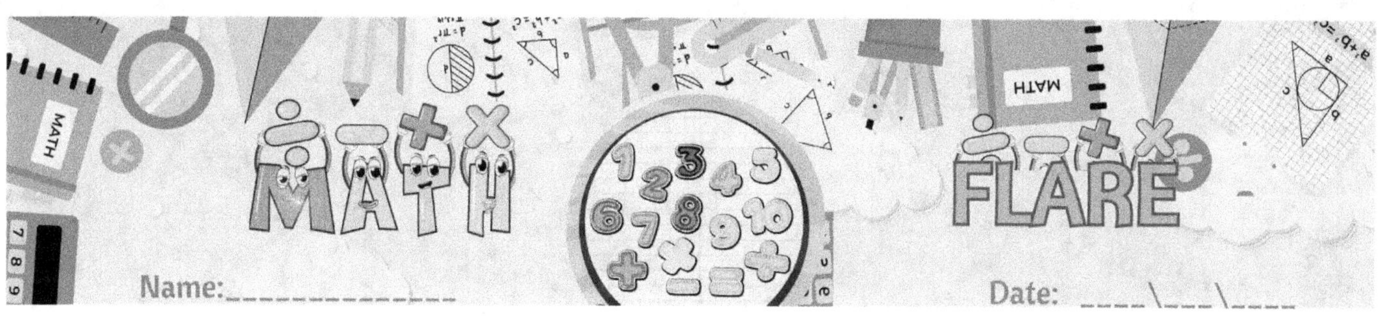

10) 56, 2, 12, 25, 1, 78

Mean = _____   Median = _____

11) 12, 70, 37, 19, 30, 3

Mean = _____   Median = _____

12) 13, 95, 24, 77, 61, 53

Mean = _______   Median = _____

13) 44, 62, 21, 13, 72, 66

Mean = _______   Median = _____

14) 60, 81, 64, 62, 89, 40

Mean = _____   Median = _____

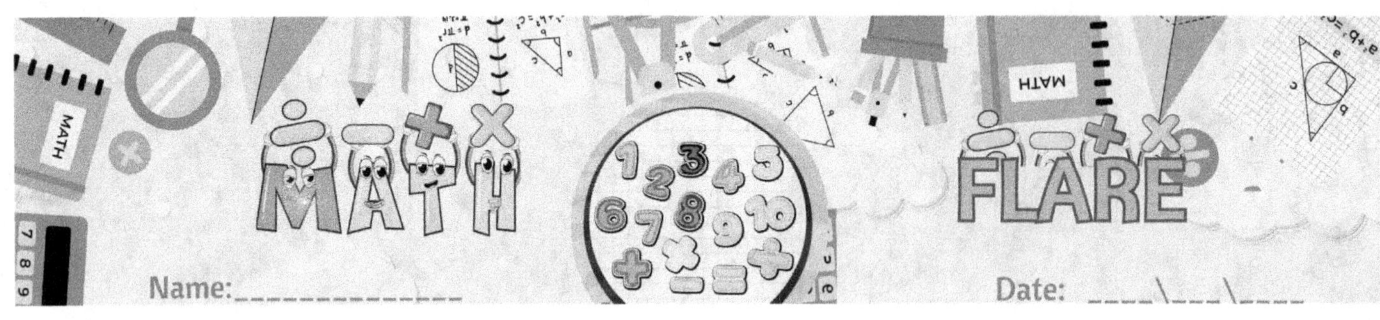

15) 82, 34, 1, 60, 23, 64

Mean = _____ Median = _____

16) 84, 87, 76, 15, 22, 74

Mean = _____ Median = _____

17) 46, 78, 64, 61, 75, 89

Mean = _____ Median = _____

18) 78, 92, 93, 4, 76, 72

Mean = _____ Median = _____

19) 93, 43, 29, 45, 64, 19

Mean = _____ Median = _____

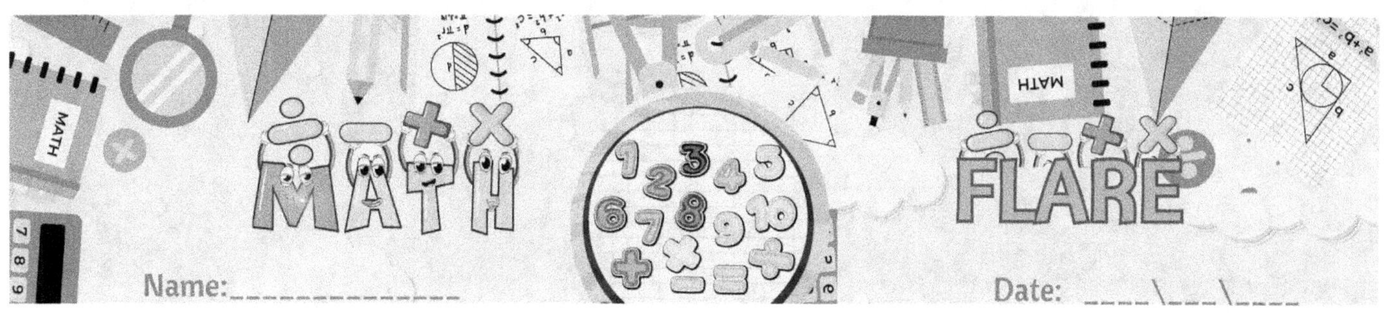

20) 15, 49, 80, 97, 36, 95

Mean = _____ Median = _____

21) 3, 52, 73, 60, 92, 74

Mean = _____ Median = _____

22) 77, 30, 41, 47, 67, 94

Mean = _______ Median = _____

23) 3, 99, 6, 74, 84, 97

Mean = _____ Median = _____

24) 47, 78, 58, 29, 67, 79

Mean = _______ Median = _____

ANSWERS

Page 1:   Long Division: Remainders

1. 9,248 R1	2. 1,636 R1	3. 2,954 R2	4. 4,002 R3
5. 3,658 R7	6. 3,355 R7	7. 6,584 R5	8. 2,116 R6
9. 3,269 R1	10. 822 R15	11. 3,508 R4	12. 3,720 R10
13. 8,516 R3	14. 17,782 R0	15. 3,130 R4	16. 6,441 R7
17. 13,623 R1	18. 4,287 R5	19. 4,192 R2	20. 9,669 R1
21. 5,206 R7	22. 4,113 R2	23. 1,919 R9	24. 15,381 R3
25. 24,650 R1	26. 5,442 R5	27. 11,581 R1	28. 2,590 R10

Page 8:   Multi Digit Multiplication

1. 208,374,270	2. 42,255,144	3. 116,963,734
4. 159,462,144	5. 502,306,357	6. 216,065,660
7. 35,672,797	8. 366,038,494	9. 91,578,660
10. 65,436,756	11. 180,752,754	12. 877,649,762
13. 188,824,392	14. 78,502,116	15. 86,572,242
16. 170,287,591	17. 641,115,442	18. 86,480,275
19. 103,632,318	20. 214,923,962	21. 459,015,309
22. 174,269,950	23. 47,576,361	24. 152,853,744
25. 297,277,074	26. 380,228,360	27. 42,606,569
28. 691,860,975	29. 174,268,836	30. 264,318,752
31. 695,953,131	32. 909,006,394	33. 21,327,312

34. 65,982,849   35. 82,540,460   36. 139,544,460

Page 12:   Multi Digit Multiplication: Decimals

1. 12,816.5625   2. 51,222.7040   3. 3,661.1695

4. 49,106.0141   5. 3,268.1616   6. 11,819.4375

7. 8,973.8955   8. 50,913.2932   9. 7,949.8048

10. 44,055.2427   11. 75,085.1850   12. 58,174.0085

13. 10,077.9354   14. 7,019.6802   15. 24,366.6752

16. 63,639.2955   17. 30,487.9666   18. 91,990.8912

19. 21,855.2397   20. 40,657.6404   21. 63,545.7440

22. 26,665.0440   23. 4,252.6617   24. 17,056.6344

25. 22,051.1888   26. 7,694.6436   27. 72,571.1208

28. 25,345.0320   29. 45,940.2736   30. 71,772.1382

31. 29,569.5655   32. 35,425.0152   33. 21,746.2551

34. 18,452.8812   35. 15,435.2504   36. 19,585.0200

Page 16:   Dividing Decimals

1. 10.97   2. 1.43   3. 10.74   4. 3.92   5. 10.44   6. 18.42

7. 1.37   8. 10.33   9. 32.32   10. 7.91   11. 3.25   12. 6.58

13. 3.91   14. 8.38   15. 18.68   16. 3.39   17. 6.56   18. 2.65

19. 10.90   20. 9.65   21. 8.36   22. 22.33   23. 4.90   24. 5.42

25. 16.84   26. 16.98   27. 6.96   28. 29.00   29. 12.90   30. 11.67

31. 13.81   32. 16.32

Page 20: Multiplication Word Problems

1. 340	2. 187	3. 156	4. 280	5. 361	6. 126	7. 220
8. 85	9. 60	10. 27	11. 48	12. 176	13. 51	14. 4
15. 270	16. 6	17. 84	18. 198	19. 66	20. 360	

Page 25: Division Word Problems

1. 53	2. 24	3. 94	4. 96	5. 58	6. 49	7. 38
8. 20	9. 73	10. 47	11. 92	12. 42	13. 4	14. 380
15. 32	16. 78	17. 71	18. 91	19. 36	20. 93	

Page 31: Place Value

1. 3 ones	2. 4 billions
3. 2 hundred thousands	4. 6 hundred thousands
5. 8 millions	6. 5 hundredths
7. 5 hundred millions	8. 7 millions
9. 1 hundredth	10. 0 ones
11. 1 million	12. 0 ones
13. 4 thousandths	14. 8 tens
15. 6 ten thousands	16. 7 ten thousandths
17. 7 ten millions	18. 7 tenths
19. 5 ten millions	20. 1 ten thousand
21. 5 thousands	22. 6 thousands
23. 7 thousands	24. 3 hundred thousandths

25. 6 tens

26. 9 hundred thousands

27. 9 ten thousands

28. 5 thousands

29. 4 hundred millions

30. 0 ten thousands

Page 35: Place Value and Expanded Notation

1. 86,951,328.0

2. 427,953,262

3. 721,739,817

4. 784,411.656

5. 5,752,768.52

6. 45,385,962.5

7. 950,603.943

8. 373,253.289

9. 45,648,173.3

10. 2,967,084.85

11. 539,650,017

12. 444,583.385

13. 275,463.503

14. 7,912,722.90

15. 4,664,351.51

16. 282,867.911

17. 8,115,570.86

18. 792,545.357

19. 9,927,905.20

20. 8,006,762.34

21. 73,492,017.8

22. 987,186,166

23. 609,038.866

24. 94,224,821.5

25. 26,987,411.6

26. 168,674,510

27. 28,725,307.4

28. 85,726,504.8

29. 582,580,812

30. 328,932.984

Page 43: Place Value and Expanded Notation

1. 2,897,917.886

2. 9,616,667,341

3. 227,506,562.2

4. 921,599,003.1

5. 13,501,387.67

6. 21,059,193.56

7. 43,497,469.74

8. 8,959,900,916

9. 8,422,200,004

10. 3,426,173,164

11. 36,404,108.87

12. 35,988,252.56

13. 1,421,480.678

14. 540,968,274.9

15. 50,326,947.97

16. 7,409,699,394

17. 9,273,691.002

18. 7,618,127,394

19. 1,842,284.877   20. 1,928,139.395   21. 3,934,997,258

22. 57,805,074.49   23. 1,076,591.023   24. 73,791,919.44

25. 6,792,538.618   26. 882,327,113.8   27. 818,914,396.1

28. 7,794,916.019

Page 50: Place Value and Expanded Notation

1. 6 hundred millions + 1 ten million + 4 millions + 5 hundred thousands + 3 ten thousands + 7 thousands + 5 hundreds + 4 tens + 1 one + 1 tenth

2. 5 millions + 6 ten thousands + 6 thousands + 2 tens + 3 ones + 4 tenths + 2 hundredths + 3 thousandths

3. 2 hundred millions + 6 ten millions + 6 millions + 6 hundred thousands + 6 thousands + 5 hundreds + 5 tens + 9 tenths

4. 1 billion + 9 hundred millions + 3 ten millions + 3 millions + 3 hundred thousands + 8 ten thousands + 8 thousands + 9 hundreds + 4 tens + 8 ones

5. 7 ten millions + 9 millions + 6 ten thousands + 7 thousands + 2 hundreds + 4 tens + 7 ones + 6 tenths + 9 hundredths

6. 2 hundred millions + 2 ten millions + 7 millions + 5 hundred thousands + 4 ten thousands + 8 thousands + 7 hundreds + 4 tens + 9 ones + 1 tenth

7. 1 billion + 6 ten millions + 9 millions + 1 hundred thousand + 6 ten thousands + 6 thousands + 9 hundreds + 6 tens + 2 ones

8. 5 millions + 7 hundred thousands + 7 ten thousands + 9 thousands + 8 hundreds + 3 tens + 2 ones + 8 tenths + 3 hundredths + 1 thousandth

9. 3 ten millions + 1 million + 7 hundred thousands + 7 thousands + 6 hundreds + 8 tens + 2 ones + 3 tenths

10. 3 hundred millions + 5 ten millions + 3 millions + 8 hundred thousands + 6 ten thousands + 4 thousands + 5 hundreds + 2 tenths

11. 7 millions + 5 hundred thousands + 6 ten thousands + 2 thousands + 5 hundreds + 8 tens + 4 ones + 1 tenth + 3 hundredths + 8 thousandths

12. 3 ten millions + 5 millions + 5 hundred thousands + 8 ten thousands + 4 thousands + 3 hundreds + 2 tens + 1 one + 6 tenths + 1 hundredth

13. 8 millions + 4 hundred thousands + 7 ten thousands + 8 thousands + 9 hundreds + 3 tens + 2 ones + 1 tenth + 3 hundredths + 2 thousandths

14. 9 billions + 1 hundred million + 5 ten millions + 5 millions + 6 hundred thousands + 6 ten thousands + 9 thousands + 9 hundreds + 4 tens + 6 ones

15. 9 hundred millions + 5 ten millions + 3 hundred thousands + 2 ten thousands + 5 thousands + 3 hundreds + 5 tens + 7 ones + 3 tenths

16. 7 ten millions + 5 millions + 1 ten thousand + 7 thousands + 3 hundreds + 2 tens + 4 tenths + 1 hundredth

17. 5 ten millions + 3 millions + 6 hundred thousands + 6 ten thousands + 3 thousands + 5 hundreds + 1 ten + 4 ones + 6 tenths + 1 hundredth

18. 4 millions + 7 hundred thousands + 5 ten thousands + 3 hundreds + 7 tens + 6 ones + 5 tenths + 3 hundredths + 2 thousandths

19. 9 millions + 4 hundred thousands + 5 ten thousands + 3 hundreds + 8 tens + 9 tenths + 9 hundredths + 3 thousandths

20. 1 hundred million + 6 ten millions + 8 millions + 7 ten thousands + 5 hundreds + 9 tens + 1 one + 5 tenths

21. 5 hundred millions + 3 ten millions + 8 millions + 9 hundred thousands + 7 ten thousands + 8 thousands + 7 hundreds + 3 tens + 6 ones + 3 tenths

22. 5 hundred millions + 2 ten millions + 8 millions + 9 hundred thousands + 4 thousands + 1 hundred + 7 tens + 6 ones + 5 tenths

23. 2 hundred millions + 4 ten millions + 1 million + 3 hundred thousands + 5 thousands + 4 hundreds + 9 ones + 8 tenths

24. 5 millions + 2 hundred thousands + 5 ten thousands + 4 thousands + 4 hundreds + 3 ones + 3 tenths + 4 hundredths + 9 thousandths

25. 7 millions + 7 hundred thousands + 3 ten thousands + 3 hundreds + 6 tens + 5 ones + 6 tenths + 1 hundredth + 2 thousandths

26. 4 ten millions + 8 millions + 9 hundred thousands + 7 ten thousands + 6 thousands + 6 hundreds + 8 tens + 7 ones + 2 tenths + 8 hundredths

27. 9 hundred millions + 3 ten millions + 5 millions + 4 hundred thousands + 3 ten thousands + 3 thousands + 2 hundreds + 5 tens + 8 ones + 5 tenths

28. 7 billions + 1 hundred million + 1 ten million + 7 millions + 4 hundred thousands + 1 ten thousand + 4 hundreds + 3 tens + 6 ones

Page 57: Factors

1. 2, 4, 11, 22

2. None

3. 2, 3

4. 2

5. 7, 13

6. 2, 4, 23, 46

7. None

8. 2, 4

9. 5, 7

10. None

11. None

12. None

13. None

14. 2, 4, 5, 8, 10, 20

15. 2, 41

16. 2, 11

17. None

18. 2, 3, 4, 6, 9, 12, 18

19. None

20. 2, 47

21. None

22. None

23. 2, 4, 8

24. 3, 23

25. 2, 5, 10, 25

26. 3, 31

27. 3

28. None

29. 2, 19

30. 3, 11

31. 7

32. 2, 4, 17, 34

33. 2, 3, 6, 7, 14, 21

34. 2, 3, 6, 11, 22, 33

35. 2, 3, 4, 6, 8, 9, 12, 18, 24, 36

Page 62: Multiples

1. 77, 154, 231, 308, 385

2. 23, 46, 69, 92, 115

3. 1, 2, 3, 4, 5

4. 2, 4, 6, 8, 10

5. 32, 64, 96, 128, 160

6. 9, 18, 27, 36, 45

7. 22, 44, 66, 88, 110

8. 36, 72, 108, 144, 180

9. 83, 166, 249, 332, 415

10. 3, 6, 9, 12, 15

11. 60, 120, 180, 240, 300

12. 24, 48, 72, 96, 120

13. 66, 132, 198, 264, 330

14. 79, 158, 237, 316, 395

15. 4, 8, 12, 16, 20

16. 91, 182, 273, 364, 455

17. 98, 196, 294, 392, 490

18. 20, 40, 60, 80, 100

19. 6, 12, 18, 24, 30

20. 67, 134, 201, 268, 335

21. 7, 14, 21, 28, 35

22. 8, 16, 24, 32, 40

23. 34, 68, 102, 136, 170

24. 25, 50, 75, 100, 125

25. 76, 152, 228, 304, 380

26. 5, 10, 15, 20, 25

27. 75, 150, 225, 300, 375

28. 93, 186, 279, 372, 465

29. 45, 90, 135, 180, 225

30. 59, 118, 177, 236, 295

31. 42, 84, 126, 168, 210

32. 18, 36, 54, 72, 90

33. 50, 100, 150, 200, 250

34. 10, 20, 30, 40, 50

35. 37, 74, 111, 148, 185

Page 67: Convert Fractions and Decimals

1. 0.996
2. 70/100
3. 17/25
4. 29/40
5. 2/19

6. 5/32
7. 21/22
8. 4/12
9. 0.75
10. 0.938

11. 0.588
12. 0.55
13. 5/18
14. 0.727
15. 0.25

16. 2/3
17. 1/5
18. 25/60
19. 0.5
20. 3/19

21. 14/1000
22. 0.929
23. 63/70
24. 0.5
25. 0.864

26. 0.667

Page 69: Mixed Numbers: Improper Fractions

1. 6 1/2
2. 172/19
3. 41/5
4. 17/2
5. 52/9

6. 39/4
7. 6 1/5
8. 21/4
9. 7 1/2
10. 19/2

11. 1 17/22
12. 93/34
13. 75/13
14. 199/30
15. 3 1/7

16. 8 1/2
17. 11/4
18. 7 8/15
19. 1 12/13
20. 8 7/16

21. 23/3
22. 24/11
23. 89/24
24. 96/17
25. 7 1/9

26. 86/11   27. 9 1/2   28. 130/19   29. 17/4   30. 51/10

31. 81/13   32. 5/2   33. 47/5   34. 5 5/6   35. 5 3/4

36. 53/14   37. 82/11   38. 7 3/16   39. 6 15/16   40. 24/5

41. 35/9   42. 9 1/7   43. 37/12   44. 53/8   45. 8/3

46. 2 7/9

Page 72:   Mixed Numbers: Addition and Subtraction

1. 15 5/6   2. 13   3. 15 5/8   4. 8 9/10   5. 8 5/6

6. 3 25/36   7. 7 11/12   8. 17 29/70   9. 19/20   10. 5 16/21

11. 3 7/45   12. 11 5/12   13. 6 1/6   14. 3 23/28   15. 13

16. 5 3/10   17. 1/2   18. 7 19/30   19. 6 3/56   20. 1 13/30

21. 11 1/4   22. 11 11/18   23. 1 13/30   24. 15 23/28   25. 1 5/9

26. 1 9/40   27. 1 1/4   28. 5 25/56   29. 8/15   30. 7 11/15

Page 77:   Mixed Numbers: Multiplication and Division

1. 5 19/20   2. 33 2/9   3. 11 1/25   4. 112/135   5. 147/172

6. 110/477   7. 10 25/28   8. 18/23   9. 65 1/6   10. 58/65

11. 11 5/9   12. 44 2/5   13. 145/196   14. 1   15. 10/33

16. 10 13/14   17. 1 11/21   18. 1 59/117   19. 49 7/20   20. 8/57

21. 63/145   22. 38 1/4   23. 400/637   24. 24   25. 315/344

26. 1 1/54   27. 7 11/15   28. 4 3/4   29. 3   30. 1 21/37

Page 82:   Multiplication with Whole Numbers

1. 4/5   2. 2   3. 3 5/9   4. 1/5   5. 1 1/3

6. 6/17   7. 2 1/4   8. 1   9. 5 1/7   10. 2

11. 4   12. 1 7/11   13. 2/5   14. 4 11/13   15. 1 1/4

16. 3 1/3   17. 4 1/2   18. 5 4/19   19. 3 1/9   20. 2 13/16

21. 4/5   22. 1 3/4   23. 1/2   24. 4 14/19   25. 5 11/17

26. 2   27. 1   28. 4 4/7   29. 4/9   30. 1 2/5

31. 1 1/4   32. 5/6   33. 1 3/11   34. 17/20   35. 6 2/3

36. 11/18   37. 2 7/13   38. 4/5   39. 5 1/7   40. 2 11/12

41. 15/19   42. 6/7   43. 2   44. 4 1/2   45. 4 7/17

46. 2 4/5   47. 4 4/15   48. 3/4   49. 1 5/7   50. 1 1/3

51. 3 1/2   52. 5 11/16   53. 2   54. 1 1/2   55. 8/11

56. 2 2/3   57. 3 1/2   58. 7 8/13   59. 5 1/3   60. 2 1/13

Page 86: Simplify Fractions: Proper and Improper Fractions

1. 1/4   2. 6   3. 3 8/9   4. 7 1/8   5. 4 13/19

6. 7 5/7   7. 3   8. 5   9. 9 1/10   10. 2

11. 1/2   12. 3 3/13   13. 8   14. 5 14/15   15. 7

16. 8   17. 7/11   18. 2 4/19   19. 7/12   20. 1/14

21. 3   22. 4/9   23. 7/8   24. 5/9   25. 5

26. 6   27. 9   28. 4/5   29. 7   30. 6 3/19

31. 5/12   32. 1/5   33. 1/4   34. 6 1/11   35. 6/13

36. 8   37. 9   38. 9 1/2   39. 8/9   40. 4

41. 1/9   42. 1/2   43. 5 3/8   44. 3   45. 6 7/13

46. 4 16/17   47. 5 1/2   48. 11/14   49. 9 1/2   50. 5/6

51. 1/9   52. 7   53. 12/19   54. 7 2/3   55. 7 3/7

56. 1/2   57. 6 3/5   58. 5   59. 2   60. 1/9

61. 3   62. 2 1/3   63. 9 17/20   64. 9   65. 3/8

66. 8 9/11   67. 2/3   68. 2   69. 7   70. 7 3/16

71. 8 6/19   72. 2   73. 1/7   74. 9   75. 4

76. 3   77. 3/10   78. 5/7   79. 8 3/4   80. 2 4/19

81. 1/2   82. 8 11/12   83. 2 1/7   84. 7   85. 7 3/10

86. 1/3   87. 3   88. 4/11   89. 1/2   90. 2 3/8

91. 6/13   92. 5 16/17   93. 2/3   94. 5   95. 3/16

96. 13/18   97. 2 1/5   98. 8   99. 1/17   100. 11/16

101. 2 5/12   102. 9 3/10   103. 6   104. 6/13   105. 6 1/2

106. 2   107. 4 7/10   108. 2 5/9   109. 8 1/9   110. 5 13/15

Page 94: Fractions Addition Word Problems

1. 5/6   2. 5/6   3. 19/42   4. 13/21   5. 29/30   6. 45/56

7. 11/20   8. 23/24   9. 3/4   10. 1/2   11. 13/21   12. 5/6

13. 4/15   14. 9/20   15. 4/9   16. 3/4   17. 44/45   18. 20/21

19. 13/15   20. 11/15   21. 2/3

Page 101: Fractions Subtraction Word Problems

1. 17/63   2. 7/24   3. 7/20   4. 13/70   5. 3/20   6. 7/15

7. 1/12   8. 8/21   9. 1/90   10. 29/72   11. 7/20   12. 1/6

13. 17/40   14. 3/20   15. 1/4   16. 2/9   17. 1/10   18. 2/15

19. 2/21   20. 1/3   21. 1/4

Page 108: Fractions Multiplication Word Problems

1. 2   2. 1/9   3. 3/5   4. 9/4   5. 10/3   6. 3   7. 8/3

8. 5/9   9. 3   10. 4   11. 16/5   12. 14/9   13. 3/7   14. 4/3

15. 1/20   16. 12/5   17. 1   18. 1/3   19. 1   20. 25/7   21. 50

Page 115: Area and Perimeter: Rectangles and Triangles

1. P=43.2 A=89.79

2. P=23.42 A=23.4

3. P=50.94 A=162.0162

4. P=48.9 A=109.80

5. P=44.40 A=93.4812

6. P=34.70 A=75.2250

7. P=37.0 A=64.07

8. P=45.98 A=90.17

9. P=24.38 A=25.56

10. P=27.52 A=46.2528

11. P=28.32 A=49.4864

12. P=42.8 A=87.66

13. P=40.20 A=85.5360

14. P=25.84 A=36.0864

15. P=40.1 A=59.75

16. P=25.62 A=28.08

17. P=67.14 A=180.1278

18. P=32.2 A=33.25

19. P=46.92 A=89.91

20. P=40.21 A=68.75

21. P=22.1 A=22.82

22. P=57.60 A=149.0048

23. P=35.29 A=52.325

24. P=27.80 A=32.2

25. P=27.76 A=36.0288

26. P=40.11 A=68.82

27. P=61.74 A=237.1680

28. P=55.83 A=133.38

29. P=31.8 A=48.65

30. P=38.7 A=72.06

31. P=57.44 A=114.7584

32. P=44.38 A=122.8234

33. P=16.6 A=9.96

34. P=64.26 A=193.7520

35. P=15.2 A=8.71

36. P=25.72 A=27.88

37. P=61.92 A=204.2901

38. P=35.0 A=58.89

39. P=46.52 A=91.635

40. P=26.5 A=26.4

41. P=16.0 A=11.99

42. P=27.15 A=31.5

43. P=25.51 A=27.39

44. P=41.52 A=85.2372

45. P=28.70 A=35.2

46. P=36.40 A=51.3850

47. P=43.87 A=82.56

48. P=28.61 A=34.5

Page 127: Area and Circumference

1. C=113.04 cm A=1,017.36 cm²

2. C=31.40 cm A=78.50 cm²

3. C=69.08 cm A=379.94 cm²

4. C=62.80 cm A=314.00 cm²

5. C=106.76 cm A=907.46 cm²

6. C=12.56 cm A=12.56 cm²

7. C=18.84 cm A=28.26 cm²

8. C=25.12 cm A=50.24 cm²

9. C=119.32 cm A=1,133.54 cm²

10. C=75.36 cm A=452.16 cm²

11. C=6.28 cm A=3.14 cm²

12. C=100.48 cm A=803.84 cm²

13. C=125.60 cm A=1,256.00 cm²

14. C=43.96 cm A=153.86 cm²

15. C=56.52 cm A=254.34 cm²

16. C=37.68 cm A=113.04 cm²

17. C=50.24 cm A=200.96 cm²

18. C=81.64 cm A=530.66 cm²

19. C=87.92 cm A=615.44 cm²

20. C=94.20 cm A=706.50 cm²

21. C=125.60 cm A=1,256.00 cm²   22. C=75.36 cm A=452.16 cm²

23. C=37.68 cm A=113.04 cm²   24. C=106.76 cm A=907.46 cm²

25. C=43.96 cm A=153.86 cm²   26. C=37.68 cm A=113.04 cm²

27. C=18.84 cm A=28.26 cm²   28. C=31.40 cm A=78.50 cm²

Page 132:   Measuring Angles

1. 100° Obtuse

2. 50° Acute

3. 120° Obtuse

4. 60° Acute

5. 90° Right

6. 130° Obtuse

7. 70° Acute

8. 110° Obtuse

9. 90° Right

10. 140° Obtuse

11. 120° Obtuse

12. 150° Obtuse

13. 160° Obtuse

14. 170° Obtuse

15. 30° Acute

16. 90° Right

17. 60° Acute

18. 70° Acute

19. 30° Acute

20. 100° Obtuse

21. 170° Obtuse

22. 140° Obtuse

23. 80° Acute

24. 140° Obtuse

25. 160° Obtuse

26. 60° Acute

27. 40° Acute

28. 50° Acute

29. 40° Acute

30. 30° Acute

31. 160° Obtuse

32. 70° Acute

33. 100° Obtuse

34. 40° Acute

35. 50° Acute

36. 120° Obtuse

37. 110° Obtuse

38. 20° Acute

39. 80° Acute

40. 20° Acute

41. 90° Right

42. 130° Obtuse

43. 140° Obtuse

44. 100° Obtuse

Page 143: Metric Conversion

1. 1,320.860	2. 0.000	3. 0.528	4. 1,056.688
5. 2.485	6. 0.003	7. 0.015	8. 8.818
9. 0.002	10. 1.864	11. 528.344	12. 0.621
13. 0.007	14. 1,849.204	15. 0.009	16. 0.015
17. 1.849	18. 0.006	19. 4.971	20. 0.007
21. 0.008	22. 0.002	23. 8.818	24. 0.009
25. 0.528	26. 0.015	27. 0.004	28. 0.004
29. 0.009	30. 0.000	31. 0.008	32. 0.010
33. 0.000	34. 0.002	35. 3.728	36. 0.011
37. 1.864	38. 0.006	39. 0.006	40. 4.971
41. 0.001	42. 0.007	43. 0.015	44. 0.004
45. 2.205	46. 6.614	47. 2,113.376	48. 0.000
49. 4.350	50. 1,585.032	51. 1,056.688	52. 11.023
53. 528.344	54. 2.205	55. 4.350	56. 0.528
57. 0.621	58. 6.614	59. 2.485	60. 0.000
61. 0.004	62. 0.000	63. 0.528	64. 0.000
65. 1.321	66. 0.007	67. 0.013	68. 0.004
69. 0.528	70. 0.011	71. 11.023	72. 0.015
73. 3.107	74. 0.001	75. 0.000	76. 0.000
77. 15.432	78. 15.432		

Page 148:   Metric Weights and Measures

1. 88,000	2. 0.082	3. 84,000	4. 0.028	5. 98,000
6. 72,000	7. 96,000	8. 0.034	9. 0.079	10. 0.041
11. 0.062	12. 57,000	13. 0.047	14. 17,000	15. 0.069
16. 40,000	17. 0.072	18. 0.012	19. 22,000	20. 0.024
21. 85,000	22. 64,000	23. 0.063	24. 20,000	25. 0.041
26. 0.026	27. 0.067	28. 91,000	29. 0.019	30. 76,000
31. 38,000	32. 0.039	33. 56,000	34. 82,000	35. 92,000
36. 11,000	37. 0.045	38. 0.016	39. 32,000	40. 0.047
41. 0.040	42. 76,000	43. 0.059	44. 14,000	45. 0.045
46. 0.020	47. 0.029	48. 0.044	49. 0.032	50. 0.049
51. 0.017	52. 60,000	53. 13,000	54. 28,000	55. 0.031
56. 0.018	57. 67,000	58. 0.057	59. 41,000	60. 0.070
61. 0.064	62. 0.050	63. 0.027	64. 18,000	65. 23,000
66. 57,000	67. 0.079	68. 0.010	69. 0.076	70. 0.063
71. 0.091	72. 49,000	73. 0.034	74. 0.086	75. 0.060
76. 37,000	77. 0.080	78. 57,000		

Page 153:   Mean and Median

1. Mean = 60.5, Median = 69.5

2. Mean = 54, Median = 47

3. Mean = 62.167, Median = 72.5

4. Mean = 68.167, Median = 66.5

5. Mean = 62.167, Median = 62

6. Mean = 66.833, Median = 69.5

7. Mean = 56.667, Median = 60

8. Mean = 71.333, Median = 86

9. Mean = 41.333, Median = 44

10. Mean = 29, Median = 18.5

11. Mean = 28.5, Median = 24.5

12. Mean = 53.833, Median = 57

13. Mean = 46.333, Median = 53

14. Mean = 66, Median = 63

15. Mean = 44, Median = 47

16. Mean = 59.667, Median = 75

17. Mean = 68.833, Median = 69.5

18. Mean = 69.167, Median = 77

19. Mean = 48.833, Median = 44

20. Mean = 62, Median = 64.5

21. Mean = 59, Median = 66.5

22. Mean = 59.333, Median = 57

23. Mean = 60.5, Median = 79

24. Mean = 59.667, Median = 62.5

www.ingramcontent.com/pod-product-compliance
Lightning Source LLC
Chambersburg PA
CBHW060510120726
48002CB00011B/3109

* 9 7 9 8 8 6 9 3 0 3 0 2 8 *